After the Crime

After the Crime

The Power of Restorative Justice
Dialogues between Victims
and Violent Offenders

Susan L. Miller

NEW YORK UNIVERSITY PRESS
New York and London

NEW YORK UNIVERSITY PRESS
New York and London
www.nyupress.org

References to Internet websites (URLs) were accurate at the time of writing.
Neither the author nor New York University Press is responsible for URLs
that may have expired or changed since the manuscript was prepared.

Library of Congress Cataloging-in-Publication Data

Miller, Susan L.
After the crime : the power of restorative justice dialogues
between victims and violent offenders / Susan L. Miller.
p. cm.
Includes bibliographical references and index.
ISBN 978-0-8147-9552-1 (cl : alk. paper) — ISBN 978-0-8147-9553-8
(pb : alk. paper) — ISBN 978-0-8147-6143-4 (e-book)
1. Restorative justice—Case studies. 2. Victims of crimes—Case studies.
3. Criminals—Rehabilitation—Case studies. I. Title.
HV8688.M55   2010
364.6'8—dc22   2010041974

New York University Press books are printed on acid-free paper,
and their binding materials are chosen for strength and durability.
We strive to use environmentally responsible suppliers and materials
to the greatest extent possible in publishing our books.

Manufactured in the United States of America

c 10 9 8 7 6 5 4 3 2 1
p 10 9 8 7 6 5 4 3 2 1

In memory of Kristen Klint,
beloved friend
and the first person to urge me to help victims

In memory also to my Uncle Harold,
Glenn H. Miller.
You are both so missed

And to my son, Connor,
who gives me great joy

Contents

Acknowledgments

The people in this book are survivors in the truest sense of the word, and I feel proud to know them. Throughout our time together, their determination, courage, and resiliency have been admirable and inspirational. That these survivors wholeheartedly shared their feelings and experiences so that others might benefit from their situations humbles me. I hope that this book honors their tenacity and allows them to feel that they finally have a voice and are being heard. Their fortitude and buoyancy reflected within this book reveal that there are many paths to closing chapters and opening new ones. I wish them only the best as they continue on their journeys.

This project was several years in the making, resulting in a forging of connections and incurring appreciation to many individuals. Most important, my heartfelt thanks go to the program participants, victims and offenders, and the key support people in their lives, without whom there would be no book. A host of other people, friends, family members, and students, were involved in various steps of the project. My undergraduate students at the University of Delaware, Tracy Levin, Rachel Kallmyer, and especially Diana Filkins, helped with data transcription, and Stacy Nelson introduced me to the Victims' Voices Heard program featured in this book. Friends and family members provided innumerable support, including listening, vacationing, and debating: my parents, Marilyn and Ken Miller, Connor Rhys Miller, Lisa, Joe, Joey, Toni, and Samantha DeRosa, Claire Renzetti, Lisa Bartran, Janna Lambine, Michelle and Morgan Meloy, special thanks to Nancy Getchell and her wonderful family, Ronet Bachman, Tammy Anderson, Maggie Andersen, Aaron Fichtelberg, the Becker family, Susan Caringella, Carol Post, Dan Atkins, Jessica Schiffman, Judy Schneider, Debbie Hegedus, and Frank Scarpitti.

My writing has benefited from the eyes of many people who provided comments on multiple drafts, with special thanks to my sister Lisa and friends Lisa and Janna, the early readers of some of the stories, for their enthusiasm and feedback. I also thank my dear friend LeeAnn Iovanni and also Dana Britton for their support, generous giving of their time and superior editing skills, and many engaging discussions we have had about social justice issues. My work is enhanced by their input; all mistakes are solely my own. I further appreciate all of the support and assistance from People's Place, an agency with which I am honored to conduct research. Thanks to the correctional administrators who helped facilitate my prison interviews, especially Paul Howard and Tom Carroll; thanks as well to Nancy Quillen for all of her secretarial support and good humor. Much appreciation to the comments raised by the reviewers, particularly Professors Kimberly J. Cook (UNC-Wilmington) and Angela Gover (CU-Denver), and to my editor, Ilene Kalish, and her skillful assistant, Aiden Amos, at New York University Press for their belief in this project and for expertly shepherding the book through the publishing process.

Guiding the survivors and the offenders through the restorative justice program was a challenge but one nonetheless welcomed by Kim Book. Kim does not accept praise easily, but the survivors and offenders resoundingly credit her listening skills, open heart, and nonjudgmental mind for navigating them through the process that led to a face-to-face meeting between the victims/survivors of a violent crime and their offenders. Her insight, her compassion, and her grace facilitated healing for all involved. None of this research would be possible without Kim Book, who supported my writing project, answered every question with patience, and always kept her focus on the welfare of her participants. Thank you Kim.

Because of Kim's centrality to this project, I end this section with her own acknowledgments:

> To my husband and best friend, Ray, thank you for being the anchor in my life. None of this would have been possible without your love and support. To Jane Brady and Stan Taylor, I offer my most sincere thanks. You took the time to listen and help the victim of a crime and gave me a gift that would propel me into not only healing myself but helping others to heal. To Diane Glenn, who has always been there to support and listen to me and has become my closest friend, I offer my love, admiration, and thanks. Thank you to People's Place. You enabled me to do what I love, and I am proud to have an association with an organization that does so much good for others. To Susan Miller, who took on the massive task to author *After the Crime* and who saw VVH and its potential to help heal victims and offenders, my deepest gratitude. Just as I am blessed to know you, so are the participants in this book, for in telling our stories you have given us a

voice and empowered us, making us twice empowered, twice blessed. And most importantly, thanks to God, who shared Nicole with me and who is the author of my life.

—Kim Book

I

Foundations

Introduction

We are a country fascinated by the minutiae of movie stars' glamorous lives and scandals. We are glued to news and TV shows about crime, eager to digest the gory details. Newscasts and magazines understand this fascination, responding with daily stories of mischief, mayhem, and murder. We love to consume other people's troubles and embarrassments, and this makes sense because hearing about other people's problems makes us feel better about our own. Since we do not know these people, we live vicariously and judge them with no strings attached. We become armchair quarterbacks—deciding what people ought to do or ought not to have done. It is common for people to attach blame to strangers—this helps to reinforce the sense that we are not as vulnerable as they are because *we* are not like *them*; we would not make similar choices. Believing that we are different, or wiser, provides us with the illusion that we have some control over our own lives.

This attitude changes when something terrible happens to us or to a family member or cherished friend. Becoming a victim of a violent crime is terrifying. Your entire world changes in moments, and events throw you unwillingly into uncharted places that are unscripted, unimaginable, and painful. The immediate circumstances are understandable: when violence is sudden, unpredictable, and horrifying, you might react with shock, denial, anxiety, fear, guilt, anger, and terror. If you are religious or spiritual, you may find solace in your faith or beliefs and use them to help you through the pain, or you might doubt your faith in a God who allows bad things to happen to good people. Whatever your feelings, you find that in order to function, you must compartmentalize your utter despair and grief because there are practical matters to handle or because you need to answer questions from police, detectives, medical personnel, lawyers, and victim services workers or because you have other people looking to you for reassurance. Quite possibly, depending on the crime, you might have to arrange a memorial service or funeral or to find a temporary safe place to live or to deal with Child Protective Services. Even given this array of circumstances, all victims share a common experience: the life they once knew changed instantly, and not only is the new place in which they find themselves terrifying, but there is no map to guide them in navigating a course back to a "normal" life.

No one asks to be a part of this journey, and no one is aware of the complicated emotions it will unleash or how it might affect other people in his or her life. Unresolved questions can trouble victims—on a good day these questions might feel like the proverbial pebble trapped in a shoe, but on a bad day they are more like a crushing boulder. Many victims feel rage, though they do not necessarily know why. Anger sometimes strikes at the oddest moments and can be (mis)directed at beloved family members or friends. Self-doubt, self-blame, self-hatred, or self-destructive acts are all part and parcel of the aftermath of violent victimization. With them comes fear, which limits victims' autonomy, and a pain so deep that victims describe feeling as though their hearts are ripped apart. These responses reflect what social psychologists call "shattered assumptions," a phrase that describes how victims feel when their equilibrium is thrown off balance and nothing they try can fix things.[1] Victims wonder whether they will even survive the incident, asking themselves questions like, "Can I live with this, or will it destroy me?" Kathleen O'Hara, a psychologist whose son was murdered, asks, "Can we, despite our tragedies, in spite of the horror in the world, still believe it is a good place? Can we either maintain our general optimism or learn to develop it, after disaster strikes? . . . An even greater tragedy would be to allow violence to keep us from joy; then truly, it has destroyed us."[2]

The people whose stories appear in this book have something in common— they could not come to terms with crimes that changed their lives profoundly, despite their various attempts to confront the situations, to grapple with them by talking to people or trying therapy and even by moving on and accomplishing other things such as getting married, having children, earning degrees, or getting new jobs. Something lingered that was unresolved, taking its toll on their daily lives, preventing them from finding peace. Grief, anger, and revenge fantasies can be immobilizing in the short term; they can be devastating in the long term. The victims/survivors[3] portrayed in this book experienced a range of crimes—child sexual abuse (father-daughter incest and grandfather-granddaughter molestation), stranger rape and attempted murder, marital rape and battering, deaths of loved ones killed by drunk drivers, and murder. Although these incidents occurred from six to twenty-eight years ago, the aftermath of the trauma and violence continued on a daily basis, often in baffling ways. Even the people they loved most did not understand their feelings of unease and of being unsettled, and many among their family and friends no doubt wanted to forget about the terrible things that had happened and move on.

But for many victims this is impossible. They may appear on the surface to have emerged "on the other side," since most are functioning adults who hold down responsible jobs and are actively engaged in parenting and other activities. Inside, however, they are stuck. Being "stuck" is the moment when others' initial sympathy turns to impatience and victims feel isolated in grief that seems as fresh to them as when the crime first occurred. It is a common enough process: victims initially receive our sympathy; over time, however, we become weary, and compassion fatigue sets in. We wonder why they do not just "get over it" or do not "try harder" to heal. Sometimes we might come to believe they are using their victimization as an excuse or to get attention. We wish that victims would reach some kind of closure and move forward, if only to allay our own impatience or guilt about their pain. We urge them to embrace life again and not to dwell in darkness. But finding this kind of closure is elusive for many victims of violent crime. Kathleen O'Hara writes about this kind of grief, which she calls "a grief like no other": "There simply is no closure. It is never over—you are never healed. It is more true to say that you *are* moving on, as an ever-changing process; that you are putting your life back together again in new ways, but that these ways are laced through with tender memories of your loved one, not just the violent act that you have been submerged in for so long."[4]

Victims commonly talk about being misunderstood, silenced, or stigmatized by people in their families and social or work networks who cannot fathom that, after all this time, they are still not "over" it. Thus, victims' experiences often weigh heavily on others, becoming the proverbial elephant in the room, surrounded by silence and denial.[5] Though family members, friends, and co-workers may see the lingering consequences of the crime, they refuse to openly acknowledge it, or they simply grow tired of talking about it and wish the victim would tire too. Weariness may even give way to silencing, trivializing, or victim blaming, which reinforces the mistreatment many victims have already received in their dealings with the criminal justice system.

Resiliency eludes many victims. When one has experienced the loss of a child or the pain of rape or some other deeply traumatic and severely violent event, it is common to feel a sense of loss or hurt so deep that moving forward with one's own life seems impossible. Yet some victims of horrific crimes astonish us by their ability to surmount the seemingly insurmountable. For instance, many Holocaust survivors who lost parents, siblings, spouses, and children chose to embrace life and begin again, although they could not have imagined rebuilding their shattered lives at the time. Other victims speak of how the experience of surviving trauma or violence leads them to want to help others. In fact, this motivation on the part of one victim to turn pain into solace for others is the springboard for this book.

An offender's act not only affects a victim's life; it also inevitably affects a host of people in both the victim's and offender's lives. Family members and friends of the offender often recoil with horror upon hearing about the brutality of the crimes committed. They may also be overwhelmed by helplessness. Children of offenders are greatly affected by losing a parent to prison, in addition to the financial insecurity and shame that accompany the arrest and incarceration of their parent. Anyone connected to a victim also reels from the initial shock of the crime, as well as the long-term consequences that shape the victim's life. Even the best case—arrest, a successful prosecution, and a punishment—rarely completely mitigates the effects that crime has on victims' or offenders' families, friendship networks, or the community. But importantly, just as bad stuff affects everyone in the victims' and offenders' orbits, so too will good stuff. Offenders' expressions of accountability, for example, may help to heal and restore their victims. And the healing of victims, in turn, may bring peace to their family. What is clear from the stories of both the victims and offenders is that while the devastation is widespread, so too can be the healing.

Victims' Voices Heard

In the chapters that follow, I describe an approach used by a program, Victims' Voices Heard, to help victims reassemble lives shattered by severe violence. The participants in this particular program—both victims and offenders—based on their positive experiences, were eager to share their insights with a larger audience, with the hope of giving other victims and their loved ones another tool to help in their recovery. In the many, many hours I spent interviewing them, the victims/survivors used words such as "life-saving" and "transformative" to describe the program, and the offenders expressed deep gratitude for the opportunity to be a part of their victims' healing process

Victims' Voices Heard (VVH) is a victim-centered restorative justice program that brings victims into face-to-face contact with their offenders to receive information, to tell offenders about the consequences of their violence, and to help them regain the control over their lives that was taken from them, first by the offender and then by the criminal justice system. It is a therapeutic program designed to help victims with their healing and recovery; it is *not* designed to affect the outcome of criminal cases. In fact, the offenders I discuss here were already incarcerated (or, in two cases, had finished a prison and probation term), and offenders received no incentive (such as parole or clemency appeal considerations) for their participation. The real people featured in this book, both victims and offenders, have chosen to use their private experiences and the knowledge and peace achieved through the VVH program to give a gift to others whose lives are affected in similar ways. This sense of purpose was something that developed as they participated in the VVH program; it was not a direction that either victims or offenders ever thought they would take prior to their involvement in the restorative justice process.

My hope is to present the stories of the participants in the VVH program in an accessible way, sidestepping the minefields of academic jargon. Since restorative justice models are relatively new, I do raise conceptual issues and research dilemmas that seem essential to a clear understanding of the goals of programs like these. However, I focus most directly on the motivations, processes, hopes, and outcomes of the victims and offenders who invested so much time, emotion, courage, and effort into the VVH program. Readers seeking a more in-depth discussion of research related to restorative justice should see appendix A. Appendix B provides additional information on the research methodology, and appendix C offers more details of the VVH program itself.

Restorative Justice

Victims' Voices Heard, the program that is the subject of this book, is one of the many creative restorative justice (RJ) programs that have developed around the country and worldwide in response to growing concerns that victims' needs are unmet by the criminal justice system (see appendix A for a more detailed description of the types and range of RJ programs). Howard Zehr, one of the founders of the RJ movement, contrasts criminal justice and restorative justice. In the traditional criminal justice model, crime is a violation of the law and is committed against the state. Breaking the law means that guilt must be determined through the adversarial system, and punishment must be imposed; the focus is on offenders receiving the penalty deserved for their harmful actions. However, in the contest between the offender and the state, victims' voices and needs are peripheral to achieving justice for the offender. In contrast, the restorative justice model sees crime as a violation of people and relationships. This violation creates obligations to make things right; the focus is on meeting victims' needs and facilitating offenders' responsibility in order to repair the harm.[6]

Most restorative justice programs, including the one explored in this book, involve some kind of encounter between the victim and offender, a meeting that occurs only after extensive preparation.[7] Sometimes letters are exchanged in preparation for a face-to-face meeting, and often victims and offenders select a support person to accompany them to such a meeting. Trained facilitators oversee these dialogues and use their skills to balance the concerns of all parties involved. Face-to-face meetings, letter exchanges, and other practices provide the opportunity for participants to explore what happened, for victims to receive answers to questions and assurances of safety to tell their stories and express their feelings, and for offenders to tell their stories, take responsibility for their actions, and display genuine remorse. Restorative justice provides a context for forgiveness, but there is no pressure to choose this path.[8] The personal journeys related in the chapters to follow show the range of emotions and actions that victims/survivors experience. As they confront their unrelenting grief while working with the dialogue process, the victims choose courage over fear. During these journeys with VVH, they honor themselves and their loved ones while finding a path that provides them with greater peace. Their stories of transformation are inspiring.

In the chapters that follow, I place the VVH program in a context of both its general and specific significance. In chapter 2, I explore the rise in popularity of restorative justice programs in the United States and other countries and draw the contours of some of the debates about using such programs for addressing the needs of victims/survivors of severe violence, particularly for the crimes of child abuse, domestic violence, and sexual assault. Chapter 2 also describes more specific details involving the nuts and bolts of VVH. In chapter 3, I describe the foundation and catalyst for VVH, as it was shaped by the tireless and compassionate efforts of its founder, Kim Book,[9] a mother whose teenage daughter was murdered. I emphasize the power of storytelling and how personal narratives can create life-changing moments for the people involved as well as for the people who hear their stories. Chapters 4 through 12 tell the stories of the victim-offender pairings. Chapter 13 provides an analysis of the themes and patterns that emerged in the multiple data-collection sites—the interviews with participants, the case files, the interviews with the program facilitator(s), and the viewings of the victim-offender face-to-face dialogue videos. The final chapter explores unfinished business related to VVH specifically as well as to therapeutic restorative justice programs more generally. It also offers an update on the victims' and offenders' lives since the completion of the VVH program and what transpired since my initial interviews with them.

2

Tossing Turkeys and Other Stories

What Do They Say about Crime and Punishment?

A flying frozen turkey careened out of a speeding car, hitting a woman's windshield, bending her steering wheel from the sheer force of the blow and then shattering every bone in her face, nearly killing her. A teenage kid out joyriding with his friends had thrown the turkey out a car window as a prank, an unprovoked, thoughtless act for which his victim paid dearly. Despite all odds and following many, many hours of surgery, she not only lived but also avoided almost inevitable brain damage. Yet rather than expressing anger and a desire for revenge at the teenager's sentencing hearing—where the penalty imposed could have been twenty-five years in prison—she embraced the sobbing teen, hugging him as he choked out the words, "I'm sorry, I'm sorry, I'm sorry." Her whispered response to him was, "It's OK, it's OK. I just want you to make your life the best it can be."[1] Why did she offer him this gift of forgiveness, which resulted in six months' jail time and five years' probation, rather than push the prosecutors to go for the maximum punishment?

A number of years earlier in New York, a young woman named Kendra was killed in an instant when a mentally ill man who had stopped taking his antipsychotic medication pushed her in front of an oncoming subway train.[2] Her family sat through every day of the first two trials and intended to sit through the next trial, the third in seven years, until the schizophrenic man finally pled guilty to manslaughter on October 10, 2006.[3] At the time of the incident, the man had been discharged from a psychiatric hospital because the state would only reimburse for twenty-one days of treatment. Since Kendra's death, her mother has lectured across the country on the need for better treatment for the mentally ill and spearheaded "Kendra's Law," passed in New York in 1999. The law allows for families of mentally ill people (and other knowledgeable people in their environment) to petition courts to require treatment for people who otherwise might not take their medication.

How could this survivor, a mother who lost her daughter, turn her grief into activism?

In another incident, early in the morning of October 2, 2006, an armed man entered a one-room schoolhouse in Lancaster County, Pennsylvania, sent the boys out of the building, and took the girls hostage. He eventually killed five girls and injured five others before turning a gun on himself. While the rest of the country watched with horror as the story unfolded, by that evening, an Amish neighbor had visited the family of the gunman and offered forgiveness to the family. Another Amish man, whose three grandnephews were inside the school during the slaying, said of the gunman's family, "I hope they stay around here and they'll have a lot of friends and a lot of support."[4] This act of forgiveness demonstrates some of the basic religious beliefs of the Amish, an order dating back to the 1600s.[5] Yet offering forgiveness so quickly and for such a heinous crime astonished many Americans. Donald Kraybill, a scholar of Amish life, explains that retaliation and revenge are not part of an Amish vocabulary. The phrase "forgive and forget" is commonly used in responding to those who break Amish rules, as long as they confess their failures—a practice extended to outsiders, even killers of children.[6] As another expert on Amish families contends, "The hurt is very great, but they don't balance the hurt with hate."[7]

These examples raise complicated questions about crime and justice. What do victims of unspeakable crimes, or those who speak for their lost loved ones, want from the criminal justice system? Should their anger, their rage, their despair, and their pain be part of the calculus of punishment? How much of victims' recovery and healing is contingent on having a voice in the process? What liberates victims from their victimization and brings them to a place of surviving or even thriving? For offenders, when, if ever, do they understand the harm that they caused, and can they play a role in helping victims in the recovery process? And finally, how can a community heal?

These questions drive our search for meaning in the current system of justice, in which voices and rights of victims and offenders compete to be heard and the issues are complicated by legal and criminal justice processes. Too often, we hear stories about miscarriages of justice—for victims or offenders—or complaints about how the formal criminal justice process silences victims. In fact, these concerns paved the way for the victims' rights movement, which developed to challenge the invisibility of victims and the deprivation of their rights in the criminal justice arena. One alternative model developed to better address victims' needs is known as restorative justice

(RJ), an umbrella term that covers a variety of efforts designed to assist victims in healing, to encourage offenders' accountability, to promote reconciliation, and to support communities who seek more efficacious responses to crime. The restorative justice movement began as a way to deal with the crime problem beyond the current "war on crime" strategies of containment and control.

The earliest programs (some of which are still in operation today) had a decidedly offender-centered focus. Given that most offenders eventually leave prison and rejoin society—usually angry and lacking the skills to begin a law-abiding life—I myself have been troubled by the nation's heavy reliance on punitiveness rather than on rehabilitation and by a criminal justice ideology that refuses to address the social structural arrangements and institutions that allow crime to flourish. At the same time, however, an overemphasis on offenders' needs exacerbates victims' feelings of isolation, silencing their experiences or treating them as secondary to offenders' concerns. Consequently, many restorative justice programs now integrate victims' needs as a central focus. Restorative justice is intriguing on a number of levels: for the potential benefits for victims, the rehabilitative potential for offenders, and the prospects for healing communities. I invite readers who wish for a more complete discussion of the theoretical and empirical complexities involved with restorative justice to read appendix A.

Although most scholars make comparisons between the formal retributive justice system and restorative justice processes, there is no universal agreement about the definition of RJ or even whether it is a process or an outcome. Both approaches agree that wrongdoing needs to be addressed, but the manner in which they respond differs.[8] For my purposes, I favor a definition that focuses on repairing harm done to victims and facilitates offenders' accountability while including healing and its potential for people and relationships affected by the crime. I do not believe that this approach necessitates restoring a reconciliation of personal relationships but, rather, that it conveys the disapproval of the wrongdoing while affirming the intrinsic value of all those most affected by the situation.

The incidents that begin this chapter draw our attention to the role that victims may play and the input they might wish to have in the pursuit of justice. Since victims' experiences and needs vary enormously, there is no single way to tailor a program to meet all their wishes, nor might that be necessary or even constitutionally permissible. However, one promising method that may accommodate victims' needs *and* social/criminal justice concerns involves programs with restorative justice features.[9]

Types of Restorative Justice Programs

There are two types of restorative justice programs: those that are *diversionary* and those that are *therapeutic*. In some ways, this distinction is like comparing apples and oranges. *Diversionary restorative justice programs* are designed to operate in lieu of the formal criminal justice process and provide alternative outcomes—thus, they are more offender centered. Advocates of diversionary programs contend that the criminal justice system operates with bias and that some crimes and some offenders are more effectively handled outside the formal process in a program that does not compound the systemic bias and that facilitates offenders' rehabilitation and reconciliation with their victims and their communities. *Therapeutic restorative justice programs*, on the other hand, operate after offenders have been convicted; their primary goal is to empower and heal victims. For many restorative justice advocates, the therapeutic goal of helping victims heal and recover is an equally important, if not the most important, aspect of the criminal justice process. Focusing on the therapeutic aspect of dialogue, a process that *supplements* formal criminal case processing, is qualitatively different from RJ programs that focus on diversionary efforts.

Therapeutic restorative justice programs can operate at any point in the criminal justice process, and reconciliation between victims and offenders is not the ultimate goal. Rather, through a dialogue between the victim and offender, victims can reach resolution of troubling questions such as, Was I specifically targeted? Did the offender know at the time or learn later the consequences of his or her actions? Is the offense going to be repeated?[10] These questions are of vital importance to a victim's sense of safety and closure. For instance, Victims' Voices Heard, the program explored in this book, operates at the end of the criminal justice process, often many years after the sentencing of defendants. The victims interviewed for this book felt strongly that their offenders needed to be held accountable by the criminal justice system. They did not wish to sidestep that aspect of justice and punishment, but rather, the victims wanted the opportunity to meet with the offenders after the conclusion of the criminal justice process to obtain more information about the crime as well as about other aspects of the offenders' current state of mind.

Many of the crimes that are part of the VVH caseload are crimes of sexual violence or crimes committed between people who know each other. Incest and child sexual abuse, intimate-partner battering, marital rape, and rape committed by a stranger or an acquaintance are known as crimes of "gendered violence" because men are generally the offenders while women and girls are overwhelmingly the victims. Many scholars and practitioners maintain that restorative justice mediation programs are ill suited to handle crimes in which women and children are hurt by the men in their private lives (fathers, husbands, boyfriends, ex-partners) or in which men commit stranger rape, because the gendered nature of the violence exposes the unequal power relationship between victim and offender. Diversionary programs do little to disrupt this power relationship and risk revictimizing women and children.[11] This is not the case for *postconviction programs* such as VVH, in which offenders are already adjudicated and under correctional control. I argue in this book that the Victims' Voices Heard program demonstrates that therapeutic restorative principles and practices can be effective in handling crimes of gendered violence.[12]

Most of the objections raised against using a restorative justice model with crimes of gendered violence surround the 1980s version of victim-offender mediation (VOM) programs, which operated as a diversionary process in lieu of involvement in the formal criminal justice system and stressed equality between victims and offenders and their reconciliation.

Recently, however, proponents of RJ have countered with a defense of the way specific RJ *therapeutic* practices, but *not* diversionary practices, might be useful in handling domestic-violence cases as well as some sexual assault cases. The focus of therapeutic programs is healing driven, rather than outcome driven, and because therapeutic-oriented RJ programs such as VVH are not offered at the beginning phase of the criminal justice process, nor are they in lieu of a harsher punishment, they escape many of the problems in using a restorative justice model for crimes of gendered violence. In fact, there are many aspects of victims' needs that illustrate the potential success of using RJ with gendered violence cases, rather than showing their incompatibility.

For instance, a battered woman may have many lingering issues related to the violence and abuse with which she must deal after the batterer is behind bars. She may have to rejoin the workforce, establish credit in her own name, begin divorce proceedings, deal with issues related to children, and so forth. But she may also feel a sense of safety and respite from fear and intimidation and abuse for the first time in a long time. This respite could reinforce positive feelings about herself and the future direction of her life and the lives of her children, for she is no longer under the batterer's immediate control. Being able to communicate to the offender the effects of the things he did to her may be remarkably empowering for a survivor of domestic violence. The offender is under the control of the corrections institution, a guard is often present at the dialogue, and if the offender has been released to parole or is on probation, he or she remains controlled (with the threat of prison for noncompliance) under the auspices of the criminal justice system. This chance to express anger, hurt—whatever consequences a survivor would wish to convey to the offender—within a safe space has the potential to be empowering not just for victims of battering and rape but also for victims of other sexual assaults and child abuse. In addition, because therapeutic RJ practices typically include the presence of other people during the process, they offer the opportunity for heightened condemnation of the crime in a public forum. Victims might feel a greater sense of validation and receive more assurances that they are not blameworthy, while offenders' backgrounds and reasons for the crime might be better understood since RJ offers a more holistic examination of their behavior.

Victims' Voices Heard—A Therapeutic Model of Restorative Justice

The specific *therapeutic* approach of Victims' Voices Heard (VVH) differs from *diversionary* restorative justice practices. Rather than trying to affect case outcomes, VVH concentrates primarily on healing. In this way, it incorporates a therapeutic RJ approach, and it was designed neither to divert cases from nor to provide an alternative to the criminal justice process or sentencing.

The Victims' Voices Heard program is a *postconviction* program designed to bring victims/survivors of severe violence face to face with their offenders to receive information, answers to questions, and so forth; it does *not* let offenders off the hook for the crimes they committed. Only twenty-five states offer dialogue programs for victims of severe violence, although there seems to be growing interest in such programs. Victims of sexual assault/rape, child abuse, and battering (as well as other crimes) are eligible for the program, although for all victims extensive preparation is required. Victims themselves must initiate the process, rather than police, victim services workers, prosecutorial screening procedures, or correctional programs; offenders cannot establish first contact, nor can their support groups of friends or families make attempts on their behalf. In fact, upon an offender's conviction, it is typical for a victim and the offender to abide by statute to a no-contact order, so even if there were a desire for contact, the law would prevent it.

Because the VVH program operates at the postconviction stage—with most offenders behind bars or under the control of the probation department—the offender neither is promised nor receives any benefit such as a reduced sentence or any leniency. Typically offenders have already served several years of the sentence imposed, which often has given them time to move beyond the anger of being apprehended, convicted, and incarcerated, and they may have begun to work on personal growth. Some of this change might become manifest in voluntary participation in prison rehabilitative programs, such as pursuing education or vocational skills. Offenders might also become involved in self-help groups while incarcerated, such as Alcoholics Anonymous or Narcotics Anonymous, or anger-management groups, or they may forge religious connections with faith-based prison groups. Still others may seek to develop empathy for their victims and engage in victim sensitivity workshops or programs.

Because of the commonly issued no-contact orders between victims and offenders and the dearth of research conducted on inmates' feelings about their victims, we do not know much about how offenders think about their victims, whether they feel remorseful or want to apologize to them or to explain any circumstances of the crime—or even to seek revenge upon release, which is typically a victim's fear. Victims usually do not know whether offenders participate in rehabilitation programs or attend victim sensitivity programs while incarcerated. The general public may feel that offenders are generally callous and disregard victims' feelings or pain (or they would not have harmed them in the first place), but some offenders feel or grow to feel genuine remorse and may desire an avenue through which to apologize to victims or to seek forgiveness.

The victim-offender dialogue in a program such as VVH occurs at a later point in a victim's life, at a time when he or she may be more able to really know what it is he or she needs to talk about with the offender or to have answered. He or she may be better able to hear what the offender has to say in a way that would not have been possible when the pain was so fresh. Since the offender is under the control of the correctional system, the dialogue becomes a more symmetrical process: the victim who is free on the outside is more empowered than the offender who is locked up. This inverts the power relations in which the offender exercised control over the victim. In fact, especially for survivors of rape and battering (or other gendered crimes committed by an intimate partner or family member), the validation a victim receives when showing an offender that she and her life were not destroyed by his actions—and that she is better off for being rid of him—may be invaluable.

When offenders are approached a number of years following the criminal act that led to their incarceration, they may have had the time needed to develop empathy. Because there is no expectation of reward for participating in VVH, the only incentive the offenders may have is to try to help their victims. Although some offenders might express an initial interest because they are motivated by boredom or seek a way to tell their story or profess their innocence, such motivations would get them screened out of the program; offenders must accept responsibility for the crime they committed to be eligible for VVH. These various requirements for an offender's participation strip bare impure motivations, making any apology or remorse uncoerced, not "compulsory compassion."[13] By learning more details about the crime through the offenders' eyes, victims may receive direct evidence to challenge any feelings of self-blame they have internalized. In cases of rape and battering, victims also may learn about or remember their own resistance, knowledge that could serve to empower them. Moreover, victims' fear about what the offender might do to harm them upon release could be addressed and dissipated. In other cases, those who lost loved ones to the violence of drunk driving or murder get the opportunity to fully express the short- and long-term consequences of their loss.

Not only is offenders' accountability a requirement for participation in VVH, but it is also something that victims embrace. In the context of the processes of the formal criminal justice system, offenders get little opportunity to express their remorse or to take responsibility for their actions. Not much is done to encourage them to understand the consequences of their acts for victims or to create any empathy for victims. In fact, the adversarial process encourages offenders to fight vigorously for their innocence or to provide reasons to mitigate and minimize their punishment upon conviction (or when agreeing to plead guilty). The legal process and prison experience effectively serve to heighten offenders' sense of alienation from society.[14] RJ questions the limits of the traditional criminal justice process to develop offenders' acceptance of responsibility and their empathy for their victims. Punishment fails to hold offenders truly accountable to victims; it mainly satisfies the state. RJ advocates believe that offenders need to understand the impact of their behavior and to attempt to make things right to the extent that they can. And the RJ philosophy takes this idea one step further: "If we expect [offenders] to assume their responsibilities, to change their behavior, to become contributing members of our communities, their needs must be addressed as well."[15] Addressing these needs could include therapeutic support, encouragement for substance-abuse treatment and support for integration into the community, and skills building, These supports exist alongside offenders' willingness to take responsibility for their actions and to address their victims' needs.

The National Picture

As of October 2009, twenty-five states have victim-offender dialogue (VOD) programs for victims/survivors of severe violence: Alabama, California, Delaware, Iowa, Kansas, Louisiana, Maine, Maryland, Massachusetts, Minnesota, Mississippi, Montana, Nebraska, New Hampshire, New York, Ohio, Oregon, Pennsylvania, Tennessee, Texas, Utah, Vermont, Washington, West Virginia, and Wisconsin. New York has the oldest program, which began in 1990; seven other states started their programs in the 1990s, and the remaining states did so in the 2000s.

At present, Delaware, where VVH is based, is the only state in the country whose program is not corrections based. Thus, since VVH's founder and coordinator, Kim Book, has an office located outside the state prison, she has greater autonomy. It does not mean that her work is independent of correctional input: with the cooperation of the state correctional commissioner, Kim developed a memorandum of understanding that fully outlines the expectations of the VVH program in cooperation with the prisons. Victim-offender dialogues (VOD) take an enormous amount of time, with some programs spending more time than others on preparing the victims and offenders before their face-to-face meeting. As the chief facilitator, Kim meets with both parties separately for at least six months on a weekly or biweekly basis. This is an intensive commitment that not all states duplicate. For instance, in the state of Pennsylvania, program facilitators typically meet with the victim and offender separately only once before the face-to-face meeting between them. The number of completed cases varies by state. As of 2009, California, which established its program in 2004, has completed 2 cases. Iowa's program has been running since 1993 and has completed 37 dialogues (with 52 other cases completed without a face-to-face meeting). Ohio and Texas have the most cases, with 113 and 356 (of which 259 were face-to-face meetings, and 97 were creative alternatives) completed, respectively.[16] Approximately 660 cases were completed nationwide from 1990 to 2009.[17]

In most VOD programs, after the offender agrees to participate,[18] the program coordinator meets with the offender's counselor and any staff member with whom the offender has had contact during incarceration, including mental health staff (for the offender's mental health screening). Preparation usually takes between a minimum of six months and one year. A number of other states' VOD programs have long preparation processes, but at least eight states (Alabama, Iowa, Louisiana, Maine, Minnesota, Nebraska, Pennsylvania, and Washington) prepare only for two to four sessions. Most states allow the presence of support people for both victim and offender. Delaware allows both victims/survivors and offenders to identify one support person to be present during the dialogue. The rules governing this procedure vary by state; in Delaware, only a chaplain or counselor who works with the inmate is considered an appropriate support person for the offender, whereas in Minnesota, offenders can request family members or friends. Only the Texas program specifically discourages support people, with the belief that only the principal players should be in the room. Most states allow audio-video taping with approval of both participants. Most states also have media-contact restrictions; the Delaware protocol states that during the preparation and dialogue both parties must sign an agreement to refrain from any relationship with the media.

Follow-ups and debriefings also vary; they are required in all states but can happen immediately or later. In Delaware, the VVH facilitator conducts private debriefings with the victim and offender immediately following the dialogue and then conducts follow-up meetings with both parties two weeks following the dialogue and again in two months; evaluation forms are given to both the victim and the offender to complete and return when they feel they are ready to do so. A final case report is completed on each dialogue and is included in an end-of-year report, with all completed dialogues sent to the Department of Corrections and the Department of Justice.

It is clear from the mission statement and the accompanying protocols that the Victims' Voices Heard program is thorough and well developed. Although victims' safety and empowerment are paramount, the program integrates other restorative justice methods and goals that facilitate healing of the larger web of people affected by the crimes, such as offenders, the friends and/or family members of victims and offenders, and the key community support people whose lives are intertwined with the victims and offenders.

The Victims' Voices Heard program recognizes the importance of the offender component in its design, believing that offenders have something positive to gain by their involvement in the program (as the larger community perhaps does as well, if the offender does not reoffend). But VVH remains at its core victim centered.

The VVH Program

Victims' Voices Heard began in 2002 with Kim as its full-time coordinator/facilitator; a volunteer facilitator was added two years later. As of early 2008, fourteen cases have completed dialogues. Twelve of these cases have involved face-to-face meetings between victims and offenders in Delaware, one was a letter exchange only, and another was jointly facilitated with a RJ program in Pennsylvania. Since the program's inception, 320 people have contacted it for information, and forty-one victims have received intake services. Over twenty potential dialogue cases have been closed without a face-to-face dialogue because after interviews with victims or offenders, Kim determined that contact would be inappropriate. In these cases, victims were too angry to participate, or offenders might not have been willing to accept responsibility for the crime or to express remorse.[19]

Victims' Voices Heard is organized under the auspices of the Center for Community Justice, formed by People's Place II, Inc.[20] It is a severe-violence dialogue program offering victims the opportunity to speak directly to the person who has caused them harm. It is described in three pamphlets for potential participants and criminal justice professionals. The first explains the general goals and guidelines. Its mission statement is simple: "Victims' Voices Heard is committed to assisting all victims/survivors of crime close another chapter in the healing process. We advocate for all victims as they seek to find the answers that will enable them to feel empowered and move forward with their lives."

The initial rules presented in the pamphlet are clear: victims must request the dialogue; their request for a victim-offender dialogue does not guarantee that a dialogue will happen; and the face-to-face dialogue is a one-time event. A section labeled "What It Is!" explains that the program is an opportunity both for the victims to have access to a structure for their grieving and healing that allows them to ask questions and receive insight and for offenders to express remorse, admit guilt, and take responsibility for their actions. It also outlines the potential benefits, which include expressing anger and pain, learning new information about the crime, seeing remorse in the offender, and ultimately feeling more powerful and in control of one's life.

The pamphlet also explains that after the victim contacts VVH, the coordinator will contact the offender to determine if he or she is willing to participate in the dialogue program. A trained dialogue facilitator will then meet with the victim and the offender separately to decide if victim-offender dialogue is suitable for both parties. Once it has been determined that a victim-offender dialogue is appropriate, the victim and offender will meet in a safe and secure place within the correctional institution where the offender is incarcerated. The pamphlet also makes it clear that the program is not a retrial of the criminal case, a form of plea bargaining, or a place for victims to get revenge on the offender.

The second pamphlet focuses on the questions that victims/survivors frequently ask, such as why they would choose to participate in the program.

This pamphlet explains that, although all victims are different, many feel that they have not been given a voice through the justice system, and many feel the need to express their anger and pain and hear offenders express remorse for their crimes.

Finally, the third pamphlet is designed to answer questions typical of offenders, including why they would choose to participate. The pamphlet says that offenders choose to participate in the VVH program because they want to do something to help their victim, and it explains that taking responsibility and having remorse not only will help their victims but will also help them feel better about themselves. For greater detail on the specifics of the VVH program, see appendix C.

Kim feels strongly about the potential of the dialogue process to help offenders and the community. She writes about this on a restorative justice website (victimsvoicesheard.org), where she outlines the VVH program:

> Usually offenders are not forced to face up to their rationalizations and stereotypes. They are never made to assume full responsibility for their crime. Offenders need to understand the human consequences of their actions and be encouraged to make things right to the extent that it is possible to do so. Offenders should participate in finding ways that this can be done. That is real accountability.

In addition to completed dialogues, Kim provides a wide variety of services that have included arranging for a victim to be taken on a tour of a prison, obtaining pictures and other information about offenders and crime scenes, arranging for a victim to participate in a victims' impact panel, arranging meetings with the family members of offenders, coordinating contacts between state agencies and victims, and assisting with writing letters to offenders. Kim also notes any "affirmative agreements" reached and signed by victims and offenders after their face-to-face dialogues. These agreements are not legally binding, but they represent the hopes of both victims and offenders for the future.

The VVH program permits a *one-time only* meeting between the victim/survivor and the offender, recognizing that continued contact would not be beneficial to either the victim or the offender. In addition, the Department of Justice lifts the no-contact stipulation between the victim and the offender only for the time of the VVH process; once the dialogue is completed, the no-contact order is reinstated by the judge (and can be requested by other criminal justice officials, if needed), stipulating that the offender can have no further contact with the victim, the victim's family members, and anyone else the DOJ has requested the judge to include. Kim fully concurs with this regulation, believing that it offers the best protection against any unforeseen circumstances that could develop with continued contact between a victim and an offender.

The next chapter tells the story of Kim Book, the woman whose personal tragedy inspired the creation of VVH and who ably coordinates the program and works as its chief facilitator. I explore her path from grieving mother to victims' rights advocate and describe my own personal introduction to her and to the restorative justice program embodied in VVH, as well as the effect on my own university classroom when Kim and several of the program participants spoke to my students.

3

Getting Personal

The Power of Storytelling

One of the best parts of university teaching is when I get to witness students' epiphanies—those "Aha!" moments when something clicks in their mind or touches their heart, leading them to see the world in a different way. Since I routinely teach classes about child abuse, sexual assault, interpersonal violence, and other kinds of victimization, it is very easy for the students (and for me) to become overwhelmed. The social and cultural patterns and institutions that contribute to these problems, the consequences of crime for victims, and the fears it raises—particularly for women—very easily give rise to impotence and depression about the scale of change that would be necessary to end the violence. What I strive to find are rays of hope—programs or legal reforms or even inspiring case studies which convey to students that they can make a difference, though perhaps only one small step at a time.

Like the victims themselves, college or university students taking criminal justice or criminology courses do not hear a lot about the needs of victims or how they fit into the criminal justice process. The focus in both case solving and college classrooms is on offenders. Consequently, after a victim comes forward to tell the police that a crime has occurred, all efforts switch to apprehending, charging, prosecuting, convicting, and punishing the offender. Victims report being ignored, having their needs trivialized, and being blamed for contributing to or causing their victimization. They often see the criminal justice system as exacerbating their original harm through its standard operating procedures. Given the typical victim's experience, it is no wonder that reporting rates for crimes are low, particularly for those that involve sexual or interpersonal violence.[1]

The good news is that some of this is changing. Since the inception of the victim rights' movement in the 1960s, victims and their allies—including practitioners and politicians at the local, state, and federal levels—have worked hard to enact victim-friendly legislation and policies. More importantly, victim advocates have worked tirelessly for greater inclusivity and victim input into the criminal justice process. In the decades following the 1980s, when then-president Reagan appointed the first presidential task force to study victims' needs, much has been put in place to ensure that victims' voices are not sacrificed at the expense of upholding offenders' constitutional rights. Various legal reforms have been instituted that include victims in the process, such as laws permitting victims to explain to the court the extent of the financial, physical, and emotional losses they have incurred.

While most provictim policies and programs are well intended and necessary, their effects are uneven and incomplete. Policies overlap and conflict and vary dramatically across jurisdictions. This band-aid approach to solving social problems confuses my students, who frequently get stuck in feeling helpless as we discuss the sheer number of victims and the consequences of their victimizations on their daily lives and the lives of their loved ones. Thus, I try to create opportunities in the classroom for students to hear or read stories of victims' resiliency or to learn about successful programs to assist victims.

One such attempt involves a required assignment in my "Crime Victims and Victims' Rights" course. My students must conduct an interview with a victim/survivor or a victim advocate or a criminal justice or social service professional who works with victims. This assignment allows them to connect course themes and discussions with the real-life experiences and perceptions of people actually working on the same issues. In 2004, one of my students asked if she could invite her interviewee, Kim Book, the coordinator of a program that connected victims of severe violence with offenders, to speak to our class. This sounded interesting, so I emailed Kim to inquire about her program and ask whether she would come to campus to talk with my students. She readily agreed and asked me if I wanted her to speak about her daughter's murder or the program she ran. Without knowing anything more I said, "Both." Since that first visit to my classroom, Kim has returned several times to talk to my students, and on different occasions two of her program participants have come with her. Another victim/survivor who participated in VVH, Leigh, has visited my classroom twice on her own.

This chapter is about storytelling and the way people's personal experiences can change their lives. In the first part, I explore Kim's story in-depth and offer some highlights from the other guest speakers to describe the power of "the story." Kim's experiences as a mother of a murdered child and her difficulties with the criminal justice system moved her to tell her story to others; her story influenced her own career trajectory and current life's work in the process. In the course of her work, her story creates mutual under-standing and empathy for other victims who have experienced tragic losses. The second part of this chapter describes how hearing these intensely per-sonal stories interrupted and reshaped my students' prior understandings of their social worlds—how Kim and Leigh (and other guests) were catalysts for transforming some of their unexamined assumptions about victims and offenders.

Kim's Story

March 23, 1995, will be forever seared into Kim Book's memory. This is the day her only child, Nicole, was murdered, viciously stabbed by a sixteen-year-old young man she knew. Nicole was only seventeen years old, and Kim describes her as vibrant, compassionate, and often mischievous. Pictures of Nicole show dancing eyes and an impish grin.

Kim and Nicole's father, Jason, had divorced when Nicole was ten. As she matured, Nicole experienced fairly typical teenage troubles, experimenting with drugs[2] and rebelling against authority figures. Until she was fifteen, Nicole lived mostly with Kim and Kim's second husband, Ray, but they had clear behavioral expectations for Nicole that she found too difficult to follow, so she moved in with her father full-time. Nicole had been diagnosed with bipolar disorder as a teenager, but her behavior was well controlled by medi-cation. Like many people who take Lithium—the typical treatment—Nicole did not like feeling as though her emotions were dulled, and Kim struggled with Jason—who did not believe in the utility of psychological counseling or drugs—to get Nicole to take her medication and receive further mental health care.

Nicole dropped out of high school with her father's permission (although she later began attending night school). During the two years between the ages of fifteen and seventeen, Nicole and Kim remained close, frequently talking on the phone and spending time together. Kim believes that Nicole was secure in their relationship and knew that Kim loved her uncondition-ally, even if Kim did not agree with some of Nicole's life choices.[3]

The day of Nicole's murder, Kim and Nicole had talked on the phone, arranging to meet later that day, but as four o'clock came and went, and Kim got a funny feeling in her stomach that something was not quite right; it was not like Nicole not to show up. At 4:30 she received a phone call from Ray, who, according to Kim, "said we need to come down to the hospital because Nicole is there. And I said, 'What's wrong? What happened?' but Ray didn't know."

The hospital was only a few blocks away, yet the ride seemed interminably long. Kim felt a sense of doom. When they got to the hospital, Jason told Kim that his fiancée, Vicki, had found Nicole on the floor in a pool of blood and had called the police. The doctor then explained in a monotone voice that Nicole was in the operating room, that her heart was not beating when she was brought in, and that she had been stabbed in her carotid artery and in the heart. Kim asked if her daughter was dead and remembers thinking, "God, I don't know what's going on. I have no idea. But I know You know, and I'm just going to trust You on this."

Kim describes this as a pivotal moment for her, "a point of surrender because I was helpless and only God could help me through. I knew I couldn't do this on my own." At that point, the nurse picked up the phone and called the chaplain. Kim knew that the worst had happened, even though the words had not been said aloud. But she still needed desperately to hear the words. Another doctor finally came out to talk with them, and he just kept saying, "I am so sorry, I am really sorry." So with that, Kim knew.

In cases of severe crime and trauma such as Nicole's murder, it is common for a victim services worker to make contact with the family to act as a liaison with the criminal justice system. In this instance, Carole, the victim services contact, came to the hospital, introduced herself, and then stepped away. Kim appreciated that brevity—she wanted some space; she did not want to have to worry about meeting anyone else's needs or to accept consolation from even well-meaning people. She also did not wish to see her daughter; that was not the way that she wanted to remember Nicole. Thinking back, Kim says, "If I had seen her body, I don't think I would be where I am right now today." Kim and Ray went home and got busy with the difficult and draining tasks of making phone calls and handling funeral arrangements.

The next day, Kim urged Ray to go to work, knowing that she needed the solace of an empty house. Kim remembers feeling that she did not have the strength to take care of anyone but herself and could not worry about anyone else's feelings: "The first day is the worst. Your mind is trying to wrap itself around what happened." She sat at home all day long, listening to the phone ring and the more than fifty people who left condolences on the answering machine. Then Carole, the victim services contact, called and started to leave a message. This was the one call that Kim knew would provide information rather than raw emotion, so Kim picked up the phone. Carole told her that the police had caught Nicole's killer, a young man named LeVaughn, and that his capture—and a photo or live tape of him—was probably going to be on the six o'clock news. With a heavy heart, Kim turned on the television. And when she saw LeVaughn being put into a police car, angrily mouthing words to the camera, she thought to herself, "Why are *you* angry? You just killed my daughter, and you're mad. What are *you* mad about?! I'm the one who should be mad."

The next day, and for many days after that, Kim was barraged with many newspaper articles with pictures of Nicole, LeVaughn, and her house. Her voice cracks as she talks about how the articles kept repeating LeVaughn's statement that he turned Nicole over and saw that her eyes were still moving, so he "finished her off." Although Carole, who worked closely with Kim, was stymied in her attempts to get some of this information for her before the newspapers published it, the pain became even more unbearable as reporters continued to repeat these details as they followed the story. For weeks following the murder, Carole played an integral part in helping Kim obtain answers to some of her questions and was sympathetic to her emotional needs.

A week after Nicole's death, the district attorney called Kim to arrange a meeting to outline the case strategy. In particular, he wanted to determine how members of Kim's family felt about requesting the death penalty for LeVaughn, which is allowed in Delaware for first-degree murder. Although Jason, Vicki, and Ray all said they believed in the death penalty, Kim did not.

Kim says that being asked by the prosecutor about her view on the death penalty was initially a very satisfying moment. She finally felt as though something she said about the case processing of her daughter's murder *mattered* and would be taken into account. For a prosecutor to give a victim a voice in the process is profoundly empowering. Kim's sense of empowerment was short-lived, however. She found out a few weeks later that the prosecutor was moving ahead with a capital trial, ignoring her opposition to capital punishment. This information totally deflated her. Both Kim's initial feeling of empowerment at inclusion and her disillusionment and dismay when she found that her voice did not matter are common frustrations echoed by many victims. This silencing remains a sore point with her: "I told him how I felt, and I will always think to myself, 'Why did you ask if you are still going to try the case your way?'"

Kim's opposition to capital punishment is difficult for many people to understand. For most, the murder of a loved one stirs up a visceral reaction of rage, anguish, and vengeance. Kim explained her beliefs in a letter to the editor of the state newspaper a few years after Nicole's death:

Murder is murder. Taking a life cannot be justified. "Thou shalt not kill." If we say we abhor murder, how can we support the death penalty? Why can't society see that if we let those who murder turn us to murder, it gives more power to those who do evil? I could not change my beliefs because my daughter was murdered because to do so would give power to the one who killed her.

Until the trial a year later, Kim says she was in a fog, and she was having panic attacks which continued for two years. The one thing she does remember is her growing concern for LeVaughn's mother. She wondered how it was going to be for her to listen to everything in court and what it would be like to be in the courtroom with her: "I wanted LeVaughn's mother to know that I wasn't angry with her." Kim also started seeing a therapist, who helped to prepare her for the upcoming trial. Kim says she felt nothing toward LeVaughn, not anger, not vengeance. Meanwhile, the state moved forward with its plan to seek a capital murder conviction.

Sometime during the fall of 1995, Kim received a phone call requesting her presence at the prosecutor's office to hear some new details about the case. The D.A. had finally received the toxicology report on Nicole and wanted to tell Kim about it because LeVaughn's public defender would likely use it at the trial. The prosecutor told Kim that Nicole had a lethal dose of cocaine and speed in her system when she was killed, news that shook Kim to the core. Kim knew that Nicole drank alcohol to self-medicate, but she did not know that Nicole was doing drugs. The terrible irony is that this information ultimately proved to be incorrect. Ten years after Nicole's death, the lead detective in the case told Kim that Nicole had no more drugs in her system than someone who had been using occasionally. "Yet for ten years," Kim says, "I repeated the information from the prosecutor to other people, thinking, 'How could Nicole be so out there and we didn't know it?'"

The trial lasted a week. Kim asked the court to shield her from having to see the autopsy pictures, and the judge complied, having screens positioned so that her view was blocked. Kim had support people with her, but says it was still incredibly difficult to be there. This was particularly so when LeVaughn took the stand to testify, when the prosecutor played his taped confession of how he killed Nicole, and when the neighbor across the street testified about seeing LeVaughn as he raced out of the house and into Nicole's car to get away.

According to the defense's story presented at the trial, Nicole was living at her father's house when LeVaughn, who had been her classmate, came to the door. A butcher knife rested on the kitchen counter next to a chocolate cake that Jason's fiancée had baked, and with it, LeVaughn stabbed Nicole to death during an argument. Nicole's body lay on the floor. When Jason's fiancée came home and found Nicole, Nicole's pet Rottweiler was curled up against her side.

After LeVaughn stabbed Nicole, he panicked and ran out to Nicole's car but then came back into the house to get the tape in the answering machine. He had left a message earlier that day that included a poem about how much he loved Nicole, and he knew Nicole's father would recognize his voice. LeVaughn was terrified of Jason; they had once had a physical confrontation, and Jason had warned LeVaughn to stay away from Nicole. Jason was unimpressed by LeVaughn's character and behavior and also did not like that he was black and involved with his daughter. In LeVaughn's panicked state, he could not get the tape out of the machine. He threw the machine against the wall so hard that the force of the impact made a hole in the wall. He then fled in Nicole's car, with her blood splattered all over his T-shirt. He drove to Philadelphia, only to return the next day because he had no money. In fact, LeVaughn's inability to pay a turnpike toll was what led to his apprehension by the police, and after he was taken into custody, he broke down and admitted everything. One year later, LeVaughn was convicted of second-degree murder and sentenced to serve thirty-eight years in prison without the possibility of parole. The jury deliberated for eleven hours before returning its verdict, also finding him guilty of possession of a deadly weapon during a felony and theft.

Over time, LeVaughn's account of what happened went through many changes, and he later claimed that he ended up stabbing Nicole in the stomach by mistake instead of stabbing her pet Rottweiler, which had attacked him. At another point he claimed that a drug-running gang from Philadelphia was responsible, since Nicole owed them forty-three thousand dollars, but the jury did not believe these new versions.

After LeVaughn's conviction, a sentencing date was scheduled for the next week. The prosecutor told Nicole's family members that one person could make a victim impact statement that could be read at the sentencing hearing. They were warned against speaking to LeVaughn directly, and comments had to be directed to the judge and the court. Kim, who decided to make the statement herself, initially agreed to these rules, but things changed once Kim got into court. Kim was adamant about wanting to speak to LeVaughn directly: "The judge and the court did not kill Nicole; the young man sitting next to me killed her. Shouldn't I have the right to speak to him? Shouldn't he hear from me, since it was my life he had changed?"[4]

When Kim was called to the front of the courtroom to deliver her victim impact statement, she says that something shifted in LeVaughn's tough-guy demeanor. Kim ignored the prosecutor's and judge's instructions not to address him:

> I told him that he changed my life forever, and every day I am going to think about him and what he did. I told him I wanted good things for him and that he had become part of my life forever. I didn't say the words "I forgive you," but he knew that's where I was going with this and that I wasn't trying to throw anger at him, and he just started smiling at me. He looked at me in disbelief as if he could not believe I was saying that to him.

Kim told him that when she thinks of her daughter, she is forced to think of him: "But I will not let your anger become a part of me."[5] Kim also told the judge that her compassion for LeVaughn "does not excuse the fact that LeVaughn killed Nicole": "I expect this court to hold him accountable."[6] Kim remembers leaving the courtroom afterward, walking outside into the sunshine, and feeling a sense of relief that it was over. "As soon as I was walking down the street, I thought, 'I have forgiven this kid. Now I need to move on.'"

That Kim could find it in her heart to forgive her daughter's killer astonishes many people. Yet she is emphatic about the need to forgive in order to move on without letting the anger take over. In a way, she believes forgiveness affirms the needs of those left behind in their grief. She is clear that forgiving does not mean forgetting. Several weeks after Nicole's death, in a letter to the editor of the local paper, Kim wrote, "I'm not bitter or angry about what has happened to my daughter, for I know that anger serves only one purpose—to destroy the person who has it."[7]

About a month after LeVaughn's sentencing, Kim called Carole with what even she described as a "crazy" request. Kim realized that she needed to see the prison where Nicole's murderer was incarcerated. In order to close that chapter—the one in which thoughts of "where is he?" kept gnawing away at her—Kim needed to physically see the place he was being held. To Carole's credit, she told Kim that she was *not* crazy and that she would do whatever she could to make this happen. Carole made a flurry of phone calls to the Department of Corrections, the Department of Justice, victim services personnel—anyone who she thought could be helpful. Carole had no success; most of those whom she contacted thought that Kim must still be angry and wanted to yell at LeVaughn or satisfy herself that he was being punished. Carole understood, however, that Kim's request was about filling in an empty spot with information so she could move on. Finally, after about nine months, Carole called the then state attorney general in Delaware, Jane Brady. During her years as the attorney general, Brady had become a strong supporter of victims' rights. She recognized the salience of Kim's request, contacted the commissioner of corrections, Stan Taylor, and arranged a tour for Kim.

Both Jane Brady and Stan Taylor, along with the then deputy warden of the institution, Michael Deloy (now the warden), accompanied Kim, showing her the compound, the building where LeVaughn was housed, the cell on the floor below his cell, the visiting room, the chow hall, and the chapel. As in most prisons, inmates were everywhere, yet Kim says she felt neither fear nor intimidation; she was at ease, calm, and relaxed. At the end of the visit, Kim thanked Brady, Taylor, and Deloy for their efforts, telling them that she had forgiven LeVaughn and wanted good things to happen at the prison so he could turn his life around. Tears glimmered in Taylor's and Brady's eyes, and they thanked Kim. Kim also said that she had a feeling, one that foreshadowed her work years later, that one day she would be back at the institution doing something constructive.

Kim returned home, relieved to close that chapter and to be able to picture what prison life was like for LeVaughn. Brady and Taylor always remembered Kim, and when she turned to them for help with getting the VVH program started, they helped make it possible. They knew Kim and trusted her because of their earlier intense connection at the prison, and they took a chance on her program despite the fact that Kim was not a correctional or Justice Department employee. It was Brady who ultimately facilitated the lifting of no-contact orders during the VVH process, and Taylor gave Kim unfettered access to the correctional institutions in the state. Today, Kim maintains that if it were not for their support and belief in her and the program's potential, VVH would not exist.

In a guest opinion spot in the local newspaper two years after Nicole's death, Kim explained her feelings in greater depth. She said that her faith as a Christian helped her to forgive and also to become closer to God through forgiveness: "Forgiving LeVaughn has set me free. When we forgive someone, it ends. It puts a stop to the anger we feel. It's over. We are then free to live our lives in peace."[8] Kim says her message to victims about forgiveness does not focus solely on religion. Rather, she says she has found that in forgiving her daughter's murderer, he no longer has the power to hurt her, even if he "messes up" in prison (or in his life). Kim also believes that offenders need to forgive themselves so they can "find inner peace and embrace more productive lives."[9]

Kim speculates that much of her way of relating to people "where they are" reflects the way that she was raised, particularly the value her father placed on being nonjudgmental. Her parents had what she describes as a wonderful, long marriage. Her father was a respected and well-loved Methodist minister. He was diagnosed with AIDS in 1990 and died a horrible death nine months later. It was at this point that his secret was revealed: he had lived a life as a gay man while at the same time being married and raising Kim and her older brother. Kim and her mother stood by her father, nursing him to the end. Their love for him never wavered. As Kim says, "I think I learned a lot about forgiveness through all that, because my mother just was so supportive of my father."[10] Kim feels strongly that judging what people do in their lives is something between a person and his or her God. She tells offenders, "I'm not here to judge you and to say what you did was terrible. I'm here to see if you want to meet with your victim and take responsibility. If you can do that, I will help you in whatever way I can."

Ironically, although Kim now facilitates face-to-face dialogues between victims of severe violence and their offenders, she has never talked to LeVaughn except for her few words at the sentencing hearing. Kim thinks that LeVaughn might one day want to reach out to her if he were ready to talk, particularly since he knows that she forgave him. He is forbidden to do so, however, because of the no-contact order imposed by the court, which stipulates that offenders cannot contact victims. But Kim realizes that often situations can change, and she has no way of knowing if LeVaughn still refuses to take responsibility for Nicole's murder. In 2005, a volunteer facilitator from Kim's program met with LeVaughn in prison. He still denies the crime and is eager to meet with Kim to convince her that he did not do it. He told the facilitator the following: "Nicole was a really, really sweet person, and that's probably why she got killed, because she was always doing good things for everyone." Although Kim is disappointed, she also believes that understanding how she feels about his refusal to take responsibility gives her empathy when she meets with other victims who want to meet with their offenders but whose offenders deny the crime. Kim can relate to victims' frustration and disappointment. Kim intends to try again to reach out to LeVaughn in another five years or so.

The Path to Victims' Voices Heard

Today, more than a decade after Nicole's murder, Kim is an energetic and effective victims' advocate. Her life's work is a testament to honoring Nicole and exemplifies Kim's refusal to let this tragedy paralyze her. The first thing you notice upon entering Kim Book's office is a large sign that exclaims,

"CHOOSE JOY." This sign captures Kim's philosophy perfectly. The other frames adorning her walls hold citations such as the 2001 Governor's Outstanding Volunteer Award, the 2002 Prison Fellowship Ministries Appreciation Award, and the 2005 Delaware Victim Rights' Task Force Outstanding Professional Award. There are photographs of her daughter, Nicole, and other family members and friends and a pile of copies of Howard Zehr's *The Little Book of Restorative Justice*. The room is bright and cheerful, with posters of flowers and water scenes. The atmosphere is soothing, a perfect environment in which to meet with program participants. It is easy to forget that as the mother of a murdered daughter, she is herself a survivor of a violent crime. Yet she does not see herself as a victim. She is a tenacious strategizer and an intense listener, and she never avoids eye contact. She brings all this to bear as the coordinator of Victims' Voices Heard.

Shortly after LeVaughn's sentencing, Kim's dissatisfaction with the justice system led her to accept an invitation to participate in a Prison Fellowship ministry, and during one of the Bible studies, an offender incarcerated for killing his girlfriend came up to Kim and said that he really wished he could tell the family of his victim how sorry he was for what he did. Kim believed in his sincerity but knew that offenders had no opportunity to relay such messages to their victims or their victims' families. She believed that offenders who felt the way this man did could really be accountable and play a part in victims' healing. In fact, she credits this experience as "setting off a light bulb" in her head that would later develop into the VVH program.

About a year later, Carole, Kim's original victim services contact, called her to ask if she would be interested in going into prison to talk with a long-term offender, which led to her giving regular talks to inmates around the state. This experience invigorated Kim's desire to help victims more directly and cemented her realization that victims and offenders are inextricably connected and can learn from one another. She went through mediation training in 1998 and became a volunteer mediator for the Center for Community Justice, handling cases involving minor offenses. It was gratifying for her to try to bring people to the table who were angry and had very different perspectives in order to iron out a workable and healing solution for all involved. Then one night Kim happened to catch a *60 Minutes* segment that focused on a severe-violence mediation program in Texas. Kim was spellbound watching a meeting between a woman and the man who stabbed her daughter to death. Rather than focusing on the pain she shared with this mother, she asked aloud, "Why can't we do this kind of mediation in our state?" She presented this idea to her supervisor, who encouraged Kim to research the programs in Texas, Ohio, and Minnesota. In turn, her supervisor promised to write a grant proposal to try such a program in Delaware. Kim did the legwork, and they applied for and received a national grant through VOCA (Victims of Crime Act) funding. Kim read Howard Zehr's book *Changing Lenses,* which she said was very significant for her. Kim trained at out-of-state institutes, including the Restorative Justice Peacemaking Institute in Minnesota, to be a mediator for victims of severe violence who wished to meet with their offenders, and in 2000 she participated in training for dialogue facilitation of severe violence cases conducted by well-known restorative justice scholar/practitioner Mark Umbreit. The coordinator of the model victim-offender dialogue program in Texas, David Doefler, sent Kim that program's design (including worksheets and exercises for victim and offender sessions).[11] By 2002, Kim had launched Victims' Voices Heard. Today, the program falls under the auspices of the Administrative Office of the Courts in Delaware.

Kim feels that when she left the sentencing courtroom on that sunny day more than a decade ago, she became achingly aware that the state "could do more for victims of crime and also to hold offenders accountable in a way that teaches them not to reoffend, to understand the full consequences of their actions."[12] Kim also feels strongly that victims need to express their feelings, despite the reactions they may receive from well-meaning others. She maintains, both for herself and also for *all* victims, that she is not there to judge either them or their feelings, an approach that came out clearly in the interviews I conducted with victims. They insisted that Kim was the only one who did not ask them, "Why aren't you over this yet?" or "How can you still be carrying this around?" Today, when Kim talks about the work she does, she understands it in this way: "I can do this kind of work because I listen with my heart and not my head. When I talk to my clients, I try to hear what they are saying. That is what keeps me from judging offenders, and it helps me find out what victims are really looking for in the process—where the healing needs to take place."

Kim's and Victims'/Survivors' Presentation to My Students

In Kim's first visit to my university classroom, she presented an abbreviated version of her story. She focused more on the dialogue process between victims and offenders and how this use of restorative justice principles could help heal and empower victims and even aid in the rehabilitation of offenders. The feedback I received from the students was tremendous—they talked about the program for weeks afterward. During the following semesters, I invited Kim to my class again, and she began bringing program participants with her who wanted to share their experiences. Donna, a woman raped by a stranger who broke into her home, talked to my class about that awful night, and she captivated my students with her eloquent and inspirational speech (see chapter 4). Another program participant, also a woman raped by a stranger, visited my class during a different semester.

During Kim and Donna's joint presentation, my students were spellbound—appalled at the sadistic violence they heard about, curious about how these women found the courage to move on with their lives, and unsure how they felt about a program that seemed antithetical to much of the current social policy surrounding crime. My students are not that different from most college and university students these days: they have been raised on "get tough" policies, and many embrace "three strikes, you're out" crime-control philosophy without questioning its consequences.[13] Although a few struggle with issues such as the death penalty, most justify such a punishment on grounds such as retribution or efficacy arguments of economics or deterrence, regardless of empirical evidence to the contrary. The stories from participants in the VVH program challenged my students' perceptions that all victims are out for offenders' blood or that all victims are unable to move beyond the injuries and harm they experience. They were flabbergasted and outraged that for all the popular rhetoric about the importance of victims' rights, many victims receive very little information about the crimes committed against them and are allowed minimal participation in their cases as they weave their way through the criminal justice system. Two of my female students and one male student had tears in their eyes during the presentation.

After class ended, several students came up to me to thank me for inviting Kim and Donna into our classroom. I also received a handful of emails. The students wanted to know more about the victims in the program—they felt somehow connected to Donna, who had, as one student put it, given them a gift by trusting enough to share such an intimate experience with total strangers. In particular, they wanted to be sure that Donna had supportive people surrounding her as she moved closer to the face-to-face meeting with her offender. Their concern was not paternalistic—they felt Donna was strong and ready—but the presentation had touched them deeply. My class kept asking me about VVH, Kim, and Donna. I asked if they wanted to write anything to Donna, and promised I would mail their notes to her. I was proud of my students' compassion and thought their notes to Donna would be meaningful to her.

My students' earnest wish to thank our guest speakers and wish them well in their lives surfaced every semester that Kim or other VVH victims/survivors came to talk with my classes. The general tenor of the students' messages after these presentations reflected their respect for the victims' courage, not only in facing the lingering demons that affected their daily lives but also in their willingness to share their experiences. Some students offered prayers to a victim who talked about her faith, and still others offered advice, no doubt reacting to some of the guest speakers' words of doubt and fear—speaking about such a private experience in public or wondering who they should tell about their life-changing events.

Excerpts from my students' notes over the semesters to the victims/survivors demonstrate these feelings clearly. One of the strongest themes in the student letters is inspiration: "Your story reminded me that victims can be strong and persevere even under horrible conditions, and I thank you for bringing that to mind. I'm touched and honored to have been among a group of strangers with whom you shared your story." Other students told the women how their stories forced them to reexamine some of their own past assumptions about offenders: "The way you dealt with your situation made me look at offenders in a different way. . . . It was very powerful to hear that you had the strength to forgive the offender and still keep in contact with him."

Contrary to the women's concerns about how the male students in the class would respond to their victimizations, it was clear that the men could now better understand how women feel about being victimized. Those who planned careers in law enforcement felt that this understanding could translate into practical knowledge about what victims might want from them. One student wrote, "I plan on becoming a police officer, and hearing of your pain can only make me a better person and policeman. Thanks." Ultimately, the letters spoke to the women's courage to endure and to confront their lingering fears, anger, and other issues; many of my students expressed a connection they felt to the women's experiences and how it touched their own lives.

When Leigh, a mother whose nineteen-year-old son was killed in a drunk-driving crash (see chapter 9), came to talk to my class about her experience with VVH, her story resonated just as strongly as had the rape survivors' experiences. My students wrote, "I called my mom immediately and told her how much I loved her and that I would *never* drink and drive" and "Your words will continue to speak louder than any individuals that choose to yell at me or call me names because I've decided not to serve them [in the bar I work at]. For this, I thank you." The storytelling by Kim, Donna,

Leigh, and others was compelling and moved my students out of their comfort zones to really think about justice issues related to victims and offenders.

The next nine chapters tell the stories of each pair of victim and offender (to the extent that both were available and willing). Using interviews conducted separately with the victim and offender, interviews with Kim, and VVH case material including the viewing of videotaped dialogues, I relate their experiences and explore the details of their participation in the dialogue process. For most of the participants, the face-to-face meeting was the most important part of the VVH program. Their experiences of these dialogues were inevitably powerful and, for many, life changing.

Victim and Offender Stories

Donna and Jamel

Living in Different Prisons

Facts of case: In 1996, while on probation from a juvenile facility, seventeen-year-old Jamel forced his way into Donna's home with the intent to commit burglary. He assaulted and raped Donna, who was forty-nine years old. Jamel was caught quickly, and he confessed. He was initially charged with kidnapping, unlawful sexual intercourse, robbery, burglary, assault, and criminal mischief; he pled guilty and received a twenty-three-year sentence. Ten years after the rape, Jamel and Donna met through VVH while he was still incarcerated. This chapter reflects my interviews with Donna and Jamel, access to their case file and letters they exchanged, interviews with Kim, and the videotape of the dialogue.

After years of trailer living and saving money for a house, Donna and her husband, John, finally found a house they felt they could afford and in which they could be happy for years to come. It was a "handyman's special," as Donna called it, but their imagination had helped them look past the narrow windows, the tiny rooms, and the yard full of rubbish and weeds to the potential that the house could become their home. Donna loved the big front porch, which soon became a place to sit and sip iced tea, to yell out to passersby and neighbors, and just to relax after a hard day of working on the house. Donna and John tore down walls and replaced all the windows, ensuring that sunlight would flood into the rooms. Donna loved sunny days and the outdoors. Her garden was a source of joy, as Donna slowly turned the neglected yard into a cozy patch of grass and flowers. They spent a lot of time perfecting a rose garden, tending to it daily. Both Donna and her husband had jobs: Donna worked in the afternoons and evenings at a local bowling alley, and John was a long-distance trucker, so Donna and her dog were often alone at night while he was out on long hauls. This did not concern Donna, since the house had an alarm system and they lived two blocks from the police station.

Before moving to Delaware, Donna and John lived for many years in Massachusetts and raised her only son from a previous marriage. In 2006, when I interviewed Donna, she was fifty-eight years old; she is a tiny, petite woman, with very long gray hair, eyeglasses, a contagious laugh, and lots of spunk. Before the rape, Donna says she was an exceptionally trusting person; she is less so today. Donna and John were active foster parents when they lived in Massachusetts, and she believes children are essentially good: "We used to take in foster kids when we lived in Massachusetts; these were children that went through the Department of Youth Services, so they were kids that had been in trouble. . . . I had no fear then. I trusted people."

This belief in finding the best in people remained strong through the years. With John away driving his truck for days at a time, Donna's job ended each night with her driving home in the dark to an empty house. The evening of the rape, Donna had gone to Wal-Mart to purchase the Holiday Barbie for her granddaughter for Christmas. This was a tradition; she started to look for the coveted doll every year in the early fall. It was October, with a chill in the air, and close to midnight. Donna unwound after her long day at work by watching a little TV. She was half asleep on her husband's recliner when she heard a knock at the door. The knock was not unusual—despite the late hour—because her husband often arrived home at odd hours and rapped lightly on the door before coming in. Usually their dog stayed inside the house, but on this night, of all nights, he was outside.

When Donna heard the knock, she "didn't think anything of it":

I answered the door, and this boy is standing there, and I still wasn't afraid. He just said, "Does so-and-so live here?" and I'm like, "No, you have the wrong house." I went to shut the door, and he grabbed the door. He grabbed the door and me that quick. . . . I couldn't really say what he looked like because I didn't have my glasses on; it was dark in the house [except for the light the TV gave off]. He had gloves and a heavy coat on.

The man did not have a weapon, but after forcing his way in with his hands around Donna's neck, he roughly knocked her down and pulled off her pants. He moved so quickly that Donna had no time to react. As he began to attack and sexually assault her, Donna believed she was going to die:

How I got away from him was, I have asthma and emphysema, and I started gasping, and I said, "I can't breathe." . . . I don't know what he was thinking, but I said, "I need water," and this request briefly took his attention. And I told him, "The bathroom is right there." He hesitated for a minute, and I knew I needed him to take only a second to get his hands off of me, because I knew how much distance I had to my front door. And that's all it took.

Donna seized that second of opportunity, ran out the door, and jumped off the porch. He ran out and went the other direction. Then, although she was terrified and afraid he was going to come back, Donna could not bring herself to show up at her neighbor's door "butt-naked":

Instead, I ran in the house and covered up and dialed 911. But I slammed the door shut and locked it first. . . . I knew I had to get away from him, because I thought if I didn't, I could die. I really didn't know what his plan was; I knew what he was doing to me and trying to do, but I didn't know how I could end up. I mean, this guy was, you know, way bigger than me, 'cause I'm small, and he was way taller than me.

Fear, coupled with the unknown, is the worst, "because you don't know what's going to happen": "The thought that entered my mind is that I'm going to die in here. You know, and I can't do that. I have too much to live for, too many people." Donna believes that that by asking her attacker for water, somehow it touched some humanity deep inside him. "We found out afterwards that someone in his family was asthmatic. . . . And so, I said the right thing."

Donna's experiences with the police, the prosecutors, and the hospital where she was examined and underwent a rape evidence-collection kit were very positive: "Everyone made me feel really great. Even the police treated me like I was their mother or their grandmother. Nobody ever looked down at me." Consistent with research findings, the supportive nature of the criminal justice response could reflect the facts of the rape: a young African American male stranger had raped an older white woman who was a stranger to him.[1] The police worked quickly and responded to the crime very seriously; helicopters searched the area almost immediately. The rapist, Jamel, was caught quickly and confessed. His confession revealed that his plan was to randomly knock on doors until he found a woman living alone and then to rob and hurt her; Donna's house had been the first one he tried. The chief prosecutor kept Donna informed about the case. She was willing to testify at the trial but was concerned that she would be unable to positively identify her attacker, as it was dark at the time and she was not wearing her glasses. In the end, there was no need for her testimony since Jamel pled guilty. Donna later found out that he was seventeen years old at the time. He received a sentence of twenty-three years. He will be in his midthirties when he is released after serving about seventeen of the twenty-three years of his original sentence.

The Aftermath

Donna continues to be disappointed by her neighbors' reluctance to get involved that night, even though two of her neighbors heard her screams. The family across the street just chose not to get involved, but the couple next door struggled about what to do. They were new to the neighborhood and thought perhaps the screams they heard were part of a private quarrel in which they should not get involved. They were horrified to find out what had really transpired, and the wife avoided Donna for a long time afterward. Donna finally confronted her: "The only thing I told her was that I wasn't mad at her, but she had to promise me that the next time she hears anyone screaming, she'll get involved."

Donna's husband had a very hard time dealing with what happened; when she told him, she says it was the first time she had seen him cry. John felt that he had let her down by not being there and not protecting her. Donna reassured him, understanding his anger and even finding some humor in his punching a hole in one of their walls—at least it was not one of the walls they had replaced. "But he took it bad. He wanted to quit work 'cause he felt that if he had been there, it wouldn't have happened."

Following the rape, Donna tried counseling but felt that the experience offered her just a "band-aid" and never helped her much. Several things troubled her on a daily basis, to the point where, as she describes it, she was living in a prison herself. For instance, a casual acquaintance wondered aloud why Donna answered the knock at the door at such a late hour. When she heard this, she says, "it just spiraled me right down to 'oh my God, it is my fault.' It took a long time to undo that statement." Another well-meaning person casually said, "Well, I would have fought my hardest to prevent being raped." This comment led Donna to question her own behavior in response to the rape: "I felt as though I didn't fight hard enough." These feelings of guilt followed Donna for years, despite her positive experience with the criminal justice system. Another acquaintance wondered aloud if Donna thought Jamel had been stalking her (one of the officers who responded the night of the rape also speculated about this possibility) and if he would try to find her after he got out. This thought terrified and haunted Donna.

For the initial four years or so after the rape, Donna appeared to be handling things well. But inside, she was not well at all. Donna has never been able to add another Holiday Barbie to her granddaughter's collection—somehow, the rape was all wrapped up into that package: "Even though everyone thought I was doing really well emotionally, they didn't see what I had shut down. So I was in prison as much as he was, only mine didn't have bars." Donna and John's home remodeling projects came to a stop; they found that their hearts just were not in it.

In the horrible period of years following the rape, Donna's everyday fears were magnified, and her sense of autonomy was destroyed, limiting where she wanted to go and when she wanted to go. "I didn't know who I was afraid of, and it was like when you are a child and you were afraid of the bogeyman: you don't know who it is—snakes under the bed, the bogeyman in the closet, whatever. Well, that was me." One counselor she saw wanted to give her medication to dull the ache, but Donna was not willing to erase what happened or to lose even more control over her life. Donna felt like she was just treading water. Self-doubt, fear, and emotional paralysis were daily companions.

A Life-Changing Public Service Announcement

One night in the fall of 2003, Donna was watching television, and a public service announcement flashed on the screen. A woman named Kim Book was talking about a new program called Victims' Voices Heard for victims/survivors of severe violence who wanted to meet with their incarcerated offenders. Donna called Kim the same day. The idea of meeting with Jamel immediately appealed to Donna: "That's something I wanted to do because I need to know some answers." After Donna called Kim, Kim approached Jamel, who was immediately receptive. Kim ultimately believed that Jamel genuinely wanted to do whatever he could to help Donna heal.

Donna entered the program with a lot of questions that she wanted Jamel to answer. In particular, she wanted to know "Why? Why me? What did I do?" She understood that he would also be going through six months of preparation before they would meet face to face. Donna admits, however, that apart from her closest family members, no one understood why she would want to meet her offender and talk to him. Even John and her sister were not completely sure this undertaking was a good idea, but they believed in Donna and became supportive. In my conversations with Donna, she repeatedly emphasized the important role that her sister, son, husband, and brother-in-law played in keeping her feeling as safe as they could.[2]

As part of the VVH preparation process, both victims and offenders spend enormous amounts of time with Kim, exploring their most private feelings with her over six months. This emotional intensity is difficult for all parties, yet it is the cornerstone of the transformative process. Donna considers Kim to be her friend, someone who really cares, or, as Donna succinctly puts it, "She's got such a light to her that you just don't see that often." Although Kim is very religious and Donna respects Kim's faith, Donna says she did not feel any need to embrace religiosity in the same way. Donna believes that a victim's having faith or having an absence of faith does not affect the potential for success with VVH. As Donna said, "Kim doesn't try to push her beliefs on me."

Donna has compassion for Jamel, but she does not confuse this with relieving him of responsibility. "I don't feel sorry for him. He did it to himself. I mean, I didn't ask for my life to be altered. I can't be as forgiving as some people, but I can forgive him to the point for showing me that he understands the wrong of what he did." She believes that inmates must recognize and understand why they are locked up and not just spend their time in prison programs: "I don't like the idea that we sent someone to prison, and they are going to get a college education. . . . No, I don't think that's fair. I highly object. Nobody gave me a free ride because I was a victim."

Achieving Empowerment through VVH

Getting information and answers to questions from the offender himself proved to be the key for Donna. Besides the self-blame she experienced after her friends' questions, Donna had other questions about the crime. She desperately wanted to find out information beyond the cursory information contained in police reports; the answers could only come from the rapist. Donna wanted to know if she had fought back, and she wanted to know if he had known her at all and had been stalking her. She feared that she and her husband would have to sell their house and move before Jamel was released from prison, so that he would not be able to find her again. Prior to her involvement with VVH, Donna intended to be present at every single parole hearing to voice her opposition to Jamel's release. She was terrified of him and worried that he could be released and she would never know. But today she "wouldn't stop him from getting released." Donna is very relieved about this change, at least in part because she can now stay in her renovated home. It now surprises Donna when well-meaning people ask why she did not move: "Move where? How do you know who is living next door to you?

Sex offenders aren't the ugly, scary, snaggle-toothed people you teach your kids to be afraid of; they are people that look like you and me."

Even before she met with Jamel, simply learning the details of the incident, especially those she had blocked from her memory, really helped Donna to feel empowered. For instance, Kim told her that Jamel said she had fought very hard. This led Donna to realize, "Yeah, I did. I mean, I kicked over a huge coffee table. . . . I found out, when I looked back, yes, I did. I fought as much as I could fight, considering my size. I'm proud of myself now, whereas before, I was just terrified." Kim was also able to obtain a photograph of Jamel, something that was very important to Donna because she wanted to put a "face to her fear." The offhand remark made that night by one of the responding police officers, that Jamel must have been stalking her, also continued to trouble her. Kim was able to ask the police and discovered that Jamel had not been stalking her, that the attack was random. The sheer relief of getting this information was key to Donna's regaining strength, extinguishing fear, and feeling more empowered. Most scholars of rape understand the act to be mostly about power and control and less about sex; the victim is often a symbolic target of the offender's anger. Donna understood more about this as time went on; she had never understood why a seventeen-year-old boy had raped a fifty-year-old woman. "I thought, 'Oh my god, do I look like someone that a young kid would want to bother? There are all those young girls out there to date. Why rape me?'"

Donna and Jamel did not have their face-to-face meeting until fall 2006. At the time of my interviews with them, they had exchanged letters, and Jamel had also written individual letters of apology to Donna, her husband, and her family. During the preparation process for a dialogue, participants work on a series of exercises designed to get them thinking about their feelings and emotions and to answer questions about various aspects of their lives before and after the crime. Most offenders never hear about the impact of their actions on their victims, or at the very most they might learn about the impact during the sentencing phase if the victim/survivor contributes to a victim impact statement. Through Donna and Jamel's letter exchange, Donna was able to tell Jamel about all the daily and long-term consequences of that night. In the first letter Jamel ever wrote to Donna, called his "letter of apology," he apologized for the pain and suffering he caused Donna. He also wrote about what he said he truly understood: "The crime I committed against you absolutely devastated your life and also the people who love you the most, your family. Mrs. Brenner, I do not want you thinking that you did something to provoke the sexual assault from me." He expressed his deep regret and enormous guilt and said that he was using his time in prison constructively: "You will not ever have to worry about me ever hurting you again in any way! When I write this I mean it with every fiber of my being, the amount of guilt I feel is enormous, this is something I never want to feel or put someone thr[ough] again in my life."

Donna's reaction when she first read Jamel's letter of apology is not surprising: "I kind of took a 'we will see' stand. Of course, I wanted to believe him, and part of me relaxed some by what he wrote, but the 'on guard' part of me still wanted to hold judgment till I talked to him." Since receiving the letter of apology, Donna has had many months to process her feelings and has also exchanged more letters and has received the answers she needed from Jamel. For Donna, the key to reclaiming herself is simply her belief: "He no longer controls my life."

Race and Punishment

Interestingly, despite over three hours of deep conversation that Donna and I had, I was not aware that Donna's rapist was African American until Donna mentioned this in the final half hour of our talk. His race simply was not something that influenced her feelings about the crime. However, Donna confided that her husband's reactions were a little more complicated. John had a hard time reconciling his feelings about the offender's race because it was a rape: "But I really think that it becomes a point whether it was red, yellow, black, or whatever. I think the race plays into it second, and the first, the action plays into it. If he had been a long-haired hippie, John would've been pissed off at all long-haired hippies. So it only came into play because you give it a visual."

It is well established by legal scholars that offenders in cases involving stranger rape receive much harsher penalties than those in nonstranger rape. In addition, it is also well documented that the most draconian penalties are reserved for interracial rape, particularly when the victim is white and the offender is a person of color. The fact that Donna is white and was a victim of a stranger rape by an African American male could easily explain the very long sentence imposed in this case. In addition, she was a stable member of the community, owned a home, and was attacked in her home by an angry youth who had been in and out of juvenile institutions throughout his young life. His prior record also played a role in the sentencing.[3]

Two weeks before Donna and Jamel were supposed to finally meet face to face in 2004, Jamel got into trouble in prison. Another inmate challenged him, and an altercation ensued. He was placed in lockdown and was in twenty-four-hour custody. But he remained totally committed to meeting Donna and finishing the dialogue-preparation process. Kim believes "he sabotaged the meeting by acting out because he got scared." When Kim went to talk to him during this time, officers brought him down the hall in an orange jumpsuit, shackled hands and feet, head down. Kim recalls, "He came inside and sat on the stool. And I had never seen this child cry, and he sat right down and cried because he was down in the hole for the first fifteen days. . . . I said, 'Jamel, I am not giving up on you. You can do this. I know you can.'"

When Donna heard that Jamel was sent to lockdown, she was disappointed and sad but not angry. It did not change her desire to meet face to face with him. She asked Kim to tell him to "straighten up" for her and hoped that he would realize that this time he had responded in a different and more mature way than he had in the past when he let people down; this time he faced Kim (and by proxy, Donna), and he admitted that what he did was wrong. Donna emailed Kim a letter to give to Jamel following his disciplinary infraction, telling him that she was disappointed about what happened but encouraging him to respect others and also himself. She told him, "Treat life like you want life to treat you. And please stay out of trouble, because every step you slide back, you take us with you."

Donna also believed that no one in Jamel's family had taught him to like himself, and when they were emotionally abusive or absent, he learned not to depend on them. She hoped that his time in lockdown might make him realize that some people will not give up on him and that he should not abandon his efforts to change his life. Hearing Donna talk about this situation and reading her letter to Jamel struck me deeply. The way that Donna responded to Jamel's backsliding—with understanding and empathy—provides the clearest illustration of how far she has come in her own healing. Ultimately, Donna concluded, "I've been really lucky. If you can make a little bit of light out of any kind of tragedy, it's all good. It happened, but it only made me stronger; it didn't kill me." In a VVH newsletter from March 2006, Donna wrote, "You are only a victim as long as you choose to stay a victim. Gather strength from this and you will grow from it. Please don't stay a victim as long as I did."

Donna believes that VVH has been a life-changing experience for her: "I've become a new person. I'm not saying I'll ever have the trust back that I did, because I don't think you ever do. . . . But, as far as anything else, I'm a lot happier. I'm a lot more at ease. I can sit out on my porch now, even at nighttime."

Donna's porch sitting symbolizes the new claim on her life and happiness. For years before the rape, her favorite activity at dusk was sitting on the porch, conversing with all her neighbors. "It ended that day. I never went out again. But, now, I go outside, and I'm getting reacquainted with the neighbors."

Donna hopes that sharing her experience with other rape victims can be healing for them. One of her most inspiring transformations—one that will no doubt have particular resonance for other rape survivors—is Donna's complete disavowal of shame related to the rape. Most rape victims internalize a lot of self-blame, often reinforced through victim blaming by others. But Donna refuses to accept any responsibility for the rape. She does not hesitate to discuss the rape and its aftermath fully and feels no qualms about using her own name in connection with these descriptions. She integrates this experience into the story of her life with no apologies: "It's just who I am, you know?" Donna has a keen sense of the damage that rape victims get from social messages. And though she herself had a very positive experience with the criminal justice system—the police and prosecutor respected and believed her—she can only imagine how much worse it is for victims without that level of institutional support.[4]

Donna also talks frankly to her granddaughter about her own experience as well as about the dangers of online sexual predators. In these conversations she reinforces the message that victims are not to blame for anything that happens to them—talking about victimization defeats the shame that victims feel in our victim-blaming and rape-tolerant culture. From her granddaughter's responses to her counsel, Donna says, "I think she's become a little more savvy because of what I've been through."

For the first time in her life, Donna now ventures into youth detention centers to talk to young men about the consequences of their crimes. The juveniles often do not care, she says, because, as with the "boy who raped me—he had been through all the systems, all the juvenile facilities—they don't stop to think of the repercussions of it." Most of all, Donna is worried that juvenile delinquents do not see victims as real flesh-and-blood people whose lives are greatly affected by their callous actions. "They don't see what if their mother or their sister or their grandmother were the victims." This service to the community is similar to her much earlier experiences as a foster parent to kids in trouble, and she feels rejuvenated by the opportunity to help others again: "I enjoy life now. Even though I can't get back life as I had it before, now I have a focus for other things, for helping other people."

Donna is still affected today by the rape—the damage to her health from long-term stress was done, and there is no getting that back. Her attitude about her poor health, however, is amazingly resilient: "Thinking back on the rape, I think, 'I could've died.' . . . I'm just happy to be here. You just take what life gives you, and you run with it." Donna believes that she has gained some perspective; she takes a little more time to "smell the roses," has a little more patience for certain things.

Donna surprises herself with another personal change—one that never would have been possible before the rape occurred: she is now an avid public speaker. She is eager to help others find the kind of peace that she has found through the VVH program. Though gregarious with friends and family, Donna had never done any public speaking. And she does it well. Alongside Kim, Donna has participated in several victim vigils as a speaker. Donna finds that this gives her a purpose—to share a story that can help other victims. Ultimately, Donna says, "I lost a certain drive that I had. But I gained another. So it makes a difference." Donna takes pride in herself for making something good come out of bad: "There's just so much I'm proud of, . . . of what I've done and what I can tell people. I'm not saying I'm proud of what happened to me, but I'm proud of the recovery of me." The day that Donna opened the curtains in her house for the first time in many years was a watershed moment. "Now that I have my curtains open and the sun shines in and I sit out on the porch and I talk to my neighbors, it's just so great."

Though Donna might have been interested in an RJ program such as VVH at the time of sentencing, she does not think that her offender would have been ready or willing to take responsibility for his actions. "For a few years, he was so angry at being caught that he probably couldn't have seen daylight in understanding. But I think that if *I* had met Kim years before, I could've saved myself a lot of years of needless—I don't want to say suffering because I didn't even know I was suffering, because how do you know when that is becoming your life? I didn't know what I was doing to myself till I stopped doing it."

Jamel's Story

In September 2006, I traveled to prison to interview Jamel. Although the correctional staff intended to move him back into a cell with the general population that evening, at the time of our meeting Jamel was still in the secure housing unit. This meant that Jamel was shackled at his wrists and ankles, and our conversation occurred with a wall of glass between us. The actual face-to-face meeting between Jamel and Donna did not take place until he returned to the general population. Kim meanwhile continued to work with him; the dialogue occurred about one month after I conducted my first interview with Jamel. After the dialogue, I talked with him again, with both of us sitting in a small room together.[5] Jamel is tall and well built, but he is gentle in demeanor and exceedingly polite. One of the first things I noticed about him was his keen interest in the world around him and curiosity about my research and my students. A cynic might say that Jamel only appeared to be curious and interested because he was lonely and bored in prison. However, he was the only offender I interviewed in connection to this project who asked questions about things that had nothing to do with VVH, victims, or the criminal justice system. Jamel is a reflective thinker and expresses himself well. I knew that he had not gone past the seventh grade in formal schooling, yet his communication and language skills were well developed. Jamel credits his ability to express himself and think analytically with the considerable reading he has done since his incarceration. He realizes that prison time could be spent destructively and cultivate bitterness; instead, he has chosen "to do a lot of reading and a lot of thinking." Jamel also credits his conversion in prison to the Muslim faith as something that has brought him more structure in his life.

Prior to receiving the introductory letter from Kim about VVH, Jamel had not thought much about his victim. He concentrated on getting his life turned around. But "when I received that letter from Kim, it had me thinking that it's a good thing, to contact my victim, to express my remorse to her." Jamel is no longer a seventeen-year-old boy, strung out on drugs and running wild in the streets, uncaring about what happened to himself or anybody else. It has been ten years since Jamel committed the rape and another seven years before he will be released at age thirty-four.

In Jamel's first letter to Kim, in 2003, he stated that he wanted to do anything he could to help Donna. Although he expressed concern about Donna "tee[ing] off verbally," he wrote, "I want to ease my victim of any agony she may be feeling by answering any of her questions," and said, the opportunity to "apologize is sufficient enough for me." He also included details about his own childhood, writing that his mother passed away when he was twelve years old, that he never knew his father. He was raised by his great-grandmother and grandmother, who both loved him and raised him in a positive environment where he was not abused. He also included some details about his prior drug use, writing, "Hard drugs wasn't my thing; I indulged in marijuana, but I was a heavy drinker at a young age."

Reflecting on the young man he was at age seventeen, Jamel describes himself as "a lost individual, like most seventeen-year-olds." Jamel used drugs and alcohol to hide his pain, self-medicating so he would not have to address the loss of his parents. Writing about his childhood in some of the VVH "homework," Jamel said that a piece of him died when his mother died, and he lost his conscience. He was kicked out of school, and he remembers feeling frustrated by wearing hand-me-down clothing and the taunts he got as a result. Jamel started dealing drugs and continued to use drugs and alcohol to try to "fill up the void." He sees now that by choosing drugs and his delinquent friends over compliance to his grandmother's rules he was taking the "easy way out." High on pot or alcohol, Jamel also started to commit robberies. These robberies occurred mostly when he felt angry and ready to explode; overpowering people and taking their money gave him an adrenalin rush.

The night of the rape, Jamel says he was angry. He had never been able to express himself verbally and, in fact, protected himself from letting people inside to see what he was thinking or feeling. Jamel says, "The easiest way to express things was physically, by lashing out, shutting out anyone whenever they tried to approach me." He had been running the streets all night with his friends, drinking and smoking pot. Jamel had been home earlier, at 8:30 p.m., because he knew that he had to check in with his probation officer by phone at 9 p.m. His friends came back for him after that call, and he left with them to continue partying. When they dropped him back home later, after midnight, Jamel could see his grandmother's light on. His friends left, but Jamel did not enter the house. He knew that he had missed his grandmother's curfew again, and rather than deal with her disappointment and anger, he decided he would rob someone. He started to look for a house to burglarize. He remembers feeling angry with himself for messing up again. Jamel maintains that rape was not his initial intent, and when he first saw Donna, he had only decided to rob her.[6]

Jamel agreed to the conditions of participation in the VVH program and in fact embraced them. In his heart, he had already taken responsibility and was remorseful. Even before working with the VVH preparation paperwork, Jamel had realized that his crime affected many people's lives. When Kim initially met with Jamel in prison to explain the process, he was ready to confront the hard emotional work involved: "I was open. Basically, whatever needed to be done, I wanted to do it."

Jamel fully understood that the process was going to churn up emotions for him about his behavior. He acknowledged this somewhat philosophically, when asked if he thought that other offenders might want to talk to their victims: "Some might. . . . Some people sincerely regret what they did." He agreed that the program has to be victim driven, because "it safeguards the victims from harm. And not everyone is going to have pure intentions, and contact might relive the crime over them. But if the victim has to contact the offender, then the victim keeps control over it." Kim worked with Jamel for months on the paperwork.[7] Jamel reflected on his childhood and his crime and faced challenging questions from Kim about the rape. He realized that Kim needed to spend time with him to assess his sincerity to ensure that he was not manipulating the situation or holding back. Jamel recollected that the most difficult aspect of the preparation was opening up initially: "That did not come easily, telling her about me—my crime and shame. You don't open up to too many people, not in here. That was the most difficult part of the process for me."

By the time Jamel wrote the letter to Donna, he felt more confident about how he could fully express himself: "how I felt about how I hurt her, things I wanted to do to make it right, how I put my life together, what I hoped to accomplish during the mediation process." He believes now that talking to a stranger helped him confront issues more fully, as the exposure of a "worse self" to a person one does not know breaks down a lot of barriers and hones in on culpability issues. The key, he felt, was that Kim did not judge him. Jamel also wrote to the other important people in Donna's life, something he felt strongly about wanting to do. At the same time, he was troubled, knowing that they had every right to judge him. Jamel is very clear about how terribly the rape affected anyone who loves Donna.

During this time, Jamel also received a letter from Donna in which she told him about her loss of trust in strangers and expressed the hope that he would change. She told him about her own son's troubles with the law in his youth and wrote, "I don't hate you and the anger has long since passed, at least for me. The hurt and fear I am left with is the hardest." When Jamel received the letter from Donna, he felt humbled and stunned: "It was a real extraordinary situation. I had committed an atrocious act against her, and she basically bore me no harm. All she wanted was to know was if I had pulled my life together and that I wasn't going to hurt no one else."

Jamel felt confident that Donna would meet a different person than the selfish hothead he was as a teenager. He recognizes that most seventeen-year-olds running the streets, strung out on drugs, fail to realize that their actions have an effect on others. Jamel also worries that because of the rape, Donna is probably suspicious of all young black men. In the preparation paperwork, Jamel stated his regrets that his own violent behavior perpetuates negative stereotypes of all black men. Jamel believes that rehabilitation is key and that particularly for African American men, "it's like circumstances are out to get you, not as an excuse, but you need support, aftercare." He hopes that he will become part of the solution once he is released and that he will be more proactive in telling young black males that they can make a positive difference in society.

Contacts since Letter Exchange

During the time before Donna and Jamel's face-to-face meeting, she asked him if he would write a letter that she could use in her work with incarcerated male juvenile delinquents to express his perspective about criminality and victimization. Jamel readily agreed and believed that it was important to tell the youths the consequences of their crimes: "from an individual who has been there and done that, that they have to get it together real soon, or they will be headed where I am now." He believes that this kind of information needs to come from someone like them, even if other speakers may have good intentions. "Otherwise, it doesn't seem as real. The kids would feel, 'Well, you don't know what I know' or 'You didn't experience what I know, so how would you know how I felt.'"

In Jamel's letter, he describes his crime and expresses his hope for the young men: "Take advantage of your opportunities now so you will not end up where I am." He explains that their crimes have a "ripple effect" that extends far beyond the immediate victims and encourages them to "imagine how it would impact your family if someone shot your father, raped your mother, or robbed you of everything you may posses on this earth." He concludes by stating, "It is not too late to begin impacting people's lives in a positive way," and urges the young men to "break the cycle of violence." It has been both heart-lifting and heart-breaking for Donna to see the impact of the letter on the young men locked up in the juvenile facility. "It was like half the room paid attention, while the other half may as well not come to listen." She hopes, however, that the sentiment in Jamel's letter has an impact on some of the juveniles, who might remember parts of it and think twice the next time they are about to do something irresponsible.

Jamel seldom has visitors, given his fractured family situation and the age and health of his grandmother, although she does visit several times a year. Much to his astonishment, his grandmother and Donna arranged to meet and talk together sometime in 2004, accompanied by Kim.[8] In fact, Donna told me during one of our conversations together that she ran into Jamel's grandmother a few weeks after this meeting, and they hugged each other.

Jamel knows that his grandmother supports anything she thinks can change the direction of his life: "If she thought participating in it was something good and changed the course of my life, she'd be happy."

The night of my first interview with Jamel, he was moved back to a cell in the general prison population. This move started the process rolling for receiving approval for the face-to-face dialogue. Because of the letter exchanges and the intermediary messages, as well as meetings with Kim, Jamel felt at ease with the prospect of meeting Donna, a feeling he attributed to his personal growth reinforced by VVH. At the same time, however, Jamel was not oblivious to some anger issues (unrelated to Donna) on which he still needs to work. He sincerely wanted to meet with Donna, yet he got in trouble inside, delaying the meeting. Jamel talks about his "screw-up" openly: "It didn't make me question the process, but I thought I had it all together, and the incident showed me that I had some more work to do on myself. Can I really get my life together liked I want to? Am I going to keep repeating the same mistakes? Am I destined to be a failure?"

Despite being in lockdown in the secured housing unit for his disciplinary infraction, Jamel was eager to proceed with the face-to-face meeting with Donna. He wrote a letter to the warden to convey why it was so important to him and to ask for permission to meet, explaining his involvement in the VVH program and how it had assisted him "in understanding the ripple effect" of his actions, "the negative aspect of them and also the positive." He thanked the warden for his time and patience, telling him, "I owe it to my victim to express my apologies verbally but more importantly thr[ough] my actions by never hurting anyone again."

There is no trace of self-pity in Jamel's words. He fervently believes that he deserves punishment for the harm he caused. Jamel believes going to prison is what allowed him to get his life together, and he strongly believes that "there's a lot of people inside here that, even though they committed a wretched crime, they regret what they done. It's not justifiable, but circumstances push a person toward a certain path." Part of getting his life together includes participation in the program to make amends.

Like many inmates, Jamel has opinions about crime and criminals and wonders whether college students would be able to put themselves in the shoes of someone who started with obstacles and disadvantages they did not face: "They don't understand that once you knock a person down, not everyone has a chance to get their life together. Most everyone gets out [of prison], and unless they have a chance to get their life together, they're going to reoffend. . . . You've got to offer some opportunities to improve their quality of life so they have different options when they are released. Or the cycle of crime will flourish." This statement does not absolve offenders of responsibility in Jamel's eyes, and he is cynical about how offenders view victims in the time immediately following the offense: "A lot of the time, when a person commits a crime against an individual, they don't really see that person half the time."

Jamel views the opportunity for victims to talk to their offender as particularly important for victims of rape, so that victims will not fear their attackers and can "get the trust and the security to move on with their life." Although Jamel is realistic and realizes that absolute certainty may be "pie in the sky," but as to Donna, he says, "I know from me she has nothing to worry about, nothing to threaten her anymore. She'll have the ability to walk in a dark parking lot knowing no one is waiting for her." Jamel hopes that he can do something when he is released to help juveniles turn their lives away from crime. But he is also cognizant of the lure of the old neighborhood and the people in it who will try to trap him: "It will be hard—they're going to pull their way, and I'll pull my way. . . . I'll have to be stronger. . . . I can't say for certain, but in my heart I know I am done. I know too much now to go back to the way I was before." Jamel acknowledges that victims would have no way of knowing that an offender has experienced such a major transformation. Even if they know that an offender has responded positively to therapy or other rehabilitation while imprisoned, it is incumbent on offenders "to follow it up with their actions."

For Donna, meeting face to face with her offender resolved many of her longstanding fears. Timing played an important role in facilitating Jamel's empathy for her and understanding of the consequences of his actions. By facing her deepest fears and internalized self-blame, the VVH process unlocked the keys to Donna's own internal prison. As she prepared to give out Halloween candy to trick-or-treaters for the first time since the rape, she knew she had conquered her fears and would not lock herself away again: "I will not let the rape steal my happiness."

——————————————————————————— 5 ——

Allison and James

From Horror to Gratitude

Facts of case: In 1981, twenty-one-year-old James broke into a family's home with the intent to commit burglary. He raped one of the daughters, nineteen years old, and almost killed her (by choking) during the assault. James was caught within a month, and he confessed. He was sentenced for second-degree rape and second-degree burglary and received a forty-five-year sentence. Twenty-five years after the rape, James and his victim met through VVH while he was still incarcerated. James was released from prison in 2007, having served twenty-six years of his sentence. This chapter follows a slightly different format because of extenuating circumstances that are discussed more fully in appendix B. It reflects my interview with James, access to his case file and letters he wrote, interviews with Kim, and the videotapes of the dialogue.

Rape is not an easy subject for most people. Victims' responses to traumatic events vary tremendously, but the crime of rape carries an even greater stigma than other crimes because of the shame, victim blaming, and layers of cultural and legal ambiguity attached to it.[1] Often the victim and family members are admonished not to tell anyone what happened—a silence that is sometimes welcomed. Unacknowledged trauma often haunts victims of sexual and intimate violence, causing responses such as anxiety, substance abuse, fear of strangers, a feeling of being dirty or ashamed, embarrassment, nightmares, and eating disorders.[2] Rape victims often feel guilty, regardless of the circumstances, and second-guess their actions. Psychologist Nicola Gavey writes about rape victims who felt empowered when they either thwarted a sexual assault against them or took steps to minimize the offender's attack; their efforts helped them reconcile their experience with few lingering emotional scars.[3] Anger can ultimately be cathartic, especially if those feelings were unexpressed at the time of the rape. However, victims seldom have control over when these feelings of anger or powerlessness surface. For instance, if criminal justice officials ask for victims' input on whether parole should be granted during the time the offender is incarcerated, victims are often reminded of the crime and their fears rekindled.[4]

In the case I examine in this chapter, the offender, James, was apprehended and accepted a plea bargain. His plea in 1981 did not include an attempted-murder charge even though he almost killed his victim. The victim, Allison, did not provide any information (contradictory or otherwise) to the court at James's sentencing. Prior to the victims' rights movement in the United States, victims and their family members might be interviewed for presentencing investigation (PSI) reports compiled by the probation department, but there was no mechanism that recognized their voices in any formal way. Except in very serious instances, cases were resolved with little or no contact between prosecutor and victim. In most states today, it is routine for victims/survivors to have the opportunity to prepare a victim impact statement or offer input to the prosecutor or directly to the judge (in oral or written form). In practice, however, the majority of victims do not pursue this option, and judges' sentencing relies entirely on PSI reports prepared by court personnel or probation departments. Pretrial prosecutor-victim contact is now part of the legal culture in Delaware, mandated by policy of the district attorney's office and the 1992 Victims' Bill of Rights.[5] James's sentence was forty-five years in prison, reflecting the breaking and entering, robbery, and rape charges. Because of good-time credits (typically, inmates receive five days off their sentence a month for good behavior), James became eligible for parole in 2007 after serving twenty-four years. He fulfilled a work-release requirement and since 2008 has been living back in the community under probation supervision.

After James had been incarcerated for a number of years, he became determined to pursue every opportunity to better himself. He read his first book behind bars and took courses to receive his GED and high school diploma. James also took part in victim-sensitivity classes, alternatives-to-violence classes, weekly groups for sex offenders, and a twelve-step program called Sexual Compulsives Anonymous, and he became well trained in virtually every construction-related skill. James also completed a two-thousand-hour State Department of Labor apprenticeship course for computer operators. In the twenty-four years that James was imprisoned for rape, he never got into any trouble behind bars and was well respected by guards and correctional administrators.

James believes he deserved to be punished for what he did to Allison and, in fact, believes going to jail probably saved him from committing more violent crimes. Before prison, James saw himself as a "walking time bomb," seething with anger and frustrated over the lack of power or control in his life. One theoretical perspective argues that feelings of rage and powerlessness are common factors in young men who commit violent and property crimes, especially those who are not closely connected to conventional social bonds such as family, law-abiding peers, and social institutions such as schools or churches/temples.[6] In James's words, "I had a lot of hate in me, and there is no doubt I would either have hurt someone fighting or maybe even killed someone." James told Kim that the night he raped Allison, he wanted to release his anger and frustration on someone: "If it hadn't been her, it would have been someone else." He had been smoking pot and drinking; he and his girlfriend had got into a fight, and she had broken up with him. James says that he felt as though he had nothing and no one who cared for him that night.[7] He tried to pick a fight at the local bowling alley, but no one accepted his challenge. He cruised around, intending to burglarize a house. He broke into one house through a kitchen window: "I walked around the whole house into every room looking for things to take; I took money from every purse and wallet I found. Allison caught my attention by moving around on the couch that she was sleeping on. I remember standing there watching her for a little bit of time, and the longer I stood there, the madder I became."

After leaving Allison's house, having overpowered, choked, and raped her, James says his anger vanished and he felt in control of his life. But he also knew that he had committed a terrible act. When he reached his car, a police car drove past him. James was not afraid of being caught and says that he was "beyond feeling anything right then." From the next day forward, he felt a lot of guilt and shame for his behavior. Once James was arrested, his grandmother, aunt, and other family members were horrified and shocked that he committed rape, and they also felt deeply embarrassed when neighbors identified them as "the rapist's family."

As James bluntly says, "I got more time in prison than I do in normal life." He was twenty-one years old when he brutally raped Allison. He was still a rebellious kid, always getting into some kind of trouble, sometimes with other guys but often alone. He explains that he was raised by his grandmother and says, "I always felt like I was an outcast, even in my own family." Around the age of thirteen, James began smoking pot and breaking into houses and stealing from people. He believes his delinquency represented a desperate cry for attention from his family—none of whom, he says, paid him any attention unless he got into trouble.[8] James never met his father and only met his mother once for about an hour. He describes his maternal grandmother as someone he could never please. During the preparation process for the VVH program, James wrote about his feelings of hurt and abandonment growing up; he felt no one cared about him and was beaten a lot "with belts, boards, paddles, switches, fists, feet, and anything that could be thrown" at him in the house.

This kind of childhood exacted a toll on James's emotional health. He told Kim that he remembers wanting to hurt the people who hurt him but felt it was easier to hurt people he did not know. It is easy to see the connection between James's childhood trauma and his rage when he writes about the rape: "At that time I had decided to rape my victim. I hated the fact her life was so peaceful and mine was in so much turmoil." He admitted in his writing that he grew up being resentful of people who had families so different from his own.[9] He describes himself at age twenty-one: "I had the mind of a kid."

The Path to VVH

In early 2005, Allison contacted Kim about VVH, and Kim began meeting with both Allison and James separately about every other week. In James's first meeting with Kim, he was adamant about feeling remorse. This was meaningful for Allison, since she never knew that James felt any remorse. Often during the preparation process, victims make requests for additional information—or information that was not provided to them at the time of the crime. For instance, some victims want updated photographs of their offender or photographs from the time of arrest. Retrieving photographs may seem trivial, but to victims who generalize their fear to all men who resemble any small part of what they remember or what they imagine remembering of their offender, a real picture that perhaps challenges their exaggerated image of their attacker can play a crucial role in alleviating their fear.

Other victims wish to read the official version of the crime as documented by the police and the court. Police policy is that only a "victim's version" of the crime report is released at the time of the crime, and this report omits a great deal of information. In this case, Allison wanted to read the original, complete police report. Kim is often able to fulfill victims' requests for photos or full police reports through her connections with criminal justice and victim services personnel. At the same time, however, Kim is cognizant that reading the words from the original police reports can be emotionally painful for victims. Historically, rape victims have experienced the most shame and victim blaming from police, who were often untrained in asking victims questions with sensitivity and in a nonjudgmental manner. Many victims experience a "second victimization" when they are asked to talk to criminal justice professionals about their trauma, despite understanding that the more information they provide, the greater the chance that their crime will be solved. The overwhelming majority of rape victims are women who were raped by men; telling another man, albeit a police officer, about the rape can compound the humiliation.

During James's preparation process with Kim, he wanted to know if his rash act of violence had ruined his victim's life. James felt relieved to learn that Allison had finished college, married, and had children. He told Kim that he wanted to participate in VVH because he was sorry and wanted Allison to know that he felt that sorrow deeply. James's first letter to Allison stated how much shame he felt over his "vicious violation" of her and how shocked he was that Allison had the courage to meet him. Mostly, James said, "I want to apologize to you and your family for all the suffering I put you thr[ough]. I deserve everything I've gotten. I know this but you didn't, and that is what bothers me the most." When Allison wrote back to James, the letter shocked him to his core. He expected her to spew anger, but she did not. He was also stunned to discover that while he received therapy in prison, she had no such help for twenty-four years.

James' Perceptions of His Crime, Prison Time, and VVH

James contends that he has never forgotten his victim or his crimes—not only does he feel guilty about what he did to Allison, but he has confronted each direct and indirect aspect related to his crime through participation in every mental health program available to him in prison. In some therapeutic programs, the correctional counselors direct offenders to role-play the part of their victims; this exercise was the closest James had ever come to comprehending, on some level, the horror of his attack on Allison. Although most criminal sentences these days routinely have a no-contact order placed to prohibit communication between victims and offenders, in 1981, when James was sentenced, there were no such stipulations. Still, James *never* thought he would ever speak to Allison and was shocked to learn that Allison wanted to speak to him.

Once the preparation process began in earnest, James found that he had a number of feelings he wished to convey to Allison. First, "to say that I'm truly sorry and to reassure her that I wish her no harm whatsoever. I'm not the same person I was then." He maintained that he "deserved to be in the hot seat" and that hearing whatever she told him about the pain and suffering he had caused her would help to fill in the missing pieces of the puzzle for him too. James also wanted to answer any questions she had about him or that night or whatever Allison needed to ask. He hoped their meeting might help him to move beyond his past and let him get a sense of peace, in addition to wanting Allison to "get her self-respect, dignity, and sense of security back." At the same time, however, James never felt that he would ever get over the guilt for what he did to her, and he does not feel that he will ever be punished enough.

During the six months of biweekly meetings with Kim, James wrote a lot about his feelings, a practice with which he had become comfortable in prison group meetings; he was undaunted by the VVH paperwork. The timing was ideal in James's mind; his parole release date was scheduled for eighteen months from the dialogue, and he hoped that the VVH process would help to ease Allison's and her family's fears for their safety upon his release. James, like many offenders, also feared that Allison's family members or friends might retaliate upon his release. He saw VVH as an opportunity to prove his sincerity about never wanting to hurt Allison or anyone again. Kim helped James understand that families are often fiercely loyal to a member who is hurt, but often when family members see the person they love who has been hurt becoming healed, it starts the healing process for them.

James did his prison time isolated from family members; he had no visitors after 1988. In prison, James actively avoided known troublemakers or inmates who he perceived were not a good influence on who he wanted to be. One of the inmates he avoided for many years was the prison barber; as a consequence, his hair hung down to his waist. When Kim first started meeting with James, his appearance was off-putting: he was unshaven, with unkempt hair, long fingernails, and disheveled clothing. Kim knew that most victims would recoil with fright or disgust if this were the first sight they saw of their offender after so many years of wondering and fear. At their fourth meeting, Kim talked to James about how people often judge each other by the way they look; he recognized that he would need to clean himself up for the dialogue to be respectful to Allison. Besides the long hair and clothes, James has a tattoo of a naked woman on his arm. Although Kim felt that it would be inappropriate for Allison to see the tattoo at the dialogue, she let James figure it out for himself. At their next visit, James was clean-shaven, with this tattoo covered up by a long-sleeved shirt and his hair cut short and neatly washed and combed. Kim also worked with James on understanding body language, such as sitting up straighter in his chair, so he would look more engaged in what was going on, and they practiced meeting a person's eyes during a conversation.

Throughout the preparation process, James learned more about Allison and how the rape had affected not just her but her entire family. He had never thought about secondary victims before. James felt that it was important to reassure the family that nothing was their fault; one of Allison's sisters thought he had intended to rape her, not Allison, since she had been visible walking in and out of their house while James was in the neighborhood working at a construction site; another sister thought she heard a scream that night but went back to sleep, thinking it was just a dream. In particular, James never had realized how truly harmful his actions were that night and was stunned to find out that "after twenty-four years Allison is still going through difficult enough times to want this meeting."

The Dialogue

The day finally arrived when Allison would meet James in person. From the letters they had exchanged, it was clear that James was remorseful and took responsibility for his actions that night and was eager to do whatever he could to help answer any of Allison's questions. But when they finally met face to face, it was as if he were a different man. In his letters and his VVH paperwork during the preparation process, James was very articulate about his remorse, yet his participation in the face-to-face meeting seemed dispassionate and unconvincing. Kim still recalls vividly how much he was sweating during the dialogue and gulping down water. The videotape of the dialogue shows that he asks for questions to be repeated a lot and looks very uncomfortable, often staring down at his hands or away from the table. There are long silences throughout the meeting.

Allison persevered in asking James questions. At times, this seemed difficult for her, but she kept talking to James despite her tears and obvious pain. At no point during the dialogue did she seem annoyed or frustrated with his responses. In fact, Allison often interpreted his monosyllabic responses with a positive spin and added explanatory detail, which he would mostly not acknowledge or reply to. James rarely used the word "I" to describe things that had happened to him or things that he did, which exacerbated the sense of his disconnection from the process.

According to Kim, in many ways Allison was disappointed and dissatisfied with the dialogue, despite her personal pride in summoning up the courage to face James and literally hear his apology. It was mysterious to Allison that James was not more engaged in the dialogue, after all his emotional writings to her and his fervent commitment to the preparation process. It turned out that something had been very wrong with James: he was sick, with an extremely high temperature of 104 degrees during their meeting, which explained why he appeared disinterested and uninvolved emotionally. However, James did not want to cancel the dialogue that had been so long in the making. James was found unconscious in his cell the day after the dialogue; Kim was told that he could very well die. Ultimately, he was diagnosed with Legionnaire's disease. Because of his illness, the corrections commissioner granted the unusual request for a second face-to-face meeting for an additional three hours. James was surprised that Allison would give him another chance.[10]

The difference between the first and second dialogue was striking. Allison and James both looked more relaxed and animated. They maintained eye contact. James was very engaged with the conversation, often interrupting Allison's flow to interject something he felt might shed some light. Allison seemed to fully appreciate his participation. At times, there was lighthearted chatter and even some joking and laughter back and forth about their personality quirks or shared remembrances of their hometown. In at least four different points during their conversation James was moved to tears and cried at some length. Allison also cried often and freely.

At the dialogues, Kim's presence is important yet subdued. Her hard work occurred in the many months of preparation with Allison and James that brought them to the point where they finally could meet face to face. One can see why her role is that of a "facilitator" rather than a "mediator" by watching her quiet, powerful style. During the dialogue, Allison read about her feelings from her personal journal so that James would understand the gamut of emotions she experienced. James told her that he needed to hear the full impact of his behavior that night and that he did not want her to protect his feelings. After reading one particularly angry entry from her journal, James said to Allison, "I wish I could take it back. I can't."

Most victims desire for offenders to understand all the ramifications of their actions. Offenders' acknowledgment of the consequences of their crime is often very validating for victims, particularly if the offenders' descriptions of the crime matches memories that victims have but have had no one to verify. It was important for Allison to know whether James knew that he almost killed her when he choked her, and James answered, "I thought I had choked you to the point you might have died. You were blacking out. That's what made me let you go." Allison seemed to visibly breathe a sigh of relief that their memories matched.

Similar to many of Kim's VVH participants, James and Allison formulated an "affirmation agreement" to be signed at the dialogue. It included five promises from James, although the agreement is "neither legal or binding, it is signed in good faith by both parties and is their hope for the future." James promised to do the following:

> write a letter to the family of Allison expressing my remorse and sorrow for the crime I committed against them; continue to do well in life and continue my education as much as I possibly can; write a progress letter, sent to VVH, twice a year letting Allison know what I am doing and my accomplishments while incarcerated and upon release from the institution; do some kind of volunteer work with Habitat for Humanity, Big Brother program or working with the elderly or assist with the Alternatives to Violence program once I am released; and, adhere to treatment programs I am required to attend, keep my mind and heart open, never intentionally hurt another person again, treat myself with respect, dignity and kindness, pray for my victim, her family and myself.

At the time of my interview with James, he told me that he now sees Allison as his central support person. This, too, shocked him: "Believe me, it's weird. I would have never expected it."

When Kim asked James in the debriefing session following the dialogue what was the most important thing he experienced, James said a sense of relief that Allison actually did forgive him: "For me, the whole time I've been in here since my crime, I've felt bad about it. I just wanted a chance to say that I was sorry to my victim and let her know that it had nothing to do with her, other than the crime itself." While the day-in, day-out routine of the prison remained constant, James noticed that he felt better about himself since the mediation. "I'd say it took a lot of weight off. I had a lot of feelings stored up. It's good to get it out." There was a particularly poignant moment when Allison asked James what justice meant to him. He replied, "I done wrong. I deserve to do the time, but I also deserve to be a person, not just a statistic or a number."

Following the dialogue, Allison and James continued to correspond, which they can do directly, rather than using Kim as an intermediary or asking the court to lift the no-contact order, since none exists." This situation is atypical for victims and offenders and is not a policy endorsed by VVH. James wrote to Allison's siblings and mother. Two of Allison's sisters wrote back to James, and the letters were very different. One was full of anger, which is what James anticipated and expected from all the letters, whereas the other one talked more about forgiveness. He answered each letter, addressing concerns and questions that the sisters had either asked him about or that he anticipated. Although he also wrote to Allison's brother and mother, he did not hear back from either of them. In the letter to her brother, James apologized for the rape and for the humiliation the boy felt at the time, when he was treated initially as a suspect; James wrote that he understood how much Allison's brother hated him. James also wrote that it was okay to be furious at him for the violation to his sister and his family. In addition, James praised Allison for her courage in facing him. Finally, he offered to do anything he could to repair the damage his behavior caused.

Thinking about Release

At the time of our interview, James was unsure about what would happen upon his release from prison. Several times, he told Kim that he wished prison better prepared inmates for reentry into society. James's concern is well founded; research documents the myriad obstacles faced by offenders reintegrating into the community, particularly those who have few prospects and have had long separations from families and communities.[12] Allison has talked with him about their writing a book together.

James's postrelease plans include finding some kind of employment in the construction field; he has learned a number of trades while incarcerated. He is very worried about what will happen to him upon release because of the crackdown on sex offenders in the state where he lives. James might have to register permanently as a sex offender, even though the rape occurred before Megan's Law went into effect.[13] James is concerned about mandatory registration because his efforts to demonstrate that he has changed and to find a job and to lead a normal life will be thwarted. He maintains, "Nowadays, all sex offenses are treated as child crimes. Or that's what they perceive it all to be. . . . All they do is put fear in people's heads."

Despite his fear of reentering the world outside prison, James holds on to some hope. Prison programs taught him to take responsibility for his crime, and he believes in himself and in his abilities more today. James wrote in his paperwork to Kim what it was imperative for him to do: "prove to myself and others that I can lead a normal life as a free person." For many offenders, the real challenge arises when they leave the prison walls and face the daily obstacles that test their resolve.[14] When I asked James if there was anything that still bothered him today, he said, "Just the fact that I did rape my victim. I hurt her. . . . I don't like that I did that, but it's something I've got to live with." A final indication of James's acceptance of personal accountability was the fact that, unprompted, he told me that he did not mind if his full name was used in the book.

James Today

Allison and James continue to correspond, even with the formal end of the Victims' Voices Heard program. Initially, they exchanged a letter about every two weeks. James is interested in the prospect of being mentored by Allison's husband, which is a task the latter wants to undertake. This kind of contact is not supported by the prison, and it is unclear how it will be addressed by the probation department in charge of supervising released offenders. Most people do not understand a victim's interest in maintaining personal contact with his or her offender, unless it is to receive reassurance that the offender is not reoffending. For some victims, it is important to know as much as they can about their offenders in order to truly stop fearing them.

James was released from prison to a work-release center housed on prison grounds in July 2007. He served twenty-six years of his forty-five-year sentence, accumulating good-time credits from good behavior and program completion. As mandated by the Victims' Bill of Rights, Allison was notified of his impending release. She spoke on his behalf at the release hearing. In November 2007, James completed work release and returned to live in the community.

Prior to Allison's involvement in VVH, she did not support an early release for James. Today, as is clear from her writings published in public venues, Allison wants more people who have experienced a violent crime to know about the VVH program. She wrote a personal essay about her experience for the VVH newsletter, which was reproduced in a similar format in a magazine marketed to inmates and their family members, *Prison Life*, and she wrote a posting for an Internet site on prison ministries. In these writings, Allison states that she believes in the dialogue process, which she sees as life changing. She is critical of a criminal justice system that reinforces the separation between victims and offenders under the rubric of protection, real or perceived, which sometimes flies in the face of what victims may feel they actually need to truly heal. Finally feeling the full extent of her emotions, processing all the fear and anger and sadness that followed the rape, and ultimately meeting with James face to face have given Allison a gift: being able to live her life more fully. Allison has spoken twice to my university classes. Her talks were inspiring to my students, and she told me that she felt empowered by sharing her story. Since that time, Allison has spoken to numerous groups in prison about victims' needs, and she volunteers as a coleader of a Bible-study group with inmates in prison (although not in the same prison where James was incarcerated). For James, Allison's movement from terrified victim to empowered survivor has given him great peace, with her forgiveness as the most surprising outcome of the VVH program. James intends to use these gifts as motivation to live a law-abiding life and to find a way to give back to society by playing a positive role in it.

Postscript (2008)

Almost all offenders face multiple and complex issues related to reentry that create obstacles to success, such as finding housing, securing employment, establishing social support, and staying away from anything that might trigger or facilitate criminal activity. James's experience was no different; it took about six months for him to find a job. His housing situation was unstable, both because his sexual-offense conviction appears in preemployment background checks and also because of his meager financial resources. Despite cautions to the contrary from VVH and the Department of Corrections, Allison and her husband have maintained close contact with James, including helping him to find housing and providing transportation to job interviews and ultimately finding him a minimum-wage job. With the help of Allison and her husband, James found an apartment, with furnishings donated by local church members. In the first few weeks that he was out of prison, James wrote a moving essay for a Bible-study group about how humbled he felt to be forgiven by his victim and to be given another chance to prove that her trust is well placed. At this point, his sole support system comprises his victim and her husband. Time will tell whether James's strong feelings of gratitude and obligation to his victim will continue to inspire him to lead a law-abiding life.

6

Laurie and Paul

Emerging from a Cocoon

Facts of the case: Paul battered and sexually abused his wife, Laurie, throughout their ten-year marriage. He was arrested for raping her at knifepoint and sentenced to serve fifteen years in prison. Laurie also suspected him of sexually abusing one of their daughters and possibly their son. Their youngest daughter—their fourth child—was conceived from the rape. I interviewed both Laurie and Paul and had access to their case files, the letters they exchanged, and the videotape of their dialogue.

Laurie loves butterflies. She loves their colors and their graceful flight, but most of all she identifies with them because, like them, she herself hid inside a cocoon and then emerged and transformed. In many ways, Laurie's story about living with an abusive husband is a familiar one. Paul exhibited most of the typical characteristics of batterers:[1] he was jealous and controlling, viewed his wife and children as possessions, and engaged in verbal and physical abuse. Because both other family members and the criminal justice system ignored Laurie's plight, she felt helpless to leave Paul. She internalized powerful social messages which dictate that women have the responsibility to nurture relationships and fix them when they go wrong. Laurie hoped Paul would change, and she wanted him there to be a father to their children. This hope persisted until the night Paul brutally raped Laurie at knifepoint and almost killed her.

Laurie met Paul when she was about twenty-one years old and living with her parents, who were very protective of her. Laurie had had several schoolgirl crushes on boys, but she had never had a boyfriend or actively dated. Through a connection at her church, Laurie landed one of her first jobs working at a steakhouse, where she met a co-worker, named Paul, who took an interest in her. Laurie was flattered by his attention, and things between them escalated quickly. She moved out of her parents' house and into an apartment with him within a few months, despite their protestations. Her parents were particularly upset that Paul was African American (Laurie and her family are white).

Paul was about five years older than Laurie, and he was very streetwise. He had grown up in foster homes and had an abusive childhood. Laurie felt sorry for him and wanted to make his life better, so when he pushed to get married, they did so quickly. Danger signs were apparent early on; Paul seemed jealous when Laurie talked to other people and possessive of her time, but she initially felt flattered by his interest and thought he was being protective.[2]

Paul constantly berated Laurie, telling her she was "totally stupid, totally incapable of surviving without him." Laurie says, "I couldn't do anything. And I believed him."[3] Paul's psychological battering succeeded in creating deep self-doubt in Laurie, which she says was reinforced by her religious background and her church's rejection of her because she married an African American man.[4] Paul's emotional abuse quickly escalated to frequent and severe physical abuse. When Laurie got pregnant, she felt that her fate was sealed. She had been raised to believe that every child needed a father, and once you were married, you were married forever.

Laurie and Paul had three children together during their ten years of marriage. It was a difficult home life. Laurie struggled to keep things intact and always stayed employed, even when Paul lost his jobs and sabotaged her job responsibilities, which involved working steadily at a local manufacturing company, twelve-hour shifts nine and ten days in a row.[5] Paul was supposed to carry his weight on the home front, taking care of the kids and the house, but "that made him feel less of a man, so he wouldn't do the housework." Paul made Laurie give him all the money she earned, but he spent her money on alcohol and pornography while their bills were unpaid and the children went without food and clothing. When Laurie grew weary of the daily stresses, she demanded that she keep her paycheck and they split the bills; it was at this point that Paul became very physically abusive. Laurie also began to suspect that something was wrong with the kids, who begged her not to leave them when she got ready for work every day. She had a sense that Paul was harming them, but she says, "I never actually saw him hit them. He didn't really abuse them too much physically. But something nagged at me for a long time that something was wrong."[6]

The abuse escalated one night in 1994 after Laurie returned home from another long day at work. Paul met her at the door, telling her that he wanted her car keys so that he could go visit a friend who was in the hospital. Paul told her it was a male friend, but Laurie suspected otherwise because he was wearing dressy clothes and cologne. Laurie was determined that "he wasn't having a woman" in her car and refused to give him the keys. Paul hit her and punched her in the head and left. Laurie dialed 911, but once the police arrived, she felt embarrassed by the way that the police treated her; the officers' behavior seemed to tacitly communicate to Paul that they would not get involved. The police did not provide information about a battered women's shelter or ask Laurie any follow-up questions after she told them that he was abusive. "I don't think they really cared. They kind of laughed about it." Unfortunately, Laurie's experience with the police is not uncommon, even with recent changes to police policies regarding domestic violence.[7] The police left without taking further action, and Paul left soon after, taking Laurie's car.

Laurie sat up waiting for Paul to come home. She was terrified, but her earlier experience with the police left her feeling that it was useless to call them for help.[8] She could not let herself go to sleep because she knew Paul was going to come home angry. "I shut off all the lights. I'm sitting there waiting for him, terrified. I couldn't pack the kids up then and there because they were all in bed. I kept thinking, 'What if he comes home? He'll probably kill me.'"

Paul finally stumbled through the door, "drunk out of his mind." He forced Laurie to go to their bedroom, where he started looking for his guns. Unbeknown to Paul, however, Laurie had heard about an amnesty period that the local police sponsored and had turned them in.[9] As Paul searched, Laurie worried that there was another gun that she had not found earlier. Instead, Laurie says,

> Paul pulled out a knife that he had hidden away somewhere. It was a switchblade. He wanted me to get on the bed and I said, NO. . . . He started hitting me and tried to choke me. He got the knife, and he put it against my throat, and he raped me. . . . He told me I'd better not call the police 'cause if I did, he would definitely come after me.

Laurie had experienced a great deal of sexual abuse prior to the night of this rape at knifepoint, and consistent with Laurie's experiences with Paul, research demonstrates that men who are physically violent with their wives are more likely to be sexually abusive as well.[10] Paul repeatedly forced Laurie to have sex with him, despite Laurie's pain and pleas to stop hurting her. He frequently watched pornography at home—usually in front of their children—and his sexual abuse of Laurie included enacting degrading scenes from pornographic movies.

The week before the rape, Paul had finally got a job. As he got ready to go to work the night after the rape, "he said, sarcastically, 'You gonna leave?'" As much as Laurie wanted to, she was not sure where to go and was too afraid to put her kids in the car and show up at the battered women's shelter because she worried about how moving to a shelter would disrupt her children's education, and she worried that Paul would carry through on his frequent threats to kill her or to kidnap their children if she ever left him.[11]

As Laurie sat in her bedroom after Paul left for work, struggling to weigh all the options, her oldest daughter, Anna, then nine years old, came into the room, and to Laurie's dismay, Anna said she had heard everything that had happened the night of the rape. Anna also finally gave words to Laurie's biggest fear: "She told me her dad had been molesting her from the time she was four years old until she was nine. It was still happening." He also threatened to kill them both if Anna told Laurie.[12]

That was the final straw. Laurie told her oldest daughter to get her brother and sister and grab some of their clothes. Laurie filled a suitcase with anything they could find, and they left for a battered women's shelter. After stopping there briefly, she took Anna to see a doctor, where she learned that her nine-year-old daughter had been penetrated. "When I heard that, a mountain of guilt crashed down on my shoulders." Laurie had suspected something was going on but could never prove it, and whenever she challenged Paul, he abused her more severely.

Once Paul discovered that Laurie was gone, he drove around every day looking for her. By chance, he spotted Laurie's car and followed her to an appointment with a social services caseworker. Laurie and the children did not see him until they were already safely inside the office, but they saw him inside the building looking for them. When they ran to their car after the appointment, Paul chased them, pounding on the car, yelling and screaming for Laurie to come back with the kids. Except for the sentencing, this was the last time Laurie saw Paul until nine years later at the dialogue.

As soon as Laurie secured a Protection from Abuse order,[13] which gave her the right to live in the house with her children without Paul, she left the shelter and moved back home. For two long weeks, she and the children lived in fear, worrying that Paul would come home any minute, but Laurie's caseworker finally told her that Paul had been arrested soon after the incident at the social services building.

Because he accepted a plea bargain, Paul received fifteen years in prison. The charge was unlawful sexual intercourse in the first degree, which carries a fifteen-year minimum mandatory sentence. Upon completion of the term of imprisonment, the sentence is required to be followed by six months of probation at Level IV (the most restrictive level), six months at Level III, and twelve months at Level II. One of the conditions of Paul's sentence was that he have no contact with Laurie or her family or any child under the age of eighteen. Because of Paul's use of a deadly weapon, the length of the sentence was longer than the national average by far—at least for marital rape. Laurie attended the sentencing hearing accompanied by someone from the state Justice Department whom she had never previously met. She was not told that she had the right to present a victim impact statement.[14]

Meanwhile, Laurie discovered that she was pregnant and struggled with the implications of finding herself pregnant from the rape that resulted in her near death and her husband's incarceration.[15] "I can't have an abortion; that's out of the question. Then I thought, 'How am I going to put her up for adoption?' Because she's got siblings, she's going to be out wondering why I didn't want her. So I kept her."[16]

Laurie continued to blame herself, and though she tried to work through the situation with various therapists, she had little success. Laurie, understandably, entertained a revenge fantasy about Paul for what he did to her and their children and felt satisfied that "he's in prison, where he has zero control over his life." Laurie regained a sense of self and felt empowered to do things that she had never attempted to do before, such as protecting her son from a neighborhood bully.[17]

Laurie's Path to VVH

About three years after Paul raped and tried to murder Laurie, their divorce was finalized, and Laurie was working at a drugstore. One day when work was slow, she was skimming through the local newspaper and saw an ad for Victims' Voices Heard. This message caught her attention; Laurie wanted to meet with Paul to tell him how he had hurt her and their children and to show him how she had changed. Laurie immediately called Kim, and they began meeting regularly. Paul agreed to participate, and they both began the preparation process. In Laurie's letter to Paul, she focused on letting him know exactly how horribly he treated her: "I wanted to describe it to see if he even understood how he treated me. He beat me, he degraded me."

Laurie's main motive was for Paul to admit that he had molested Anna, but her need to hear this admission from him presented a legal problem: he was not serving time on charges of incest, and if he admitted the abuse, the state could bring new charges. Ultimately, in her letter to Paul, Laurie stated that though she did not want to get him in any more trouble, she needed to "bring an end to the pain and heartache": "Getting some answers from you, having you listen to me and hear what I'm saying to you, will help me so much."

No one in Laurie's family and social network really understood her determination to participate in the dialogue. But Laurie had expressed a desire to confront Paul in prison prior to learning about VVH. In fact, she had repeatedly asked her contact person from the Justice Department if she could talk to him. But her contact never understood and kept acting as if Laurie was crazy to want to do that. "I couldn't explain why. I just had to. . . . It wasn't something I *wanted* to do. I *needed* to. I was filled with such bitterness, it was like a physical weight on my shoulders. Carrying it around made my whole body ache."

Laurie also wanted Paul to see her as the new, more confident person she had become. By the time of my interview with Laurie, she was in her junior year in college, finishing a degree in human services. Her dream is to work with homeless people, to give them a boost in establishing independent lives. In preparation for the face-to-face meeting, Kim recognized the symbolic importance to Laurie of looking and feeling confident, of presenting her "new self" to the very person who had beaten her down, emotionally and physically. Courtesy of the VVH program, Kim bought Laurie a new outfit and had her hair done professionally. Laurie looked how she felt: in charge of her life.

The Dialogue

Laurie had never been inside a prison and expressed some trepidation about going there and about seeing Paul, but at the dialogue, Laurie felt protected because there were correctional officers everywhere. Paul sat down at the table, and Kim started the dialogue. Laurie thanked Paul for agreeing to meet with her, and then she proceeded to tell him how their marriage was for her during the ten years.

During the two-hour dialogue, Laurie talked with confidence and control over her emotions, asserting herself without raising her voice. She chronicled the humiliation and degradation she felt about his use of pornography, the fact that he had affairs with other women in their own house, his frequent sexual abuse, and the harm he had done to the family. She told him that his constant use of force to have sex with her when she did not want it was rape, even though she had not thought of it that way at the time: "It was dehumanizing, it robbed me of my identity—I could have been an animal." Laurie maintained, "Our kids have no security—they saw me hit, the kids were hit, their mom and dad were locked up in the bedroom for ten hours, and they lived in different houses all the time." Laurie also described vividly what happened to her and the children following his arrest and how difficult their lives had been.

Throughout the dialogue, even when Laurie was describing awful things that Paul did, he remained calm. At a couple of points, he cried. When he first spoke, after thanking Laurie for asking for the dialogue and apologizing for what he had put her through, he said, "I have no real excuse but what was going on before I met you. I really loved you. But I was afraid that if I let you get too close, you'd really hurt me or abandon me, or take off, and I was scared." He then talked about his horrific childhood and the lessons he learned about keeping everything inside. Paul thanked Laurie for helping to put him in jail and told her what he had learned there: "I don't have to be afraid anymore, jealous anymore. I don't have to be afraid that you, or whoever, is going to leave. I wish I could go back and make things right, but I can't." Finally, he told Laurie, "I take responsibility for all that I've done," and he asked if there was anything he could do to make it better for her.

This gave Laurie the opening she sought. She told Paul that she has forgiven him about the rape but that the family had been decimated by the accumulated problems and stress that followed Paul's departure. Then, she said clearly, "For a year and a half later, I was a total wreck, and a lot of it has to do with Anna. I need to know something: if there is any way you harmed our daughter." Paul responded, "That answer is yes. Again, I'm so sorry." Laurie also asked about her son, but Paul denied molesting him.

One of the most poignant moments was the point in the dialogue when Paul looked directly at Laurie and said, "I can see how strong you are, Laurie, and please believe one thing: none of this is your fault, *none* of it. Don't take that burden no more." She received his reassurance that upon release from prison he would not look for her and the kids or put them in any danger.

At almost an hour into the dialogue, Laurie told Paul that she wanted to talk more about the rape. She told him that what bothered her most was his threat to cut her throat and leave her dead body for their children to find in the morning. Laurie wanted to know why Paul wanted to kill her. He said, "Let me be frank. There were three things going on. One, I thought you were going to take off. Two, I thought you had someone else. I couldn't stand that you wanted to be with someone else. And three, I didn't want to be abandoned. . . . This is not on you. I felt less of a man." Paul tried to explain to her that he was trying and that it was very hard to hear all the things she was telling him. He also acknowledged that Laurie had changed too and had got stronger.

At that point, Laurie transitioned away from the disturbing questions and asked more generally about Paul's life inside the prison. Paul seemed relieved, and the mood lightened; they even shared a few laughs. Laurie was curious if he had got into any fights, but he assured her that he does not have a short fuse anymore. He waxed philosophic about prison life, and Laurie seemed to be listening respectfully. She then described her life—focusing on more positive things such as the kids' aspirations and her interest in finding a church. Laurie's final question to him was whether he still considered the kids to be his and whether he cared about how they were doing: "Laurie, the kids I talk about 24-7. . . . I have [photos of the kids]; I think about them all the time."

Paul got the last word, saying to Laurie again that he always regretted that they never talked and reminding her that they had some fun times. However, he maintained, "I'm the stupid one, crazy, and retarded—because I had something good and I lost it."

After the Dialogue

After Laurie had the opportunity to confront Paul, the relief she felt was incredible: "I was terrified of him. He intimidated me; now, he wasn't intimidating me anymore. I told him things that would have resulted in him backslapping me before. But he could see I'm not that same person." Laurie sensed that Paul could tell that she was serious when she told him not to look for her. She did not tell him how prepared she is now: Laurie now hides a baseball bat behind her door and "wouldn't hesitate to use it."

About a week after the dialogue, Laurie wrote about the relief she felt handing over all her baggage to Paul to carry, saying that after watching herself on the videotape of the dialogue, she was impressed with the attitude she presented throughout the video. "My body language spoke for itself. I allowed silence to ensue for moments at a time and at one point succeeded in making Paul fairly nervous, a fact that will please me for the rest of my life. I could see the confidence and determination on my face, in my whole stance." Overall, Laurie is very content that Paul admitted to hurting their daughter, even though he did not admit to hurting their son. She does not believe his denial regarding their son.

At the time I met with Laurie, Paul was scheduled to be released from prison within the next year, and Laurie was trying to coordinate with correctional officials to arrange his release to the northern part of the state for work release. Ironically, the town where she now lives has the only work-release program in the southern part of the state. "Best of luck to him, as long as he leaves us alone. By the time he gets out, the local police and the state police will both have copies of the PFA. My landlord's going to have a copy of the PFA. I'll just litter them all over. I'll paste them everywhere. So the police will know that I'm serious. If I call and say, 'He's here,' they'll help me out."

Except for a meeting with Kim directly following the dialogue and another meeting about a month later, Laurie's weekly contact with Kim ended. Laurie has continued to receive validation about her self-worth from her academic success at college and the respectful relationships she has with her co-workers. She delights in the fact that her degrading life with Paul is behind her, and she is moving forward with completing her bachelor's degree and taking good care of her kids. Laurie does not hide what happened in her marriage from other people. "I feel like if I can share it with somebody, I will." In many ways, Laurie sees the almost-fatal rape now as a turning point in her life, something that was awful but finally forced her to leave Paul and enabled her to start a new life and to become independent. She no longer worries about what will happen when Paul is released from prison. Laurie says, "VVH really gave me a boost of self-confidence, and that has not gone away. It's helped me open up, to be able to talk to people. It's healthy to talk, and it's okay to be friendly, without being afraid of being accused of something. It's like, 'Oh, they like me.' Paul just had me believing that that was not possible. I have changed so much from who I was. I would have never believed it."

Paul's Story

Paul began our conversation by telling me, emphatically, why he was different from many other offenders: because "God did everything for me." He explained that although he was religious and had God in his life prior to prison, he "backslid." Paul talked a lot about the "old" Paul and the "new" one. The "old" Paul would never listen to someone else's views or needs and would make excuses, hurt someone before they hurt him first, blame everyone else, not take responsibility, think about revenge, and be full of anger. He credited his participation in the VVH program as challenging this self-destructive behavior, forcing him to be honest with himself and to stop feeling such rage and, the hardest part for him, making him walk in his victim's shoes. But he believes this discomfort only made him become more insightful about his shortcomings. Kim insisted the process stay focused on his victim, but Paul confessed, "Sometimes that gets really hard. When you go back and you think about it, you can't believe that you did some of these things that you did. I loved my victim. That's one of the hardest parts I've had to deal with: look how much I hurt my victim." Once Paul realized that he was faced with a choice about whether to transform himself and stop repeating his typical styles of behavior, he described an epiphany: "I never want to be that person again."

Paul was up-front about the main reason the VVH program intrigued him initially: he wanted to see Laurie again. He maintained, "I always wanted to talk to my victim, to ask for forgiveness, and to try to explain why I did what I did." But batterers often present a rational conciliatory side of themselves to outsiders which often conflicts sharply with the behavior that has characterized their intimate relationships. This dissonance is why many scholars criticize the use of restorative justice for domestic-violence victims and their offenders. In particular, scholars and some practitioners are wary that the batterer will use a face-to-face meeting to reassert well-honed power and control tactics (even if the mediators are unaware of the presence of these tactics because of their subtle, intimate form). Yet Kim's case notes testify to Paul's sincerity: she met with Paul over a dozen times before the dialogue, for a period of about six months. She stated that he "has worked diligently to prepare for this face-to-face meeting. . . . He has taken responsibility for the recorded offense and has expressed deep remorse for his actions; he is open to dialogue with Laurie for the purpose of helping her heal in any way possible; he has not exhibited or indicated to me any desire to harm her physically or emotionally; his attitude and behavior with me has been consistently positive and cooperative."

In Paul's interview with me, he described his childhood as an unhappy one in which he was beaten with belts, switches, and other objects by both his biological mother and his foster parents. When he was about three months old, he was removed from his mother's care and sent to live in the first of what would be twenty-two foster homes.. Paul's anger at his mother reverberated in his conversations and writings; he stated that his mother ran around with various men and told him that his father did not want him. But when Paul finally met his father when he was nine years old, he discovered that he had just been released from a mental institution. Paul's stepfather was a drinker and would often pass out in the yard and soil himself, embarrassment that Paul still recalls vividly.

During the course of meeting with Kim, Paul revealed several instances of sexual abuse he endured as a child, and at age fourteen, he was raped by a teacher.[18] When he told his family members about it, they told him to forget about it. The message he received was that it was okay to do that to a kid and that boys need to "man up"[19] and move on. His mother's response was particularly painful; she asked, "Did you get any money for it?" Paul contends that these reactions to his hurt made him unable to trust, leading him to keep everything bottled up inside. He had attempted suicide several times prior to marrying Laurie.

Paul believed that all these hard life lessons affected the way he treated Laurie. He orchestrated his first marriage at age seventeen in order to leave his foster home. His says his first and second wives cheated on him. Paul became very bitter and felt he deserved better.

> Laurie never did anything bad to me, but my lifestyle has always been about self-defense. So that's why I started doing bad things; Anna became a part of this mess. . . . I was already hurting, so I put the pain first on Laurie. I started doing crazy stuff like going after other women. . . . Everything just exploded the night that all this took place.

Today Paul is able to describe all the things he did during the marriage that let Laurie and the kids down: he did not support them and made little effort to get or keep jobs, they lived in cars and shelters, he said hateful things to the children and to Laurie, he drank too much, he watched too much pornography, and he wasted their money on phone-sex calls, although he did not acknowledge the physical beatings he gave Laurie or the kids. Although he believed that Laurie was loyal and took the vows of marriage, "until death do us part," very seriously, Paul always thought Laurie was cheating on him and wanted to punish her. He acknowledged that his extensive watching of pornography probably fueled his desire to rape Laurie. This connection is supported by research studies that find that not only is rape presented in pornography as "normal" sexual behavior, but it conveys the false message that women ultimately welcome the violence.[20]

Paul's recollection of the night he raped Laurie differs from hers, and although he takes responsibility for the rape and weapon use, his descriptions of some of the events leading up to the crime as well as his discussion of his relationship with Laurie and the children minimize his fault and the violence he inflicted. This kind of reconstruction is typical of sexual offenders.[21] Paul's portrayal of the circumstances leading up to the rape that night revolved around his anger and his ongoing suspicions about Laurie's fidelity.[22] In this rationalization, Paul aptly exemplified typical behavior of a jealous batterer who is unreasonably paranoid of his partner's behavior, suspecting sexual betrayal at every turn. He told Kim several times that he believed that Laurie even had sex with the two officers who responded to her 911 call earlier that night, and he said that he told Laurie he wanted her to do everything (sexually) that she had done to the two officers and that he yelled and screamed at her, asking why he could not please her the way the other men had.[23] Next, it occurred to Paul,

> I would need a gun. I wanted her to be scared. [I couldn't find one.] Then I remembered that the one knife was always kept on the side of my bed. In the middle of sex, I reached over and I opened it. At that point, I was so intent on just wanting to hurt her. The only thing that stopped me was when she started crying. I thank God for it. When I heard her cry, I closed the knife.[24]

It was not until Kim began the dialogue process with Paul, providing worksheets to complete and specifically asking questions about the crime, his victim, and so forth, that he began to realize that what he had done to Laurie was rape. It often takes a long time for offenders to develop empathy for their victim and to fully understand the traumatic consequences of their actions. Paul had steadfastly blamed Laurie for his abusive actions for nine years, saying such things as, "If Laurie would have let me take the car, I don't think anything would have happened." In fact, he initially maintained emphatically to Kim and others that he did not think that he had truly raped his wife; he did not force her to have sex. According to Kim's records of this conversation, she stated to Paul that he had told her he was raped when he was fourteen and then asked him how it was "that he was raped and Laurie wasn't? What was different?" This was a watershed moment. Paul began to cry and told Kim what when she put it that way, he realized that he had raped Laurie.

In my interview with Paul, neither of us mentioned anything about the sexual abuse of his daughter, Anna. Yet this topic figured prominently in his conversations with Kim during the preparation process (and later, in the videotape of the face-to-face meeting). Laurie was determined to hear him admit to the molestation, and Kim made numerous phone calls and wrote various Department of Justice employees to determine if such an admission would make Paul vulnerable to further prosecution (something Laurie did not want).[25] Paul assured Kim (and Laurie) that he would admit to sexually abusing their daughter but would not provide any details. Most of the time in his paperwork and his sessions with Kim, Paul stated that he did not know why he molested Anna, but he did confess that he was jealous of the kids and the time and attention Laurie lavished on them. He then stated that Anna reminded him of himself and that he began despising her. Anna was very attached to Paul's mother, whom Paul hated, and he felt that anything connected to his mother could hurt him. Paul's feelings about women in general exemplify his mistrust of them as well as convey his traditional ideas about gender (e.g., he stated that women should not talk dirty, work in a prison, or tell him what to do; when he saw a woman not "acting like a woman" it made him mad; women should be meek, quiet, and act like ladies).

Paul's Path to VVH

When Paul first heard from Kim that Laurie wanted to meet with him, he was very happy. The development of Paul's strong profession of faith also made him feel that he should trust the process.[26] He admitted to Kim that he was excited to see Laurie again and curious about the "new" Laurie and that he still had feelings for her that he was afraid would come up when he saw her again.[27] Paul was glad that the VVH program included the letter exchange prior to the face-to-face meeting because he saw in Laurie's letter to him that she was not going to verbally attack him when they met.

Paul says that what he received from the dialogue process was peace and the knowledge that he actually did something "for Laurie" rather than "to her." When Paul walked through the door and saw Laurie for the first time in years, he says he felt good, but he also acknowledged that the outcome was a toss up: "I had to sit there and look her in the face and hear everything that she had to say, take it all in, with someone that I've loved." Paul was prepared for how angry she was and for her wanting to tell him all the things that she went through. He told Kim that there were some things that Laurie said that he felt defensive about and wanted to challenge, but he held his thoughts because he decided that it was not necessary and wanted to truly listen to Laurie, because she said that he had never listened before during their marriage.[28]

Paul describes himself as a person who had frequently got furiously angry for little reason. He believes that this is true of a lot of offenders and that they could benefit from participating in VVH. He says, "I know it's for the victim, but you have a lot of people in here that really, really wants to be able to ask for forgiveness about their crime. We need to help the victim to heal. But offenders, we need to be healed."

Paul believes that it is harder for men to seek help because of the pressure to seem macho and under control. However, with his strong faith now, Paul says he feels less pressure to prove his masculinity through power: "I have Christ now. I don't have to be macho." This has allowed him to be more authentic and embrace roles, such as "man" and "Daddy," with dignity. His time in prison gave him the freedom to contemplate and challenge his past, for which Paul credits his reading of Scripture, his friendship with the prison chaplain, and the help of other religious-minded people involved in faith. Through church sponsorship, he made two long-term friends who visit him.[29]

Postdialogue

About a month after the dialogue, Paul met again with Kim and was glad to find out that the meeting had really helped Laurie. He explained the way it made him feel: "I don't have to be feeling so down like this; I can move on to other things. I tell people [other offenders] who say they would never do what I did: 'Do you want your victim healed? Or do you want them to carry your burden for the rest of their life?'" Paul feels he "manned up" and faced his victim and gave her what she felt he owed her.

Reflections on VVH Program Today

Paul truly believed in the VVH program, as heard clearly in his remarks to me in the early fall of 2006: "Kim's program is one of the best programs there is because it helps the victim to get through what they need to get through. But it also helps the offender to open up to see himself. So the program was really, really good." He acknowledged, "I'm no saint. I'm not special. I do get angry, and I do get upset. But what I try to do is when I start feeling myself getting in that way, I do something that will help me get out." Paul's one lingering concern was the lack of postrelease support from the Department of Community Corrections. Paul asserted, "They just throw you out there on your own. . . . When it's time to leave, they kick you out." Consequently, Paul spent a good deal of time developing resources and contacts on the outside to help him with the transition when his sentence was up.[30]

Paul's interpretation of his success aside, Laurie gained a great deal from facing her tormentor. She was able to show him that even though he had beaten her down for so many years, physically and emotionally, she was no longer the meek, passive servant to his commands. Laurie's presentation of herself at the dialogue was impressive—she was no longer afraid of him, and she was willing to take charge of the situation to receive answers to questions that were very important to her. The asymmetry of power was tilted in the other direction, toward Laurie, who found her voice and purpose in the VVH process.

In a pamphlet about VVH, Laurie wrote these words about closing this chapter in her life:

> I feel so different without all those burdens, not carefree, exactly, but in some ways, more relaxed. I feel more confident now, more able to stand up for my children and myself. I discovered that I am truly much stronger than I ever was before. I thank God every day for allowing me to experience the trouble I did because it is certainly through trials that true growth occurs. Thanks to my dialogue, I have closed the door on my past and can finally look toward the future with optimism, knowing that I never have to look back again.

Under this statement, Laurie signed with her full name, followed by the word "Survivor."

7

Melissa and Steven

Losing Innocence

Facts of the case: When Melissa was seventeen, she told her mother that her father had molested her from the age of ten until she was fifteen years old. When her father was confronted, he confessed and was ultimately arrested. He was given a prison sentence of seventeen years, which he began serving in 1999. When Melissa was twenty-two years old, she sought out the VVH program, making her the youngest victim to participate in a dialogue. I had access to Melissa and Steven's case files and the letters they exchanged. I interviewed both Melissa and Steven, though initially Melissa was reluctant to agree to participate. Melissa gave her full consent to be interviewed after she learned her father wanted to participate in this project. She felt strongly that he should not have the final word. I respected Melissa's request that I not view the videotape of her dialogue with Steven. I relied on my interviews with Melissa and Steven about the dialogue as well as Kim's impressions of it. I have also corresponded or talked with both of them since the dialogue for updates on their lives.

Melissa's parents divorced when she was just two years old, then rekindled their relationship and remarried when she was ten. Though Melissa's father was a stranger to her, Melissa was incredibly excited to finally have a father, and she remembers some early times when the family shared fun and laughter, taking family trips to Six Flags, Busch Gardens, and Hershey Park. However, Steven quickly began to rule the household with an iron fist, becoming verbally and physically abusive and controlling of Melissa, her brother, and her mother. The kindness and fun disappeared from the household unless her friends were over. Melissa recalls that Steven treated outsiders "as if they were gold" but was verbally and physically abusive and controlling of family members. These dynamics are consistent with many people's motivations to pretend to outsiders that "all is well" in their homes. With his family, Steve orchestrated a pleasant and normal front that hid the physical and sexual abuse inside the privacy of the home. Although Steven only used physical violence to punish Melissa occasionally, these bursts of violence directed at Melissa were enough to scare her and remind her of his power. Most of the physical punishments happened when they were alone; the rest of the family did not witness the acts. Melissa feels that her brother escaped such violence because Steven knew he would have fought back.

Steven's controlling behavior and bad temper flavored every aspect of Melissa's life. For instance, when she was in the sixth grade, he purchased a small notebook in which he wrote all the rules she was to follow. He attached the notebook to a string and forced her to wear it around her neck for a month, even to school. Melissa was mortified, but despite her embarrassment, she did not dare to take it off because Steven said he would come to her school unannounced to ensure that she was wearing it and that it was visible. He also forced Melissa to shower daily at 5:30 p.m. and often watched her in the shower. To make this seem more normal, he told her that he believed that most adult women shave their legs "incorrectly," so he taught Melissa to shave her legs "the right way" and inspected her efforts.

Melissa says Steven molested her for five years (there is some discrepancy between Steven's and Melissa's accounts; Steven claims the abuse lasted less than two years).[1] The abuse included instances of oral sex, fondling, and masturbation. Steven tried to normalize the incest by telling Melissa it was totally appropriate for such intimacy to occur between a father and a daughter. For instance, he told her that he talked with other adults who said it was natural for a man to take a shower with his daughter. Steven also explained to Melissa that if a man got excited and did not have sex, he would be in pain. Like any dutiful daughter—particularly one controlled by fear and physical punishments—Melissa felt sorry for her father and did not want him to be hurt.[2]

During these years, Melissa's mother was emotionally absent and struggling with her own mental and emotional health issues. Although Melissa was unaware of it at the time, she has since discovered that Steven also controlled her mother through threats, intimidation, and occasional violence. Melissa's mother was often away from the home working two jobs to keep the family afloat, and then she would come home to continue working to cook and clean for the household. Children do not always see the reality: as a child, Melissa remembers that her mother was not around, but she knows now, as an adult, that her mother was putting all her energy into taking care of her family by working long hours, while Melissa's father was uninvolved or sometimes unemployed (once for a two-year stretch) and sitting around the house playing video games.

At the time, Melissa blamed her mother for failing to protect her. Melissa did not understand how it was possible that her mother could not have known what her father was doing. Melissa's anger at her mother at this time— rather than at her father—is consistent with research that shows that children who are incest victims blame the parent who has the least power in the household for failing to protect them, rather than the more powerful abusing parent.[3] Steven reinforced Melissa's disconnection from her mother, forbidding her to talk to her mother about anything that was going on because it would upset her. Melissa and her brother learned all too quickly that when their father forbade something, they should not dare to disobey him.

When Melissa was still in middle school, one particular incident made a lasting impression on her. The sexual abuse had already started—it began when she was ten—but Melissa had not yet become a rebellious teenager. Her father began sobbing uncontrollably, a sight she had never seen before, and telling her in excessive detail how he was going to kill himself. He also told her where he would hide the suicide note so that only the family could read it and her mother could not collect life insurance. Melissa remembers how helpless she felt and how scared she was. She had wanted a father so desperately, and now he burdened her not only with the betrayal of trust associated with incest but also with the secret that he might kill himself. In retrospect, Melissa today believes that Steven deliberately planned the situation in order to solidify control over her by preying on her vulnerability and desire for a father.

Partially as a way to assert some independence and partially as a way to "get through the day," as Melissa grew a little older, she began drinking and smoking marijuana, and Steven's temper escalated into serious physical abuse. Turning to drugs or alcohol as a coping mechanism is a very common way for abused children and teenagers to anesthetize themselves from trauma and is a particularly common response for girls.[4] Melissa remembers getting suspended from school for smoking pot. As part of her punishment, Steven forced her to tell both sets of grandparents, which hurt them greatly. It was at this time that Steven's temper escalated into serious physical abuse: to punish Melissa for the school suspension, he made her drop her pants and bend over the recliner. Then he whipped her so hard that he left welts, bruises, and his handprints. Melissa remembers that for the next two weeks, she could only sit sideways on a chair. Melissa's depression about the sexual abuse profoundly affected her will to live, and she found it increasingly difficult to get out of bed in the morning. She describes herself in those days: "I was extremely angry, hurt, and confused. My rebellion was the only way I could control things. My drug use was my way of not dealing with my life—I didn't care about anything."

Telling the Secret

By the time Melissa was seventeen, things at home had escalated to the point that her behavior troubled her mother so much that she risked Steven's rage by insisting that Melissa get some help. Steven refused, no doubt out of his own desire to control Melissa and his worry that the abuse would be revealed, but her mother persevered, dropping Melissa off at a treatment center while Steven was at work. Away from the toxicity of her family environment, Melissa finally confronted the "family secret" and realized how it connected to her depression.

Melissa told both her brother and her mother what had happened. This was a pivotal moment. More than anything else, child victims need two things: they need to be believed, and they need to be safe from further harm. In retrospect, Melissa says, "I don't know what my next step would have been if she hadn't [believed me], . . . running away?"[5] Her mother parked the car at a shopping center close to home, and they talked. They decided to confront her father together. When they confronted him, Melissa remembers that Steven said nothing at first, just listened and took it all in, not apologizing or defending himself or explaining. Melissa remembers screaming at him. He finally admitted to her mother that what their daughter said was true. The last words he said to Melissa—the last time she saw him until the dialogue five years later—were, "I never thought of you as my daughter."

Within a week, Melissa's mother moved the family out of state. This was a profoundly important moment for Melissa because her mother's willingness to move symbolized that she wanted her to feel safe and protected, and Melissa was relieved that she would be able to start anew in a place where no one knew her past. Her family rallied around her, creating a cocoon of safety. Melissa's maternal grandparents flew into Delaware the day after she revealed the abuse and helped to orchestrate and finance the move, and her uncle worked with her brother and friends to get a moving van and pack up all their belongings.

Meanwhile, Steven turned himself in to the police and admitted that he committed the abuse. He refused a plea bargain, choosing to accept whatever sentence the court handed down. Despite Melissa's relief that she was safe, she was overwhelmed with guilt about his arrest and subsequent imprisonment. In fact, Melissa wrote a letter to Steven in jail, apologizing for getting him in trouble and telling him how much she loved him. Melissa's ambivalent feelings reflect very typical behavior for incest victims, who have both depended on their abusers and also been terrorized over many years; they are often terrified of the consequences when they challenge these dynamics.

Consistent with the research on victims of child sexual abuse, for the years leading up to the dialogue Melissa was haunted by feelings of guilt and self-blame about the abuse she endured. As a child, she knew on some level that what her father was doing was wrong, yet she was unable to stop him. Her helplessness then made her feel as though she was partially responsible for the abuse even as an adult, and this guilt was reinforced when people such as her husband or other family members and friends asked her why she did not say anything about Steven's behavior while the abuse was ongoing. Unfortunately, this reaction—asking why the victim did not tell anyone— is all too common. Yet the findings of research are unequivocal: regardless of age, children are never responsible for inappropriate sexual behavior by adults, even when they are uncomfortable with it or have an idea about the inappropriateness—much less illegality—of such abusive actions.[6]

The Road to Victims' Voices Heard

Melissa's moving away from Delaware and eventually knowing that her father was in prison helped put her on a healthier path. Melissa's mother worked tirelessly to find her a counselor she could trust, and Melissa received a lot of unconditional love from her mother, maternal grandparents, and brother, and from her husband. With a strong support network in place, she was able to find more solace in understanding the past, but there were still too many questions. Melissa wanted answers from Steven, but she realizes now that she was not yet emotionally ready to confront him. "I had so much hate and anger. I felt if I ever saw him, I'd kill him. . . . Then just as time went on, I matured. I didn't have as much hate for him. I just needed answers." Everyone dissuaded her from her desire to connect with Steven, but finally someone at the state Department of Justice gave her Kim Book's name and information about the Victims' Voices Heard program. Melissa promptly called Kim and explained how she was feeling.

Because Melissa lived out of state, the VVH correspondence took place by phone or through the mail. Almost every week, Melissa received new paperwork to fill out, "homework assignments" from Kim. Melissa is a very reflective person who valued the exercises, even when they made her think about difficult situations. Although it was painful for her to dredge up memories of the abuse, they were helpful for preparing to meet Steven.

Melissa and her brother remain very close, and she leaned on him for support. She felt that he understood the family situation best because he knew their father's temper and their family dynamics. Her husband was as supportive as he could be about her VVH participation, despite some difficulty understanding the situation as clearly as her brother did. It is always very difficult for someone's partner or spouse to hear that their loved one was sexually abused, mistreated, and hurt by someone else: "If you're not going through that situation yourself, it's harder. My husband was scared to death I was gonna get hurt and it was gonna put me way back to where I was when we first met."

Melissa's mother had no interest in ever seeing Steven again but rallied to support her daughter's wishes despite her own hesitations. She was particularly concerned about Steven's ability to twist things around. It was reassuring to Melissa that his success with manipulating adults as well as children reveals just how clever he was, equally manipulative with her as a trusting child as he was with adults who should have known better.

Both Melissa and Steven spent about six months preparing with Kim before the dialogue. Without this preparation, Melissa worries that she would have turned back into a little girl again, cowering before her father. It was clear to Melissa that Kim's goal was to ensure that "the victims are in the right place, that they don't end up walking out more hurt." Melissa was also relieved that Kim also understood that only the victim herself truly knows what she needs.

It was very helpful for Melissa to know that Kim was talking with Steven concurrently. For example, Melissa said that Kim prepared her to see him after so many years by asking her, "What did he look like when he hurt you?" and then telling her how he had changed, so she could readjust the picture she had frozen in her mind. Especially for survivors of incest, betrayal is a constant fear, so Melissa needed reassurance that Kim's utmost goal was to protect her as the victim. Melissa needed to feel she was safe, which was understandable given her experience with Steven's control, abuse, and betrayal.

The exchange of letters was helpful because Melissa got to hear from Steven directly and not just through an intermediary. Melissa especially appreciated hearing his recollection of the incidents of abuse. Melissa compared his writing to the tone of a business letter, rather than as she imagined a father would write to his daughter. In her own letter to him, she was able to express her feelings directly as well, as this excerpt illustrates: "I want to leave any hurt or bad feelings at the door. I don't want to take them home with me—I want them resolved."

Meeting Face to Face

Kim and Melissa arranged to meet at the prison, and Melissa had invited her sister-in-law to be there as her support person. VVH paid for her airplane ticket to Delaware for the dialogue. Melissa felt intimidated as Steven entered the room: "You sort of turn back into that scared little kid." Melissa had prepared a list of questions and comments, and she feels that Steven listened to what she had to say and cooperated by answering any questions she posed, albeit with some lack of clarity. Steven took responsibility for what happened, and Kim confirms Melissa's recollections about Steven's sincerity and sentiments expressed during the dialogue, during which he said, "You are a better person than I am. I couldn't forgive someone for this. But I am sorry. I'm sorry to you, your mom, and your brother. There's only one criminal here, but there are many victims."

What was crucial to Melissa was that Steven repeated that the abuse had not been her fault. Typical of most children who survive sexual abuse, Melissa entertained many self-doubts and blamed herself, but she now refuses to beat herself up about it. She knows that children simply do not have the tools and maturity to understand what they can as adults: "Someone you love and trust is never supposed to hurt you."

At the conclusion of the dialogue, both Steven and Melissa signed an affirmation agreement. This was very important to Melissa, and it was something that they had negotiated beforehand, with Kim's help, during the preparation process. It is not a legally binding document but was signed in good faith by both parties, and they consider it to be their hope for the future. In it, Steven stated the following:

> It is my intent to assist both sexual offenders and victims of sexual offenses whenever possible.
> It is my intent to participate in counseling, continuously from this moment forward.
> It is my intent to never victimize a child.
> It is my intent to never have any contact, in any form, with my victim Melissa, or with any of her family, from this moment further.

Melissa is glad that she participated in the dialogue, finding relief in facing Steven and showing that he does not scare or control her anymore. When she was growing up, Steven repeatedly told her that she was a "screw-up" and would not amount to anything, and she delighted in demonstrating, "I'm a better person than you. I am not what you told me I was gonna be." She wanted him to see how wrong he was and that she was no longer that scared little girl. Being able to face her fear was her greatest triumph. "Even though he couldn't hurt me anymore, I was still scared to death of him, that he might come after me or my kids. But I was able to stand up to that and face him and let him know, 'I'm not afraid of you. You don't control me.'"

I asked Melissa to reflect on how going through the VVH program had changed her life. She reported that she no longer has nightmares or problems sleeping. She also has less anxiety surrounding the date when her father gets released from prison, which is scheduled for the year 2012, when her own daughter is ten years old—the same age Melissa was when her father began molesting her.[7] This thought upset Melissa so much that she had begged her husband, a hunter, to teach her how to shoot a gun, but after going through the VVH program she is "not stressing like that anymore."[8]

Religion and forgiveness were not parts of Melissa's motivations to meet her father. She is not a religious person—her father is an atheist and influenced the family in this regard. She explained that in fact the sexual abuse has made it very difficult for her to believe in God and religion. "It just doesn't make any sense to me, the whole experience. . . . I mean, when people say that everything happens for a reason, that is crap to me. Granted, it made me grow up faster; it makes me a better parent. But still."

Melissa has tried to forgive Steven, thinking perhaps he had a sickness and that he could not help or control what he did to her. "So, on some levels, as far as that goes, I have forgiven him. But on other levels, I want to, but I can't because it's like, 'Alright, you have a sickness. You can fight it.' It's what's more important, your child or your urges?"

Long-Term Effects of VVH for Melissa

Melissa believes the dialogue process has transformed her life and made her feel more at peace today. "I'm no longer sitting there ripping myself apart that I let this happen. *He* did this, not me." She believes that the VVH process effected a change in her understanding of herself. For instance, Melissa better understands her parenting style: "Because of the crime, I'm a lot more of a protective parent. I'm absolutely paranoid when it comes to my kids, of somebody hurting them."

Other people close to Melissa have noticed changes too. Her husband has observed that the biggest change in her is that she no longer obsesses over the subject of what her father did or gets visibly upset when it comes up.

Melissa's long-term goal is to work professionally with adults who have survived child sexual abuse or with the child victims themselves. Based on her positive experience with VVH, she says she would recommend the program if the victim were ready, because it was so empowering and a relief that she could now "let a lot of things go": "I'm so glad I did it. I'm a different person. I don't have a single regret about it."

Steven's Story

Most sexual offenders minimize and rationalize their abusive behaviors, comparing their actions to other sexual offenders' and concluding that their own behavior is not as serious or damaging.[9] Steven is no different; although he acknowledges that everything he did was inappropriate, he feels that his actions were not as "wrong" as they could have been since his sexual abuse of Melissa did not include intercourse. Also consistent with research on child sexual abuse and incest, Steven characterizes the first time he "crossed the line" as an unintended innocent act.[10] Steven describes the first incident with his daughter: he was sitting on railroad ties and got splinters in the back of his upper thigh, near his buttocks. When he tried to get them out, he could not, and Melissa helped him. After she removed the splinters, he asked her to get some alcohol and pour some on him. He says that the alcohol spilled onto his genitals, and Melissa got something to help clean him up. Steven says that when she was cleaning him up, it felt good; he enjoyed it and told himself that the feelings were mutual. As time went by, he began to create occasions for physical intimacy, often asking her to rub Ben-Gay on his back.

Steven admits that he tried to encourage Melissa to enjoy the abuse so that he could continue it. According to Kim's review of the videotaped dialogue, Steven admits that he lied to Melissa, manipulated her, and conned her. Steven also explains that he believed what he was making Melissa do would bring her closer to him and help him control her better so she would have less hostility toward his rules, become more obedient, perform better in school, and stop using drugs and alcohol. Rationalizing abuse in this way is a common feature of sexual offending.[11] Today, however, Steven accepts that he irrevocably violated the father-daughter relationship, and he takes full responsibility for his actions. He was eager to help make amends. Steven contends that his participation in the program was to reassure his daughter that she was entirely blameless and that he was the only one responsible for the sexual abuse.[12]

In my interview with Steven, he described his family life and what he initially saw as his tenuous relationship with Melissa. Steven had had no contact with his son or daughter in the ten years during which he was separated from Melissa's mother. Steven explained, "When my wife and I separated, my daughter was an infant. I didn't know her. My son was older. So when [my ex-wife] contacted me about reuniting, my son was known to me as my son. My daughter—and the way I worded it was, unfortunately, because we did not grow up together, it could have been any child off the streets: 'Oh, this is your daughter.'"[13]

Steven believes that once he came to accept Melissa as his daughter, he was no longer able to abuse her. He takes a lot of pride in the fact that he was the one who recognized that what he was doing was wrong and stopped the abuse. Research on pedophiles suggests otherwise: abusers often stop their behavior when the children begin to start looking more like adult women, rather than as little or young girls.[14] Melissa was fifteen when Steven stopped molesting her. Steven's sense of himself as calm and controlled belies a struggle between what he wants people to think about him and the reality. For instance, at several points during our conversation, Steven admitted that he does not always have control over his anger, and during our interview, he asserted control over the questions and direction several times, telling me what he wanted to talk about and what he did not. He also told me how much he was giving up (e.g., time on his job) to meet with me and how fortunate I was that he agreed to meet with me. Steven says he felt blindsided by Melissa's accusations and that at first he believed that if he just went away, Melissa and her mother would not press charges against him, claiming that Melissa's maternal grandparents talked her into pressing formal charges.

Steven says he did not want to put Melissa through a court case, so he refused to try to negotiate a plea bargain. He told me, "I accepted my punishment. I am guilty. . . . I'm glad she told—not that I'm glad I'm in jail—I'd be lying if I said I was—but if it helps her get over it, I have no problem doing the time." Steven's acceptance of his punishment is ambivalent, however; he believes that although his behavior with Melissa was inappropriate, it would have been far worse to have progressed to intercourse. Thus, he believes his crime is not as bad as that of the guys who "went that far" with their daughters. Concomitantly, he asserts that his sentence was too harsh and that he should have served only four years, rather than the seventeen-year sentence he received.

A few days into Steven's jail stay, his mother told him that his wife and his daughter's family were moving to the South, following his wife's parents, who retired there. At several points in my interview with Steven, he mentioned to me, in a self-pitying way, that now he is all alone: "I'm the only one in Delaware, and I'm not from Delaware. I don't like Delaware. I don't want to be here. My mother died [while I was in prison here]." At the same time, however, Steven acknowledges that his actions violated his whole family, causing his son's ambivalence toward him now, his estrangement from Melissa, and his divorce. He says that the only silver lining is that now Melissa and his son are closer. Steven also says he felt a more acute sense of grief and loss during the VVH process, because he knew the face-to-face dialogue would be the last time he would ever see Melissa.

Steven's Experience with VVH

Kim sent the initial invitation letter to Steven on May 10, 2004. He had been incarcerated since June 1999 on a seventeen-year sentence. After about six months of meeting with Kim, the dialogue occurred on January 24, 2005. Steven's assessment of the paperwork required by VVH was quite negative. He felt that it was excessive and in some ways irrelevant to sexual offenders such as himself. "I've got a list of things that she can work on. Kim's a total control freak, without hesitation. Okay, she gives us some homework to go over. But some people in here have problems with homework because of limited vocabulary, and they can't express their thoughts that well." As he often did, Steven distinguished between himself and offenders he believes are not as intelligent, a pattern that emerged several times in my interview as well in suggestions and corrections he made to Kim's paperwork.

Despite these criticisms, Steven respected Kim's "honorable behavior" and the respectful way that she treated him. There were some areas of his past that he did not want shared with Melissa but discussed with Kim. Steven felt the information was relevant for Kim since she was working with both of them, but he felt that if she shared the information with his daughter, she might feel blamed for something. He says, "I worked very hard not to give any blame to the victim." Steven says he did not want Melissa to think, "Look at me, poor me": "I didn't want to give that chance."

Steven had difficulty writing his letter to give to Melissa prior to the actual dialogue because he did not know how Melissa would react to his words. He tried to focus on her feelings and what he wanted her to know, as this excerpt shows:

No reason, no thoughts, nothing can justify or explain adequately my actions. . . . You were a caring and loving and trusting child. I took advantage of that. I perverted something that you freely gave to me. It did not

start that way but gradually I changed that thing into my own sexual grati-
fication. . . . I remember you asking me if it was wrong and I lied to you as
it changed into something obscene. This change was created by me. You
trusted me to always do what was right, and I failed you.

Steven apologized, writing,

I regret and am sorry for what I did to you, but also I am sorry for what I
caused in you. I affected the entire rest of your life negatively when I was
supposed to be a positive influence. In no way did you ask for or deserve
what I did to you. When you gave me trust, I gave you dishonesty. You
gave me caring, I gave you abuse. I took your innocence. None of this even
mentions that I disrupted your home and family, and hurt your mom and
brother.

You were right in contacting the authorities. I know it was probably a
very hard thing to do on many levels. . . . Never think you shouldn't have
said anything, because you did what you should have done. Actually, you
did what I should have done but was not strong enough to do. You finally
did have that strength that I was lacking. Your actions helped make the
world better.

Steven had anticipated that Melissa's letter would be full of rage and was
surprised and relieved that it was written in a respectful way, despite what he
had done to her. Steven said, "In the letter Melissa sent me, it was just a very
appropriate letter, very mature—more mature than what I was expecting." As
the letter to his daughter suggests, Steven worked hard to convey Melissa's
innocence and to allay any lingering doubts she had that turning him in to
the police was the wrong thing to do. At the same time, however, according
to Kim's case notes, one of the areas in which Kim worked the most with
Steven was in getting him to understand that the dialogue was a time for
Melissa to get some answers and to facilitate *her* healing. In other words, the
face-to-face meeting was not an opportunity for Steven to talk about himself
or to try to get Melissa to feel sorry for him. Steven accomplished this goal,
addressing crucial points that he wanted Melissa to hear, without minimizing or excusing his behavior.

Kim also talked a lot with Steven about the strength of a father's power
over his daughter and Melissa's inability to prevent him from abusing her.
This fact was important to reinforce because in the early stages of the VVH
preparation process Steven had occasionally stated that Melissa could have

stopped his abuse. Kim talked at great length with him about his mistaken belief that Melissa could have stopped him, which put the responsibility on her and alleviated his own responsibility, allowing him to believe she was a willing participant and that he could continue. By the time I interviewed Steven, he expressed a much more complete understanding of this issue. In fact, after reviewing the videotape, Kim reported that Steven clearly stated his understanding at the face-to-face meeting, saying to Melissa, "I protected you from everyone but me. You have nothing to do with me being here. I'm here because of what I did. I did the crime, not you." Steven acknowledged to me that it was very hard to face Melissa, but he spoke of how impressed he was with her comportment during their dialogue, saying, "She's a very healthy person."

Long-Term Effects for Steven

After the face-to-face meeting, Steven maintains that he does not feel dramatically different because he says he had always accepted responsibility for his crime. Steven tries to spread the word about the VVH program, but only selectively. He believes that "some offenders might want to see the victim just because they want another chance to maybe control or something, especially over a family member or spouse. But some really are sincere and truly want to help the victim heal." It was disconcerting to hear that Steven believes that offenders who hurt their own family members would be eager for a face-to-face meeting so that they could continue their control; Steven fit this hypothetical scenario yet saw himself as an exception in his belief that his actions did not stem from a need to regain control over Melissa. Steven talked about his participation as a selfless act with only Melissa's needs in mind, and he also gave credit to the program for helping victims heal and letting them be heard.

Steven told me that he would like to speak to people about sexual abuse when he is released from prison, to try to educate children and parents about warning signs. He explained it this way: "I would love to go into junior high schools and hold class with them—at least when they are old enough or whatever—and just talk about things. I would like to be able to talk to parents, about 'this is how sex offenders do things.'" I probed him on this idea, asking him, "Do you mean to give them warning signs to watch for? Like 'if your kid starts getting withdrawn, you might want to ask questions'?" Steven agreed: "Things like this should never happen. Me seeing her in the shower, me seeing her naked. I broke all the rules. I would like to talk to kids . . . and explain these certain things should not happen. If these things do happen, make sure the kid knows that she isn't gonna get in trouble. She needs to tell."

I asked Steven what his plans were after he was released from prison, given the required designation as a sexual offender that would be displayed on his driver's license and his limited support network. He was resigned— and unhappy—about his prospects: "I can't get out of Delaware. I'm in here for another three and a half, three years. Then I'm on probation forever. Not really forever, but for twelve years. I'm gonna be seventy-some years old." I asked him about transferring probation so that he could go back to Arizona, where he used to live, but he was cynical about that possibility too and probably realistic: "You need family, a job. I don't have a family. I have no support system, other than my son. But so I can only get a job and residence, which are all requirements, right here in Delaware. It's such a little state to be stuck in."

Kim's letter to Steven, sent about a week after the dialogue, reminded him of his courage in what he told Melissa: "that you are sorry for the pain you caused her and she now is feeling a sense of having closed a chapter in her life that was not good. It may be painful for you but it is a good thing for her, and sometimes we must sacrifice our own needs for the sake of someone else's. You did that and I hope that can bring you some measure of peace."

For both Steven and Melissa, the VVH process and the face-to-face meeting were very significant. For Melissa, confronting her father was empowering, particularly since his last image of her was as a victim. Today, she is an accomplished, mature adult. Melissa was able to show her father that she was no longer the scared teenager who was manipulated into doing things that felt uncomfortable and disgusting. Hearing and reading his apologies helped to erase any lingering traces of self-blame or doubt that she had internalized from that time in her life. Steven was finally able to tell her directly that the abuse was not her fault and to apologize for the things he said and did to her that had violated her sense of security and trust in others. Melissa's experiences have made her a more alert parent, one who is resilient and able to succeed in her life despite her father's sexual abuse. Although forgiveness of her father was not an outcome, nor was there an expectation that it would be, what Melissa did secure was a profound sense of safety and the ability to forgive herself.

8

Scott and Bruce

Thou Shalt Not . . .

Facts of the case: When Justine was twelve years old, she told her parents that her grandfather was "touching" her. Her grandfather, Bruce, was charged with rape in the fourth degree (sexual penetration of a victim less than sixteen years old) and continuous sexual abuse of a child. He also molested Justine's female cousin. He served two years in prison for these offenses, followed by house arrest. He was released under the probation department's supervision and is registered in Delaware as a sexual offender. Justine's father, Scott, sought out VVH; Justine herself did not participate. I interviewed Scott about his participation in VVH, had access to his case file, and watched the videotape of the dialogue. Bruce, who is now in his seventies and in declining health, did not participate in an interview for this book. I was able to conduct a brief interview with Justine, who is now nineteen years old.

Whenever the cousins got together, the two girls were inseparable, running around the house, giggling, and sharing dreams and secrets. One such secret came out in the summer of 2002, when Justine was twelve and her cousin Meg was fourteen. Justine said to her cousin, "Has Pop-Pop ever . . . ," and Meg finished her sentence with the words "touched you?" and answered, "Yeah." Pop-Pop was Bruce, their grandfather. The secret was too big to keep to themselves, and since the girls were both very close with their mothers, they told them first.

That night, everyone sat around the kitchen table listening to the girls and deciding what to do with the information, speculating about their legal options and talking logistics. According to the girls, the abuse had been going on for about three years, beginning when Justine was about nine years old. Justine's aunt is an attorney, and she characterized the situation as a Catch-22: the girls would need counseling, but any counselor would have to report the abuse. Reporting child sexual abuse exacerbates an already traumatic situation for victims, as they have to tell strangers about their experiences and be prepared for the repercussions following such disclosure.[1] Scott and Jackie decided to confront Bruce with the accusations when he and his wife, Heather, arrived home from vacation the next day. Since Scott's father was a minister, they also asked some ministers they knew well to come over and support them through the initial meeting. When Scott asked Bruce about the girls' accusations, Bruce told them, "There is some truth to what they are telling you."

Jackie and Scott called the police, who quickly responded and arrested Bruce. Scott recalls that Bruce did not seem overly repentant, and Scott believes that Bruce probably would have kept sexually abusing his grandchildren if they had not called the police. The police recommended that Justine be examined at the hospital. Jackie took Justine there, where a SANE (Sexual Assault Nurse Examiner) nurse met with them.[2] When they got back home that night, in low tones in the privacy of their bedroom, Jackie told Scott what the doctor said, that the molesting involved more than touching, even though Bruce denied that there had been any penetration. "Right at the very end, Bruce got to a point where he was using his fingers. He was inserting fingers, and that's what scared Justine, because she was wondering what step he was going to take next."[3] The SANE nurse reassured Jackie that the physical examination fully supported Justine's story. Scott jumped up, angry beyond words, heading for the door to confront his father-in-law. "The only thing I could picture was his face pounding into the carpet, because that was right where I was going to put it." Jackie got between Scott and the door to detain him, saying, "Listen, you've got every right if you want to go down and beat him up. . . . But if you go down there and you do that, it will create legal trouble for you. I don't need both of you locked up." Scott looked at her face, and reason prevailed.

When child sexual abuse is exposed, family members often try to make sense of the situation. It is very common for parents to blame themselves for their inability to protect their children, but child victims often react initially to sexual abuse by withdrawing, feeling anxious, depressed, and fearful, and hiding what is happening, because they cannot make sense of it and they feel too vulnerable and afraid to tell anyone.

Scott and Jackie tried to recall any clues in Justine's behavior that, in retrospect, seemed suspicious and would have tipped them off that she was being molested. Although their family was very close, Scott and Jackie had noticed nothing strange or out of the ordinary about Justine's behavior during the time her grandfather was molesting her. The only difference in Justine's personality had been that she seemed quieter, a change her parents attributed to the recent loss of one set of beloved grandparents. In retrospect, it was easy for Scott to see how Justine's allegiances were torn; she loved her family and was taught to respect her grandparents.

After Scott's father-in-law admitted that some of the girls' accusations were true, Scott could not stomach seeing him. Scott felt horrified to learn that some of the molesting occurred on car rides to Wal-Mart, something he had encouraged Justine to do with her grandfather. Scott avoided Bruce, which was somewhat difficult because of the close proximity of their houses and the fact that Bruce was not incarcerated until about four months after his arrest. When the family met with the prosecuting attorney to discuss case strategies, they were asked to consider a compromise. Since Bruce admitted to part of what he had done and physical evidence corroborated the victims' testimony, the prosecutor raised the option of a plea bargain. The prosecutor stressed that Bruce was in his seventies and that it would be rough to put the two girls, then thirteen and fifteen, through a trial.[4] The prosecutor suggested a mandatory sentence of two years in prison, followed by one year of home confinement with an ankle bracelet. Bruce would never again be allowed unsupervised contact with anyone under eighteen and would not be permitted to see his grandchildren unless they made the choice to see him after they turned eighteen. Under Delaware law (as in most states), Bruce would have to register with the police as a sex offender and document his whereabouts for the rest of his life. The family agreed, largely to avoid the pain and messiness of a trial (though the evidence could have been used to request a sentence of 125 years). Bruce was ultimately convicted of rape in the fourth degree (sexual penetration of a victim less than sixteen years old) and continuous sexual abuse of a child. Justine was present during the meeting and agreed with the punishment proposed. Several years later, as Justine matured, she acknowledged some regret in letting Bruce get away with such a light punishment.

The situation was incredibly emotionally charged within the family, and not surprisingly, Heather, Scott's mother-in-law, felt particularly conflicted. Her initial reaction was one of disbelief; she thought the girls were exaggerating. As time went on, she realized the girls were not fabricating the events.[5] Eventually Heather conceded the truth and filed for divorce. Her determination to obtain a divorce was further strengthened by her own daughters' (Scott's wife and sister-in-law) dawning recollections that their father abused them when they were children. The time after Bruce's conviction was very tough for the entire family. Everyone was angry and uncomfortable. Scott had struggled with intimacy and expressing his feelings after his own parents' deaths, and the revelations of abuse only made the situation worse. He became even more emotionally inaccessible to his wife, who really needed his support. Scott was forced to confront the walls he had built up around himself when Justine asked if the abuse was her fault.

During the time Bruce was incarcerated, Scott says a lot of healing went on, particularly for his mother-in-law, but he does not believe that his wife and sister-in-law have healed.

Discovering VVH

Scott credits his strong religious faith for giving him the strength to handle the horrific discovery that a trusted family member was sexually abusing his daughter. Not only was Bruce his wife's father and children's grandfather, but Scott had known him since he was an infant because Heather and Bruce were lifelong friends of his parents. Scott felt that he was handling things well by himself, but meanwhile, his marriage was floundering.

This was a turning point for Scott—just when his frustration was at a peak, a good friend of his suggested that Scott talk to his pastor, who encouraged him to turn everything over to God. That night, Scott and Jackie had a very long talk, and she decided that they should hold off on the divorce and give the marriage a second chance, to—as Scott put it—"give God time to work with it." Around the same time that Scott's faith was challenged and restored, his father-in-law had completed his prison term and was sent to a work-release facility. One day, while Scott was driving to meet with his pastor, Dan, he says that he happened to hear a religious program on the radio that centered around the subject of forgiveness, which caused him to have an epiphany that changed his life. He realized that Bruce was the one person who was his big challenge, his "big hurdle to get over." Scott recognized how difficult it would be to forgive, but he also realized that he wanted to ask Bruce to forgive *him* for the ugly thoughts and feelings he had been harboring against him. Scott knew that revenge served no purpose.

Although Jackie and Justine did not fully understand the urgency of Scott's need to forgive Bruce, they offered their support for his desire to confront Bruce and explore forgiveness, as did Dan. Scott called the victim services worker who had been assigned to the case, and she provided information about the Victims' Voices Heard program. He then called Kim and told her, "I need to forgive him for what he's done. But equally as important, I need his forgiveness for the things I've said against him." Given Kim's strong faith, she understood Scott's conviction, without which he feels strongly that he could not have even contemplated sitting in the same room with the man who molested his daughter.[6]

Kim met with Bruce at his work-release location, explaining that the sole purpose of the meeting for Scott centered on forgiveness on both their parts. Before the dialogue preparation could begin, Kim needed to discern whether Bruce was willing to admit what he did and express remorse. He admitted that he inappropriately touched his granddaughters, but he denied penetration. He also maintained that his granddaughters had been his only victims, although there had been allegations that he had also molested his daughters. Bruce wanted to participate because he thought the process could help heal his family. He told Kim that he accepted the plea bargain so Justine would not have to go to the trial, and he wanted to make sure that Kim knew some of the good things he had done, such as agreeing with his wife that they should pay for Justine's (and her cousin's) counseling costs. Kim challenged him on this point, asking if perhaps he took the plea bargain as much for himself as he did for Justine so that the crime would be kept quiet and out of public scrutiny. He agreed that the decision to avoid trial also benefited him.

Kim met weekly with Bruce during the preparation process. He often wavered in his description of the circumstances, sometimes blaming his granddaughter for calling him to come over to visit. He says he interpreted Justine's friendliness as interest, indicating to him that his interest in sexual activity was mutual. Placing blame on victims or claiming that they share responsibility are common rationalizations among child sexual offenders. Kim noted that Bruce often seemed more concerned about what the situation did to *him* than what it had done to his *victims,* maintaining that the sentence imposed was too severe and unfair (he felt that his conviction should have been for "offensive touching" and not for rape). He worried about the future a lot, knowing that people would treat him with suspicion upon his release and that he would be all alone at the end of his days. During some meetings, Kim observed that Bruce would host a "pity party," crying about his failing eyesight and being ostracized from his family.

Scott and Bruce were very clear about their motivations, goals, and expectations for the dialogue, and the preparation process went smoothly. Both men began writing letters to be exchanged prior to the actual face-to-face meeting. Scott's letter to Bruce quoted Scripture about forgiveness, and he explained that, as a man of faith, the meeting with Bruce was something that he felt that he *had* to do and that he was hopeful that Bruce could use this experience to help others in similar situations.

Bruce was surprised by the tenor of Scott's letter; he had thought it would be filled with anger. Bruce wrote back a short note saying why he would agree to meet: "to express my regret for my actions." Bruce acknowledged that the letter was hard to write: "because I made such an unfortunate mistake." He also stated, "I don't want to cause pain to the family and I will make every effort to stay as far away from the family as I possibly can. I understand your wishes and I will do my best to abide by them. I hope that you would not harbor bad feelings towards me and there are none towards you."

Scott felt that this initial letter "skimmed across the surface of what Bruce had done," and he was not impressed. Meanwhile, the preparation for the face-to-face dialogue continued for a number of months. Bruce continued to express a lot of confusion about why Scott wanted to meet with him. In Kim's weekly meetings with him, she continued to assess his sincerity and prepare him for the dialogue. Ultimately, Kim wanted Scott to be prepared for any outcome. Bruce told Kim that he knew what he did was wrong, but he also believed that the devil talked him into doing what he did, especially since he insisted that he had never done anything like that before. Most sexual offenders who abuse children say the abuse was a one-time occurrence. Yet in nearly every case, child sexual offenders continue to offend until they are arrested.[7] He also stated that on one occasion when he was looking at his granddaughter, a circle appeared in front of her, and he saw the devil in the middle of the circle. At another meeting, he asked Kim if she thought his abuse was due to a physical condition, since he had family members with various hereditary diseases. These rationalizations are consistent with sex offenders' need to avoid responsibility for their own behavior. As their meetings progressed, however, Bruce more fully acknowledged his responsibility for his behavior. More and more often, Bruce mentioned to Kim that he should have known better than to molest his granddaughter, but he still did not think "people could give concrete reasons about why they do the things they do."

Scott, on the other hand, worried about his ability to make and maintain eye contact with Bruce. Kim encouraged Scott to bring a support person (Scott chose his pastor friend, Dan), and she also came up with a solution: Scott's supporter would sit directly behind Bruce. If things got too intense, Scott could shift his focus and look at Dan. Kim worried about Bruce's tendency to wander off task and developed ways to reel in his attention by asking him specific questions in an orderly fashion. Scott was also reassured by the fact that although he could ask Bruce any question, Bruce would not be permitted to ask him anything without clearing it first with Kim.

Dialogue

Kim talked with Scott about what he feared most during the dialogue. Scott said, "My initial sight of him. I'm terrified by my reaction to seeing him for the first time." When Bruce did enter the room, he looked terrible. He appeared to have aged at least ten years during the past three. In fact, he stumbled over a chair walking into the dialogue. Scott admitted that it was a relief in some ways to see Bruce so frail because it cushioned the blow, so that the only thing he felt for him was pity.

Each dialogue is unique, and the format of the conversation is guided by the wishes and needs of the victim, who initiates the process. In Scott's case, he wanted to accomplish three things: to forgive Bruce, to receive forgiveness from Bruce, and to help Bruce understand how his unique experience could be used to help others. Scott did not want to talk about the past or to rehash any details about the sexual abuse; instead he wanted to look at the potential for change and growth in the future. Bruce did not want to talk about specific details either, so Scott's expectations were easily met.

Because Bruce had been released from prison, the dialogue occurred in a classroom at the work-release center located on the prison compound. The two men sat in upholstered chairs with a small coffee table between them. Bruce did not bring a support person with him, but Scott's pastor-friend Dan sat directly behind Bruce, as planned. After Scott said a prayer asking for God's guidance during their conversation, Kim opened the dialogue by thanking both men for participating and directing Scott to begin telling Bruce why he was here and why he wanted to meet with Bruce. Scott declared, "I'm here because it is high time for forgiveness. A lot of time has passed." Bruce interrupted him and quickly spoke, not meeting Scott's eyes at first: "I would just like to say how sorry I am for all the heartache, pain, and grief that I've caused and by letting an evil spirit get into me, which I'm not quite sure how it happened. I will try to make sure things I do in the future are for the benefit of the family." He also apologized that their neighbors knew what was going on, including Justine's friends, which, Bruce acknowledged, was no doubt hard on her.

Scott then asked for Bruce's forgiveness: for "things that I have done, thought, and said in the past two years; I need to ask you to forgive me for what I've done against you. Forgiveness is a two-way street." At first, Bruce did not seem to understand his request and talked about how prison had been an eye-opening experience for him. Kim had to interject at this point to verify that Bruce understood Scott's request. Bruce assured Scott, "I'm not sure why you need mine, but you certainly have my forgiveness." Scott did not respond, and Bruce added, "But I think I'm the one that needs to be asking for forgiveness." In recalling the dialogue about a year later, Scott says he was thrilled to hear Bruce finally say this: "It was so cool. It was a really, really neat experience." In turn, Scott told Bruce, "I do forgive you one hundred percent for what's happened. I told Kim and Dan that Jesus had to hang on a cross to be forgiven. All you and I have to do is sit across a table."

Several times, Bruce tried to elaborate on his apology, and he also mentioned his hope for a reconciliation with the family. Kim reminded him that the dialogue was only between him and Scott. Bruce also mentioned several times that Scott "did the right thing" by not asking for a trial and "drag[ging] a young person through that." The implication of these two messages was contradictory; Bruce claimed that he had taken full responsibility for his actions but also admitted contemplating going to trial to fight the charges against him.

Although Scott approached the dialogue with the goals of forgiveness and finding peace foremost in his mind, he grew to want an equally important outcome, and one that eventually took precedence: to encourage Bruce to use the lessons he learned to help others. Scott stated, "I want something beautiful to come out of this. It's not just doom and gloom and the end of everything good—that's not what God would want of me or you."

Although Bruce recounted his faith "credentials" (such as how many years he had attended church or sung in the choir), he responded in a more secular vein—for example, with promises of continuing his volunteer work with Meals on Wheels—but during the dialogue, he did not ever say that he would use his "testimony" as a convicted child sex offender to help others. Scott pursued this emphasis to live a Christian life and offer testimony and help for others in similar positions, but Bruce's comprehension did not seem to go beyond "doing good things." Their exchanges were respectful, informal, and friendly. At no point was either man defensive or antagonistic. A few times, there was even some laughter, and some stories revealed a long history together, as Bruce knew Scott's parents and was impressed by his father's ministry. Scott spoke honestly about how he believes that "letting go" to give God control is difficult for men, but he shared many examples of situations in which his life was better for it, and he explained how much he wanted the same kind of bounty for Bruce.

Toward the end of the meeting, Bruce acknowledged again, "I ask for forgiveness from the families involved. . . . If there is anything I can do to make things better, I'm for doing it." Scott took this final opportunity to remind Bruce that he could make something good out of the situation; Bruce agreed, saying that he was a good communicator and that he had helped others in the past. At the end of the dialogue, Scott and Bruce signed a previously arranged affirmation agreement that stated that Bruce would do the following: "To honor not living in the same county as his victims; to agree to do something good with this; and, for the remainder of his days, that he will practice Christianity and not just give it lip service." Scott closed the dialogue with a prayer and an optimistic spirit.

Postdialogue

Scott's feelings following the face-to-face meeting were cathartic: "I truly have gotten past it and let it go." Not everyone in his family shared his sense of peace; his wife still struggled with her issues with her father, and his mother-in-law was reticent about the process. Kim had warned Scott that people outside the dialogue commonly react by minimizing the offender's ability to take responsibility and to show remorse as well as by attributing offenders' efforts to a manipulative attempt to try to better their conditions of confinement or secure release. On the other hand, Scott's daughter, Justine, wanted to know the details of the dialogue. She also felt that she might want to watch the videotape of it herself someday, though she was not ready in its immediate aftermath. Overall, Scott also realized that his naive worldviews had been challenged with the reality that crime has no boundaries; it can touch anyone, such as the way it invaded his own family.

Despite Bruce's fears about facing the future without a home or family, he felt good about participating in the dialogue. In his meeting with Kim two months after the dialogue, Bruce expressed hope that their meeting helped Scott and that something positive came out of something negative. Though he had earlier been worried about videotaping the dialogue, he now said he hoped that other relatives might watch it eventually and understand how he felt, perhaps leading to reconciliation.

Although Scott describes Justine as resilient today, she still, understandably, feels a sense of betrayal by her grandfather. She does not resent her father for forgiving Bruce, however, because she shares his Christian faith. Following the arrest, Justine developed an eating disorder, and she met with a counselor to help with this and the other effects of the sexual abuse. In 2006, Justine decided that she wanted to watch the videotape from the mediation and asked for Pastor Dan and her father to be there with her. Scott says, "Justine sat here, and she got a little teary eyed in a couple of spots, but for the most part Justine handled it real well."

Justine has grown into an independent young woman. She was seventeen at the time of my interview with Scott. Scott states proudly that she is considering a career in therapy or counseling, and he supports her decision: "Who better? She's been there and understands." One of the reasons that Justine gives for pursuing a counseling degree is that since she has been through so many counseling sessions, she recognizes that different things work for different people. Scott's mother-in-law is doing well and even dating. Justine and her grandmother are very close, especially considering Heather's early response to the charges against her husband. Ultimately, however, it was very validating and empowering for Justine to have her grandmother take her side.

Bruce's Civil Trial

After Bruce's release from prison, Scott's wife and sister-in-law filed a civil suit against Bruce, seeking restitution for the physical and emotional harm his crimes had caused their daughters. At the 2006 hearing, they were disheartened to realize that Bruce could not pay any restitution. However, they learned that they could establish the cause for restitution, and the ruling could help other sexually abused children in the same position. The judge awarded a little over $1.2 million to split between the two girls. It was just a symbolic judgment, but their grandfather had to sit there and listen to every word read by the judge.

However, both girls, now age seventeen and nineteen, had to take the stand, answering questions about how the crime affected their lives, their relationships with their families, and their friendships. It was emotionally difficult for the girls to see their grandfather again. After Justine finished testifying, her grandfather declined to ask any questions. But, according to Scott, when Meg took the stand, Bruce said, "First, Meg, do you realize that what you're accusing me of I never did? All I ever did was tickle you." The judge silenced Bruce very quickly, saying, "Guilt has already been established here," but Scott's anger flared again. He worried that the state of forgiveness he had worked so hard to achieve was in jeopardy. Dan told him, "Scott, God even forgives jerks. Bruce was a jerk." Scott takes at least some comfort in knowing that Bruce has remained true to his promise that he would stay far away from the family.

Ultimately, this case is about how a father, as the secondary or indirect victim, was able to reconcile his angry feelings toward his father-in-law for abusing his daughter. This does not address what Justine might have needed or wanted; she was under the age of eighteen, and it is not even clear if she had any desire to confront her abuser face to face. Justine supported her father's need to forgive her grandfather for his own reasons, and after viewing the videotape of their meeting herself, she found that she was able to move beyond the trauma with less anger and more pity for her grandfather. By talking with Bruce, Scott was also able to move on, freeing him up to offer more support to his daughter. The importance of the message and presentation of forgiveness superseded all other motives for Scott, who says he was fully satisfied with the dialogue. He said what he wanted and needed to say and felt a huge sense of relief and momentum to move forward following the dialogue's completion. Although Scott's motives differed from those of other victims, the similarity is that Scott wanted to have his voice heard and move forward from the crime.

Postscript

In April 2008, when Justine was nineteen years old, she agreed to talk with me on the telephone about her father and grandfather's dialogue and to update me on how she is feeling about the situation today. Justine was very open in our conversation and had a gentle but confident manner of speaking. Her retrospective assessment did not reveal a lot of conflict or ambivalence— although she thinks it was sad to see her grandfather looking so skinny and unhealthy on the videotape of the dialogue, she does not extend this sympathy to excuse or minimize his offending.

Justine fully supports her father's need to participate in the VVH program so that he could have a conversation with her grandfather and achieve forgiveness. From the very beginning, when Scott sat the family down to explain why he *had* to forgive Bruce and seek Bruce's forgiveness, Justine says she understood how important it was to him. Justine feels that it was good that her father was able to work through his anger. "I knew that Dad had to forgive him. It helped my Dad a lot." She herself has *no* interest in seeing her grandfather, however. In fact, she says,

> When I watched the video, I still had a lot of anger towards my grandfather. Even his answers made it all about him, and he acted like what he did wasn't so bad. He still doesn't accept what he did, and he thinks we made it a bigger deal than he thought it was. . . . At first, I felt sorry for him. But later in court [not in the videotape of the dialogue], when he was making fun of my cousin, it seemed like he was really selfish, and he was really mean to her.

Justine holds out some hope that the dialogue ultimately will make her grandfather better in some ways: "Maybe he'll think about what happened and understand." At the same time, however, she spoke to the general issue of the lack of credibility with sexual offenders when I asked her if there were any additional questions that she wants to ask her grandfather: "If he was asked more questions, he probably would have lied." Justine also stated that she did not think she could ever meet with her grandfather, or at least not for "many, many, many, many more years." Although she believes that the VVH program is very good for "certain people who know what they need from it," she does not think that her mother would ever seek it out because "it would bring up too much old stuff."

Justine believes the decision to avoid a criminal trial was a good one at the time, although she says she would push for one now, since she is older and more confident that she could get through it. Thinking back to the scared and hurt girl she was when the secret was revealed, she recognized, "I don't think I could have gone through a trial. I blamed myself, and I wasn't even sure of myself half the time." Her feelings of confusion and self-blame are consistent with the research about how victims of child sexual abuse characterize the abuse.[8] Justine has only positive words to say about how the police and prosecutor treated her; they made it clear that they believed what she said and did not ask her a lot of questions. She says that her family got her through it: "My mom and I got even closer. My cousin Meg—we were always close, but now we are closer since we went through the same thing." Justine was hurt at first when it seemed as though her grandmother did not believe her accusations and sided with her grandfather. But "then she came around and took our side. I'm really glad. I wanted my grandmother to do stuff with, and if she hadn't [changed her position], I wouldn't be able to." Justine also believes the punishment was proportionate; she realized, "The biggest punishment of all is that he lost his family. He lost everyone. So that's an even bigger punishment than any time in jail could be."

Justine is aware of some long-term consequences of her grandfather's sexual abuse, as she feels that it changed who she became, and she still has "trust issues." She also offers some advice for other victims/survivors of child sexual abuse: "I would tell them it wasn't their fault. I would tell them not to keep it inside." The first counselor Justine saw after the abuse came to light did not have her own firsthand experience of child sexual abuse, and Justine believes this was a barrier to her healing. This realization makes Justine more determined to become a counselor for children who have had this happen to them: "I have that experience, and I could give better advice. I wish I had someone at the time that could tell me what they did and if they felt the same way as I did. Then maybe I wouldn't have felt so weird."

Today, Justine has her own apartment but lives in the same town as her parents, and they talk nearly every day. She is working as she contemplates her next move, which she hopes will be going to college to learn more about the fields of victimology and counseling. Justine's resiliency and strength have been fortified by the open communication she now enjoys with her family, an intimacy that grew out of the dark place where her secret was revealed. Her father's participation in VVH, and his candor in talking about the issues with Justine and in sharing the process with her, have empowered her to move forward with her life.

9

Leigh and Jenny

Lives Interrupted

Facts of the case: In May 2001, a drunk driver killed eighteen-year-old Cameron. Jenny, the driver, was nineteen years old when she crashed into Cameron's car, having run a red light at eighty-two miles per hour. Her blood-alcohol concentration was 0.14. She pled guilty and was convicted of first-degree vehicular homicide (which carries up to five years of imprisonment). She received three years in prison and two years of house arrest, though she served less because of good-time credits earned. I interviewed Cameron's mother, Leigh, Kim, and Debbie (the volunteer facilitator who worked on the case with Kim) and had access to the case files, the letters exchanged, and the videotape of the dialogue. I was unable to interview Jenny. Leigh has presented in my university classes twice, and I have also corresponded and talked with her many times.

When Leigh talks about her son, her whole face lights up. Cameron was special—a bright, inquisitive young man who loved snowboarding, his girlfriend, his family, and his friends. He was the middle child of three children and had a unique ability to size up a situation, silently, before deciding how he fit into it and what he wanted to do. Remembering how special he was gives Leigh some happiness when she reflects back to that dark time, in 2001, when a drunk driver killed Cameron. He was eighteen years old, about to graduate from high school, when a nineteen-year-old young woman plowed into his car at an intersection early one morning.[1]

Leigh and Cam's father, Gary, got a divorce when their daughter was six, Cam was nine, and their oldest son was thirteen. It was an amicable divorce, and Leigh felt that they had settled into the two-family mode very comfortably. Cam did well in school, and his teachers commented on how bright he was. Leigh said, "He was just a nice kid and very devoted to his sister—but a good kid just like everybody else: he made good choices and bad choices."

Cameron was an avid snowboarder and applied to colleges out west so he could snowboard. About two and a half weeks before he died, he went out to visit the schools, finally deciding on the University of Utah. After a great deal of discussion, Leigh and Gary decided to let Cam postpone college for a semester so he could follow his dream to travel, a decision that made him "the happiest kid you have ever seen."

The Night of the Crash

The weekend of May 4, 2001, Cameron was supposed to stay at his dad's house, but his sister and her friends were over there too, so a few minutes after midnight Friday night, he walked in the door of Leigh's house. As Leigh was going upstairs to go to bed, she said, "'Love you dearly, Cam.' And he said, 'Love you too, Mom,'" Leigh did not know that those would be the last words she would hear from her son.

That night, at 2 a.m., Leigh was awakened by a phone call that jarred her out of a deep sleep. She was home alone, and a voice on the other end of the phone was calling from the hospital. Once the woman verified Leigh's name, she asked, "Do you have a son named Cameron?" The caller told Leigh that he had been in a serious accident and that she needed to get someone to drive her to the hospital. Her mind was blank, and she could not absorb it all. She called Gary, her oldest son, and a few friends and told them to get to the hospital right away.

When Leigh walked in, she strode up to the desk, announced who she was, and demanded to be taken to her son. She thought at the time they would take her to his room, and she would "pull the curtain back, and there he'd be, and I'd talk to him and tell him it would be okay." But when she saw her ex-husband and daughter sobbing, she knew he was dead. "I just fell down and cried and screamed because I lost my son, and he had been in such a good place in his life, the best place."

All they knew from the police was that Cam had been killed in a wreck and that someone else hit his car. At the time, Leigh had no idea that the driver of that car, a nineteen-year-old girl, was at the other end of the hall and that her parents were in the waiting room. She had walked right by them. Leigh recalls saying to the priest, "I don't know which mother has it harder, me or the driver's mother."

The next day, the police visited Leigh's house and told her that Cam had stopped for a red light at an intersection, and when the light turned green, he proceeded through the intersection just as nineteen-year-old Jenny McAndrew ran the red light at eighty-two miles per hour. Jenny hit her brakes about twenty feet before she hit Cameron's car. Leigh learned that Jenny had used a fake ID to have a couple beers and some shots, progressing to "Jell-O shots for a buck each," and then she left the bar at midnight for the hour drive to her friend's house. Leigh says, "She murdered him. She murdered him. And she murdered him because of her choices."

Leigh started a scholarship in Cameron's memory at his high school. Many people sent money to add to it. One condolence card that really touched Leigh had $3.27 inside, all in coins, from a little boy, and it said, "I'll never forget when you [Cameron] were nice to me and told me I had to do well in school and took me to McDonalds."

After Cameron's death, Leigh found it hard to do daily tasks, even though she was aware of her responsibilities for her other kids. Her other children "were in desperate need of someone to talk to": "I was so hurt I couldn't do it." She was numb at that point about how she felt about the nineteen-year-old young woman who killed her son, who had decided to plead guilty to vehicular homicide in the first degree. Leigh explains what she felt when saw Jenny in the courtroom: "I felt a visceral hate that I can't describe. It was horrible. And I knew I couldn't feel that way, that it was *not* something that I could live with."[2]

Jenny never tried to apologize or to contact Leigh to talk to her. Leigh did receive a letter, however, through the district attorney's office, that supposedly came from Jenny, but the words in the letter seemed hollow, somehow forced. Leigh found out later when she and Jenny met face to face through VVH that Jenny had not written that letter. Her father wrote it, in the hope of swaying the court and mitigating her punishment by generating sympathy. At that time, however, Jenny refused to play any part in her parents' efforts because, as she indicated in her VVH paperwork, she thought it was a "cheap idea" and apparently told her parents, "You're trying to make her [Leigh] feel sorry for me, and that's not right." Jenny was determined to plead guilty despite her parents' disapproval.

After Jenny pled guilty, the family was asked to write a victim impact statement describing the effects of the crime on them. Both Leigh and her daughter spoke to the judge about what it meant to lose Cam, reading from their victim impact statement letters. Cameron's fifteen-year-old sister, Cely, wrote to the judge, "I do believe that Jenny McAndrew should be given ample time to suffer her consequences, to reflect about the effects of her choices, and to make an example to others of the repercussions of drinking and driving. She took Cameron's future away from him."

Leigh wrote an equally moving victim impact statement to the court. It began by stating, "It has been said that Cameron died in a horrible accident, but there was no accident. Cameron died because of the choices that Jenny McAndrew made." Leigh implored the court to impose the maximum penalty but also to require Jenny to participate in counseling and substance-abuse classes, "so that she can contribute to society when she is released from prison." Leigh ended by saying that Jenny's youth should not mitigate her punishment since Cameron would never see his nineteenth birthday.

Jenny was in the courtroom and heard every word of these statements. She was not seated in front, so Cameron's family did not have to look at her. Leigh recalls never looking at Jenny, and she had no sense that Jenny showed any remorse. Jenny received three years in prison and two additional years of house arrest. For vehicular homicide in the first degree, the maximum penalty a convicted offender could receive is five years in prison; the minimum is eighteen months. The prosecutor could have pursued a charge of manslaughter, for which an offender could receive zero to ten years. The D.A. recommended to the family the minimum penalty for vehicular homicide of eighteen months. Leigh has lingering bad feelings about how the prosecutor's office presented the sentencing options to her, since she had trusted the D.A. to recommend the maximum sentence, but "he recommended something less than the max, which really infuriated me because I felt like I got screwed by the D.A." Making things worse, Leigh felt rebuffed by the prosecutor—rather than speaking to her directly, he left court after presenting his recommendations. Leigh remains angry about this treatment today, and her personal experience has given her insight into the ways victims' voices and needs are silenced, betrayed, and trivialized.

After Jenny had been imprisoned for about eighteen months, a feeling started gnawing at Leigh. She had to meet her. Even though her extremely supportive friends and family did not understand her need to talk to Jenny directly, Leigh felt that she had to, because "if you're so filled with hate, that's the primary thing in your life," and one cannot move forward with such hate ruling one's life.

Leigh is adamant about the fact that Jenny made bad choices that night. She is not naive, however, about similar bad choices made by many other teenagers and young adults, especially since her oldest son was arrested on a charge of driving under the influence (DUI) the night of his high school graduation.[3] "She was a kid who made bad choices, and they all do, they all do. Anybody who thinks their child isn't going to is crazy. They all do. My oldest son had been once arrested for underage drinking and driving, and so I know about bad choices."

Leigh was determined to talk with Jenny. She called the prison and spoke to the warden, who promised to help her. But he never called her back. Leigh persevered, but the continued lack of follow-through from the warden reinforced her anger and disillusionment over the way victims are treated by the criminal justice system. Finally, Leigh talked to her liaison at the district attorney's office, who told her about the Victims' Voices Heard program.

When Leigh found out that there was no other avenue she could pursue to speak with Jenny, she called Kim about VVH. Leigh was not interested in going through the extensive preparation process that the VVH program entails—she thought she was "beyond that" and had adequately processed her feelings. However, looking back, she now acknowledges that the time it took to prepare for the dialogue was extremely worthwhile. Leigh now understands that for all dialogue participants—victims and offenders—preparation is crucial. Leigh initially met with Kim, but her main facilitator throughout the process was a trained volunteer mediator, Debbie, a psychology professor in the Philadelphia region. Leigh says she "clicked with Debbie."[4]

When Kim approached Jenny, as Leigh understands it, "Jenny McAndrew said, 'I will do anything [Leigh] wants me to do,' which shows remorse and a willingness." Leigh respected this maturity. Leigh also found out that while Jenny was in prison, she took advantage of every opportunity, including taking educational classes, participating in Alcoholics Anonymous, and doing therapeutic and emotional work on changing behavior patterns. Leigh was glad that Jenny's choices in prison prepared her to be a contributing member of society. Almost a year before Jenny's scheduled release date, she applied to get out earlier; Leigh was adamantly opposed to that and wrote a letter to the judge expressing her dismay. The court ended up keeping Jenny for the full time of incarceration, minus some time she earned for good behavior. Upon her release, Jenny also had restitution payments to fulfill to Cameron's family.[5]

Leigh's preparation for the dialogue progressed. Her expectations for the process were optimistic both for herself and for Jenny: to receive a little bit of closure, to see for herself if Jenny was doing better, which would make Leigh feel better, and for Jenny not to wake up feeling guilty every day. Jenny stated that her expectations for the dialogue were to do whatever she could for Leigh. Jenny also felt that she left a bad impression in court in 2001, and she wished she could have told Leigh how badly she really felt. Jenny also told Debbie that she would not have traded her time in prison for anything and that it was the "best thing that could have happened" to her because it made her grow up and it was where she deserved to be because of what she did. As part of the VVH preparation process, Jenny wrote a brief letter to Leigh, preferring to wait until they met face to face to talk in more depth. In the letter, she told Leigh about her many attempts to write her a letter. She had written many but never sent them because she knew they would not express how sorry she was. This time she wrote, "I'll never be able to completely forgive myself for what I did to your son and to your family, but I have used what has happened as my motivation to live and make something of myself. . . . Each morning that I've woken up Cameron has served as my inspiration to not only make it through the day, but to make something of the day."

By the time Leigh and Jenny met face to face, it was about three and a half years after the crash that killed Cameron. Leigh had thought a lot about meeting Jenny. Jenny's lack of remorse is all that Leigh remembers from the courtroom, and she hoped the dialogue would change this memory into a better one.[6] During the time Debbie and Jenny spent together, they explored Jenny's feelings about who she was at the time of the crash and who she had become. Jenny learned some information about Leigh that was consistent with her positive impression of her—she admired Leigh's work with MADD and with troubled teenagers. At the same time, however, Jenny told Debbie that one of her greatest fears was to be involved in another crash, despite her adamant refusal ever to drink and drive again. She felt she has learned that she is not invincible and that her experience has made her more compassionate and aware of other people's feelings and how she can affect them.

The Dialogue

Since Jenny was on work release and no longer incarcerated, the dialogue occurred in a conference room at a private business. Leigh and Jenny faced each other across a table, and Debbie, the facilitator, sat with them. Their support people were in the room, and Kim was in the background, quietly present. Debbie opened the dialogue, telling both women how she admired them for their willingness to meet; she also praised them for their hard work in preparing for the dialogue. Leigh began by reading a statement to Jenny that detailed the impact that Jenny's choices had on her family. Leigh was very articulate in describing the grief they experienced, how impotent she felt in helping her other children grieve and move forward, and how guilty Cameron's girlfriend felt (she felt that if she had kissed him one more time or had a longer conversation, he would not have been at that intersection). Leigh also talked about how they had all done something very special with the loss of their son, brother, boyfriend. Although they would give anything to have him again, they hold him in their hearts, and they are better for loving and knowing him; and they can move on with their lives. Leigh concluded with the questions she wanted to raise: "What about Jenny McAndrew? How has this affected you? Are you the same person now as when you killed my son? What were you then? Now? What will you become?"

A long silence followed the opening remarks and questions. Jenny choked back tears as she told Leigh, "There's nothing I can possibly say that could *at all* make up for anything you've gone through." Leigh told her, "Just say you're sorry, Jenny." Jenny explained that saying sorry felt so inadequate, and Leigh responded, "But it's something." Jenny apologized to Leigh, and Leigh asked if Jenny had changed from the person she was at the time of the crash to who she was today. Jenny tried to explain, saying that she had been "irresponsible, immature, a person who worried only about that day, invincible, young." Jenny had been a political-science major in college, with aspirations to become an attorney, but she was not a serious student and preferred partying and hanging out with her friends. When Leigh asked Jenny to recount the events of May 5, the night of the crash, Jenny told her that she was going to be perfectly honest with her and was going to correct impressions or lies she had told to the police and everyone else at the time. It was at this point that Jenny dropped a bombshell that Leigh was not prepared to hear, telling her that she had been in a rush to pick up her friend: "I said before I didn't see the light because I was too drunk, but I did see it. . . . I used that as an excuse, that I was too drunk to remember." Leigh looked at Jenny in amazement, visibly shaken. Debbie called for a break, and Leigh left the room. Later, Leigh said, "I couldn't take that. To think she'd seen that red light, and she just barreled through it."

When Leigh returned to the table, she wanted to know what Jenny remembered of the wreck, and Jenny told her that she remembered everything. "I slammed on the brakes and turned my wheel, and after the collision, I kept saying to myself, 'What have I done?'" Jenny said that she asked the police and the emergency medical technicians, "Is everyone okay?": "But no one told me anything for eight hours."

In Jenny's paperwork for the VVH process, she wrote at length about her guilt and shame and about how horrible she felt about what she had done. After the wreck, she hid in her home, depressed and fearful to leave the house; she also stopped eating and slept all the time. And she wrote, "Immediately following the crash, I abused my prescriptions and drank to numb myself"— in order to forget the horrible consequences of her actions. Jenny's self-medicating to anesthetize herself is a common coping mechanism. She wrote, "I welcomed the feeling of dullness [the prescription painkillers] brought."

At this point in the dialogue, Leigh declared she needed another break. When the dialogue resumed, Debbie asked Jenny if she had anything she wanted to say to Leigh. Jenny apologized again, and Leigh thanked her, saying, "I know you didn't go out that night to kill Cameron or anyone else. You went out to party and have fun with your friends. This is the consequence that came from it. . . . I'm not here to tear you up. I appreciate your honesty."

Most victims want to know what offenders do with their time behind bars, feeling that if offenders are constructive and productive while incarcerated, they will not only confront the causes of their criminal behavior but also be less likely to reoffend upon release. Leigh queried Jenny about her program participation while in prison. Jenny provided detailed information about her activities, which included educational and occupational programs, prerelease classes, life-skills classes, addiction counseling, peer- and staff-facilitated counseling, and fund-raising for personal products for indigent inmates. Jenny also explained that although she was not mandated to attend Alcoholics Anonymous (since she was not charged with DUI), she volunteered to participate in that program in addition to living for nineteen months in a residential substance-abuse treatment center located within the prison. She said that in prison she learned to take responsibility for herself "and grow up": "Before, I'd take a job every couple of months, blow off money, and know or expect my parents to help out if I needed some money. Now, I take pride in my work; I complete things, I am responsible, . . . because I got a second chance. I guess I grew up." Leigh seemed relieved to hear that Jenny made conscious decisions and efforts to become a better person and told her so.

It was important for Leigh to know how the crash affected Jenny's life. No matter how difficult it was for Jenny to talk about what she did, she looked directly at Leigh during the dialogue. As I watched the videotape, it seemed to me that she tried as hard as she could to provide details while facing someone she had hurt so deeply and irrevocably.

At the time of the dialogue, Jenny was still under house arrest, which meant she could only travel to work and back, had a 10 p.m. curfew, and was required to meet weekly with a probation officer and to submit to random urine tests. Jenny answered Leigh's questions about her life since prison, stating that she did not drink anymore and did not miss it. Jenny was working as a bartender, and she also expressed satisfaction in having the opportunity to make sure that no one was overserved at her bar. Jenny also told Leigh that she shares information about the crime with everyone who asks, in conversations or when she explains why she cannot accompany them to places after work: "I will keep sharing my story with people so they'll think twice before they drink and drive. That's why I tell everyone."

Leigh asked Jenny if she wanted to know anything about Cameron. Jenny replied that every time she heard something new about Cameron it was very hard because it reinforced that he was so special. Regardless, Jenny told Leigh that she *did* want to hear anything that Leigh wanted to tell her: "When I came today, I was hoping to get a better idea of who he was." Leigh seemed touched by this sentiment and shared a number of funny and delightful stories about Cameron when he was a child and about his teenage pranks; she also talked about his hobbies and personality. Later in the dialogue, Leigh also told Jenny that Cameron was not perfect and that he was arrested for underage drinking when a bunch of his friends were sleeping over at one of the guys' houses when they were sixteen years old.

Jenny also frankly explained about the letter Leigh received before Jenny pled guilty, saying that it was her lawyer's idea and that she had wanted people to know at the time of the sentencing that those were not her words: "I did it. I should pay the price. I'm not going to try to make them think I'm a wonderful person. I knew what I did. . . . I didn't want people to think that I'm a little angel and I just had a slip-up that day. I deserve to get punished for this." Leigh was glad to hear this admission; it was a relief for Leigh to see a "different" person at the meeting than she had seen that day in court. Leigh also wanted to know about Jenny's future plans. Jenny stated that she wanted to go back to college and that she might still want to pursue law school, even though being a convicted felon could complicate admittance to the bar. Then, Jenny asked Leigh, "Why did you do this [the VVH program]?" Leigh tried to explain fully: "I had to see that you had gotten better. You were a kid, a nineteen-year-old child—five months older than Cameron. I didn't want two kids to be ruined by that crash." Leigh also brought out photographs of Cameron and told a few more stories about who was in the pictures and when they were taken. She said a few final words to Jenny: "You've got to be better, Jenny, every day. Some days will be shitty, but you have to try, every day. Knowing Cameron, he would be very glad I was here with you today." Then, Debbie read the affirmation agreement aloud, and both Leigh and Jenny signed it. In it, Jenny promised never to drink and drive again. She also vowed to think of Cameron each day and, "in his memory, do all in her power to live a better life, give back to society and exemplify the kindness and generosity that was Cam." After signing, Jenny and Leigh looked at each other across the table, rose, and shook hands.[7]

Following the VVH protocol, Debbie met with Jenny, and Kim met with Leigh to provide support and debriefing. Debbie says, "One of the things that I thought was the most beautiful thing to watch, that just really brought me to tears, . . . Jenny took the pictures of Cameron, and she placed them ever so gently into a pile. She looked at them, while she straightened them up, and then slid them gently into the bag. That absolutely tore me up. . . . She was so careful. It made me think that this really had an effect on her."

When Kim asked Leigh to describe how she felt right then, she stated, "Good. Jenny is going to get better, and that makes me feel good." For Leigh, the hardest part of the dialogue was listening to Jenny admit that she saw that the traffic light had turned red, but she ran it anyway. Leigh was impressed with Jenny's honesty. Jenny said she felt very glad they did the dialogue and hoped that the meeting helped Leigh. She felt as though neither she nor Leigh were as stuck emotionally and would be able to move on.

This dialogue was the first one that Debbie facilitated. Although Kim was involved initially and at the dialogue and was available to support the process, Debbie had got to know both Jenny and Leigh very well over the months that they met to prepare. In retrospect, over a year after the dialogue, Debbie talked about how powerful it was: "This was one of the most emotional things I think I've ever been a part of in terms of interaction between these two women, talking about such intense issues. . . . Afterwards, when I got in my car to drive home, I just totally fell apart. I just was drained. I just wept, thinking, 'Oh my God, this was so touching.'"

Leigh now talks to her other children about how "it's not what happens to you that counts, but it's how you react to it that counts." Leigh describes herself as a very positive person, a very happy person, who has a great deal of optimism. She believes that Cameron's death cannot be the defining moment of her own life, despite how deeply he is missed. Knowing that her family is going to make it also helps Leigh. Leigh believes that the VVH program was a great thing to do for healing herself and making her stronger for her family and her other children. She also talks to high school and university students about drinking; she speaks to driver's education classes in high schools and presents in university classes. However, though Leigh does participate in presentations for MADD and believes in its purpose and goal, she does not identify with its membership because she is not angry any longer, and she feels that too many people involved with MADD have not let go of their anger. Leigh is unwilling to be angry because she feels it robs her of feeling at peace, and she would rather use her energy to find joy and not nurse anger.

Leigh maintains that the urge to meet Jenny was not about forgiveness. She understands and appreciates that people's religious beliefs advocate forgiveness, but she feels Jenny's punishment was deserved. When Leigh was in the car, driving to the hospital that night, she "bargained with God the whole way down": "This is what I'll do if you'll save my son. I'll quit my job. I'll sell my house. . . . He's got to be okay. . . . Even in my saddest, most horrible moments, I never blamed God; I don't think God did this. . . . I think God is there for you when you need him and that we have free choice." Meeting Jenny face to face was a turning point for Leigh. She says that now her thoughts are no longer consumed by Jenny. However, her newfound peace was challenged last summer when one of Cameron's best friends came home and told his mother that he saw Jenny at a bar and that she was drinking. The friend was incensed, but Leigh responded differently: "I don't know if she was driving. She's twenty-two years old. She's allowed to go to a bar and have a drink. Why should this kid be so upset—he's also at the bar drinking, and he's twenty-two years old at that time—if she's being responsible about it and didn't get behind the wheel?"[8]

Today, there are things that still haunt Leigh, that bring her back to the darkest place of missing her son—music, especially trumpet sounds, maybe for their mournful tones. She say it depends on the time of year, like when it is close to the anniversary of his death: "I could cry at the drop of a hat, and I will feel like that easily for the rest of the week. That's just the way it is, and you grow to know that."

Leigh does not hide the fact that her son was killed. She says it is sometimes awkward at social situations when people ask her how many kids she has, but she believes that if other people are uncomfortable with that, it is their problem, not hers. She chooses to honor her son. Although Leigh will never stop missing Cameron, she continues to heal. She has finished her doctoral degree in education. When she drove up in a bright red convertible to a meeting with me, I could see the personification of her spirit of accepting change and moving forward. In this way, she is living the challenge that she gave to Jenny at the end of the dialogue: you must become better in order to bring a bit of order to the chaos.

Postscript

In May 2008, Jenny McAndrew lost control of her car while driving at a very high speed on a curving road, hitting a utility pole and a tree before overturning several times. She was killed instantly and pronounced dead at the scene. She was the driver and sole occupant of the vehicle; no other people or cars were involved. Toxicology reports revealed she was not legally intoxicated; there were no drugs in her system, and though she had consumed alcohol that day, the amount was equivalent to about half a glass of wine.

When Leigh first heard about Jenny's death, she says she was numb. She did not know what to feel. At first, she recalls being slightly angry since Jenny squandered her chance to have a better life, but this feeling quickly gave way to an overwhelming sadness for the tragic loss for Jenny's parents and brother. Leigh believes that Jenny may have lacked the resources or support that she needed to rid herself of lingering guilt. Leigh felt compelled to reach out to Jenny's family—to tell them she knew that Jenny had done what she could and that she herself had wanted Jenny to be successful and live a full life. With a very heavy heart, Leigh wrote a letter to Jenny's parents, in which she expressed her sadness and emphasized that the VVH dialogue gave her great solace and that Jenny had accepted responsibility for her actions and had shared all she had done in prison to try to become better able to make good choices. She wrote, "Jenny's meeting with me was a gift beyond value. She helped me to continue healing." She closed the letter by saying, "My thoughts and prayers are with you both, and with your son—but mostly with Jenny. I pray for her peace."

10

Julie and Kevin

In Memoriam

Facts of the case: In late 2000, Kevin was driving under the influence of alcohol and crashed into the car in which Lisa and Keith, Julie's mother and younger brother, were riding. Kevin, age forty-two at the time of the crash, eventually pled guilty and was sentenced to serve eleven and a half years in prison. Julie and Kevin's dialogue occurred on September 9, 2004. I interviewed Julie, Kevin, and the VVH coordinator and had access to their case files, letters exchanged, and the videotape of their dialogue. I have also corresponded or talked with both Julie and Kevin since for updates on their lives.

On December 2, 2000, Julie lost two of her best friends. On that day a drunk driver's car careened into the automobile carrying her nineteen-year-old brother, Keith, and her mother. They were a very close-knit family. Although Julie did not have an idyllic childhood, her mother's love was constant and kept her feeling secure, and she said that she and her brother "were closer than most brothers and sisters."[1] Although Julie's biological father did not live with them while she was growing up, he tried to help from time to time, but Julie felt, "It was more or less us three against the world." When she was just nineteen years old, she married and gave birth to a son, and her mother became a huge presence in her son's life. From the time he was three weeks old, he had an overnight at his grandmother's house each week, and he grew up adoring her and his Uncle Keith.

The Crash

Julie remembers everything about the day of the crash, down to the tiniest detail. They were celebrating her son's third birthday, and a number of family members joined them. Her mother had to be at work early the next morning so she, Keith, and Keith's fiancée left around 6:30 p.m. that night. As

Julie says, "They got up to go and never made it home." The crash happened around 7 p.m. that night. "The man was coming around the corner and hit them head on. Killed my brother instantly—the airbag deployed, and he was so short, and he didn't have his seatbelt on. He died immediately. My mother was alive, and they heliported her to the hospital; about three minutes from the landing pad she finally gave up." Keith's fiancée was in intensive care in a coma for several weeks; she ultimately survived.

Julie knew nothing of the crash until late that night, when the phone rang. Her husband answered; the caller on the other end was Julie's aunt. She told him that Julie's mother and brother were dead.

> My husband turned around and looked at me with the strangest face. You could see the color draining. I just looked at him and I said, "No. There's no way." He just dropped the phone, and of course I could hear my aunt screaming when he dropped the phone. I just looked at him, and I said, "No." He grabbed me, and I just said, "Who is it? Who's dead?" He said, "It's your mom and your brother."

The next few days went by in a daze. Julie was consumed with finding out more about the crash details and making funeral plans. It was not until four days following the wreck that they learned that it had not been her mother's fault. "It was a man, and he was drunk. His blood alcohol content was 0.225," and once he was discharged from the hospital the police transported him to jail.[2]

Kevin pled guilty to charges of vehicular homicide. Julie was told that there would be an opportunity in court for him to say something to the family as well as for the family to express their feelings. Julie's remembrance of that day is that she was unimpressed with Kevin's attempt to speak to the family: "He couldn't even look at us. His back was turned against us. . . . I wanted him to face all of us. But now that I understand the actual rules of the court, I think it was something that he wasn't allowed to do." The family then read letters in front of the court. Julie read both her own and her father's statement. She talked about how wonderful both her mom and her brother were and said, "There are not enough trees to make the paper in this world for me to express the loneliness and pain I have and will feel for the rest of my life. There will never be a sentence that will be strong enough for the pain we all will endure."

Julie was enraged that Kevin received a fifteen-year sentence, even though that was the maximum penalty the law allowed. Julie's experience as a surviving family member trying to negotiate the criminal justice system was frustrating. She was not impressed with the way her family was treated by the prosecutor's office, and her entire family felt as if they "were the offender instead of the victims." Her feelings about Kevin were unequivocal: "I hated him." From that point on, no one was spared Julie's rage, including her husband. "What really snapped was when I was literally beating the crap out of my husband on the floor, and all I remember him yelling is, 'It's not me. I'm not him. You need to do this to him. You don't need to do this to me.' And I remember kind of standing up looking at him, wondering, 'What am I doing?'"

Julie and her husband turned to a marriage counselor for help, and the counselor reassured her husband that Julie's rage and pain were the issue, not him. The abuse that Julie experienced in her childhood at the hands of her stepfather came to the surface and further fueled her rage at losing her loved ones. Julie says, "This man comes in and amputates my life. And now, everybody I've been close to has been taken away from me, one way or another. So I really had to work on my anger."

Julie felt that she had to channel her destructive energy to something that might offer her more solace, and she became involved with MADD (Mothers Against Drunk Driving), about three or four weeks after the crash. She attended meetings only a few times and found it helpful, but she realized she got too angry when members told stories about drunk drivers receiving light sentences. She waited about a year before becoming involved again.

It was during this time that Julie saw an advertisement for Victims' Voices Heard on television, and she called the number right away. Julie had been wanting to meet with Kevin: to "keep reminding him of what I miss every day and kind of let him know what my husband has to put up with, what I have to deal with." Kim told Julie that she would send Kevin a letter stating that someone in his victims' family wanted to meet with him. It took two months for Kevin to respond to Kim's letter, which Julie found very frustrating. Julie found out later that the delay in getting back to Kim was due to Kevin's desire to talk to his family and his cellmates about the process. "I think he really just wanted to know what he was getting himself into."

Kevin was forty-two years old at the time of the crash and very close to his mother. He had a history of drinking—with no violence attached to that history—and some minor drug use. Kevin had been arrested for drinking and driving, but these arrests did little to deter him. Once Kim received the acceptance letter from Kevin, the process began. The preparation went on for about eight months. Julie is very positive about that time and about those two hours every two weeks: "I actually looked forward to them because anything that would happen I would store it, and then I would come here, and I would bawl it out." Kevin and Julie exchanged letters, but Julie was most concerned about the meeting.

Kim prepared both of them for what the meeting day would be like. "The most important thing to me and also to Kevin too was that neither one of us could be verbally attacked." It was important to Julie to convey to Kevin, "He affected an entire colony of people, employees of my mother, friends of hers, high school friends of hers, brothers, uncles, aunts. I just wanted to let Kevin know what he had taken from me and who these people were. All he knew that they were passengers on the road." By the time of the meeting, Julie's motivations had little to do with Kevin personally. She wanted to let go of living "for" her mother and brother. She wanted to move on, to let them rest in peace, and to stop feeling guilty for enjoying herself. The prospective dialogue gave her hope of moving past this part of her life.

The Meeting

Julie felt that no one, not even her husband, understood her interest in meeting Kevin. But she did not want to go there alone, so her husband reluctantly accompanied her to the dialogue. As Julie, her husband, and Kim sat in the waiting room, the correctional staff escorted Kevin in. Kim opened up the dialogue by thanking them for participating and suggested they begin by telling each other why they were there. Julie described the first few moments: "I couldn't look at him, and he couldn't look at me." Finally, "I looked at him, and then I just turned my head because all I could see was Mom and Keith."

Julie began by telling Kevin that she wanted him to know about how her life had been affected by the crash. She began by reading a more emotional version of her victim impact statement to him. She also wanted to know about Kevin's life and how the crash had affected him. As Julie started to read the letter, Kevin began weeping visibly. He never took his eyes off Julie, even though Kim had warned her that his guilt had often prevented him from looking people directly in the eye. However, Kevin wanted to show Julie that he respected her by not turning away no matter how ashamed he felt. A particularly poignant exchange occurred when Julie described how guilty she felt for changing the time of the party or for not having her mother and brother stay a little longer at the party; she blamed herself for putting them on the road at the wrong time. Kevin refused to let her take any responsibility; he told her several times that she was blameless, that the crash was solely his fault, and that she should stop beating herself up about it.

Julie brought a photo album to show Kevin pictures of her and Keith growing up and of Keith with her son, as well as many photos of her mother. She told him about happy memories related to the photos, and there was no anger in her voice when she described these times. In fact, during the entire face-to-face meeting, which ran slightly over two hours, Julie's tone was never angry. At Julie's request, Kevin also brought a few photographs to show her. After the crash, Kevin received some photos of the crash site from the district attorney; one photo was of her brother, dead at the scene, although this exchange is atypical in criminal cases. Kevin did not look at these photos often, but they reinforced his commitment not to drink again. It was incredibly difficult for Julie to see them, but she reconstructed what she had learned about the crash and shared this information with Kevin.

During their meeting, Julie also expressed her relief in finally realizing that although Kevin's choice to drink and drive irrevocably changed her life, she no longer hated him. She saw him as a human being who did not kill her mother and brother on purpose. Julie recalled that her mother frequently told her that "life is what you make it" and said she now chooses to take the negative and turn it into a positive. She told Kevin that he turned her into a person she wasn't before, because now she savors life more and is able to use her loss to educate others rather than to generate sympathy. When Kevin asked Julie if she could ever forgive him, she said, "When you are out there again and have your freedom, and you can prove to me that I can forgive you, that will be the day." For Julie, this meant, "If he can go to a bar, and he can do it without drinking; if he can pass by a liquor store and not have to stop for a drink; if he can keep himself clean."

Julie thought it was positive that Kevin was following Alcoholics Anonymous in prison. He told her that he had actually stopped drinking before the fatal crash but that he had broken his sobriety when his fiancée and father had died suddenly.

At the end of the dialogue, both Kevin and Julie signed an affirmation agreement they had previously discussed with Kim. Although the document is not legally binding, both parties signed it in good faith. It covered these hopes:

> Kevin promises never to drink and drive again.
> Kevin will send a yearly progress report to VVH, who will forward the report information to Julie.
> At Julie's request, Kevin will go to visit the gravesite of her mother and brother when he is released.

After the meeting, it took a while for Julie to sort out her feelings. One of the most shocking things for her had been Kevin's clean-cut appearance. Her memory of him in court had been of a man with "hair all over him, . . . an animal." As time went on, she came to "believe that if he wasn't drinking, he would have never been capable enough of taking somebody's life. He was a very gentle person" throughout the meeting, "very remorseful." Julie was deeply touched and surprised by several of the requests Kevin made to her during the meeting, such as his desire to maintain her mother's and brother's gravesite, to help with the tending and cost of the roadside memorial at the scene of the crash, and to form an organization through which they would speak together about their experiences as both a victim and an offender.[3] They talked about doing this through MADD and speaking to kids in schools, and Julie said, "I would really love to do that with him." Julie is convinced that Kevin has the potential to be a contributing member of society, and she would like to see him released on parole, and she would also like to meet with him again.

Julie has earned awards for her activism: she won the Volunteer of the Year Award from MADD in 2005 for her public speaking, and she and her husband currently work with the county police department and members of MADD to monitor drivers at checkpoints for driving under the influence (DUI). It is rewarding to her to find even one drunk driver out of 1,167 cars, as they did one night.

Aftermath

Julie believes the loss of her mother and brother has had a profound effect on how she now relates to the world around her. She used to take things for granted, and with the unexpected loss she has a new outlook on life. "I'm not quiet anymore. I don't put up with much crap anymore. I'm a very outspoken person, and if I don't like it, I'm going to tell you." Her husband notices the difference in Julie and jokes around with her, saying, "I think I liked you better before, when you were quiet." Anger and rage are no longer her daily companions. Julie describes herself as feeling much more peaceful. "I still speak about Mom and Keith, and I'm one to preach about the drinking and driving. But anymore when I speak about them, it's not for sympathy; it's more or less for knowledge." Julie has also spoken at a statewide victims' conference and recently began working to earn a victim advocate certification. She is passionate about reaching out to other victims, and possibly to offenders too, to share her experiences.

Julie felt drawn to making a connection with Kevin's mother, as she feels strongly that Kevin will need support to help him stay sober. "I wanted, as a parent to a parent, for her to understand that I didn't hold anything against her and that I didn't hate her son and I appreciated meeting him." The meeting between Julie and Kevin's mother lasted about an hour. In talking with her, Julie realized that her own family was not the only one affected by the deaths. Kevin's mother was in her sixties and had counted on Kevin for company. She appreciated that Julie wanted to talk with her, and they hugged at the end of their meeting. It was important to her to know that Julie did not blame her.

Julie makes conscious decisions about honoring her loved ones. For a long time, she used her mother's purse. She still wears her mother's ring to feel a stronger connection to her. She put decals on her truck that display her mother's and brother's names and birth and death dates, followed by a line that says, "killed by a drunk driver." She designed a large tattoo on her leg as a permanent tribute to them. Julie finished our conversation by telling me about a concept that Kim uses that strikes Julie as most authentic:

> Going through this program is like going to meet the man who has packed his bags and moved in with you. You didn't ask him to move in with you; you didn't ask him to come live with you. He did it; now he has to suffer for it. But, you know, he's a stranger. Why not go and meet him? He's living with you in your own home. Every day. You ought to meet him.

Kevin's Story

Kevin no longer thinks of the crash that killed Julie's mother and brother as an accident. This is consistent with how MADD views DUI crashes: they do not use the word *accident* because it sounds as though drunk-driving fatalities cannot be prevented, and DUI crashes *are* always preventable. The only memory Kevin has of the crash is leaning down to pick up a cigarette and then seeing headlights and swerving. Although he has scars on this face, arms, and legs, parts of his lip are still numb, and the end of his nose was cut off and sewn back on, Kevin does not remember anything else before waking up in the hospital. He then kept asking if anyone had died but was not told about Julie's mother's and brother's deaths until a day later.

Although Kevin says, "I can never forget the lives I took, . . . the family I messed up—I destroyed," and he says that not a day goes by when he does not think of the people whose lives he irrevocably changed, he had never thought about trying to contact the family members before receiving the letter from Victims' Voices Heard. Kevin was terrified at the prospect of meeting with his victim face to face, but he says, "I felt in my heart, if I could help her, and maybe help myself too in some way."

At the sentencing hearing, Kevin planned to express his sincere sorrow about his actions to Julie's family. However, he was so overcome with emotion that he was unable to tell them about his remorse fully. Kevin was stunned that Julie wanted to meet with him, because he felt, "If someone had killed my family, I would not want to meet with them and would look at them as someone who had ruined my life." At the same time, however, Kevin wanted to help his victim get whatever she needed from him in order to heal. This focus on helping Julie, rather than feeling sorry for his own situation, came out clearly during the face-to-face meeting; whenever Julie asked him how he was doing, he deflected, saying, "Don't worry about me; this is about you." He also believes that one of the things a victim wants most to hear from an offender is that he is not going to do it again. For Kevin that was an easy promise to make. To fulfill his promise, he says he will rely on his inner strength and everything he has learned since that fateful day: "As far as going back to drinking or anything, that's over with."

Kevin's commitment to full participation included persevering with the paperwork he had to complete and responding with openness. He does not like to write much, but he forced himself: "You've just got to be open and honest. I didn't agree to do it just to do it. It had a purpose and a reason. The exercises put you in the victims' position and their footprints. It opens you up a lot more to things that you probably hadn't seen yourself. It's long, and Kim's tough, but it's a worthwhile process. It helped the victims more than me, but it helped me in some ways too." About six months into the VVH preparation process, Kevin and Julie exchanged a letter. For Kevin, this gave Julie "an apology, showing the remorse" he felt: "how I thought about what I did to her." In his letter he apologized for what he had done and wrote about why he agreed to meet with Julie: "so you can understand why this happened, and that it was none of your fault whatsoever and so you can tell me about yourself and your family. I need to know who they were."

Kevin's Life before the Crash

Kevin is no stranger to the pain of losing beloved family members. He believes his experience with loss helps him to understand some of the deep sense of loss Julie has experienced. In the year before the crash, Kevin's father, who had been sick for a long time, passed away. This was devastating to Kevin. Then, about eight months after his father died, Kevin's girlfriend of almost six years had an aneurysm and died instantly. Worse still, Kevin was the one who found her in the bathtub; there was nothing anyone could have done to prevent her death. Although they were not formally engaged, there was an understanding that they would eventually marry.

Kevin received his first DUI the night of his girlfriend's death.[4] Rather than reach out to friends and family to help him sort through his feelings and deal with the pain of these major losses, Kevin withdrew and lost himself in drinking. People close to him noticed his isolation and tried to reach out to him. His mother knew he was upset and even suspected he was suicidal. Kevin says that on some level he understands the pain that Julie is going through because when his fiancée died, it was sudden, "just like that [snaps]. Gone." But he understands the difference between these deaths, too: "I did it to her [Julie]. My girlfriend, she just passed; the Lord took her."

Kevin blames himself for his withdrawal from the world and describes how he started getting drunk regularly. This was a change for Kevin, who describes himself as a social drinker for most of his adult life and who seldom drank because his fiancée did not drink. After about a year of anesthetizing himself with liquor, Kevin decided to stop. He had almost stopped drinking when he went to a local bar to pick up a cooler a friend had borrowed. "The bartender drew me a beer, and I said, 'Well, I'll just have one.' And then some other women came in, they started talking about aunts and uncles, and fiancés, and my girlfriend. It was just hard. I started feeling down about it. So I drank some more then." Kevin recollects that he had ten beers over the five-hour period that he sat at the bar and remembers little else about that night.

As the time approached when Kevin and Julie would meet face to face, he grew apprehensive. "After going through the program for six months, it seemed like everything's good. Julie knows I'm sorry and remorseful and take responsibility. But, in person, you wonder, is she going to act different? Her husband was going to be in the room too, and another officer. Was her husband going to say something?"

The dialogue took place in 2004, about two years before Kevin's interview with me. Kevin recalls, "It was kind of awkward at first. We kind of got into it a little bit, talked a little bit more—lots of crying. I cried a lot. It was hard to look at her and see what she was going through." Julie read a letter to him that she had written to the court at the time of sentencing but that the judge did not permit her to read. It was a very angry letter. Kevin says, "I told her, 'I don't blame you for feeling that way. I felt that way myself. I shouldn't be sitting here. If I could trade places with your mother or brother I would. They should all have been sitting here with you.'" He felt he deserved every word of that letter. The hardest part of the dialogue for Kevin was facing Julie. Kevin forced himself to look directly at her. Reflecting back, Kevin's impression of Julie was that "she's a sweet little person," and he was surprised that she wanted to hug him at the end of the dialogue. After the dialogue, Kevin was escorted back to his tier in the prison. In some ways, he just went back to his daily routine. In other ways, his life was different: "It was there; she was there. I knew who she is; she knew who I was." At the dialogue, Kevin and Julie agreed to exchange reports every six months: "like give her a progress report about what I'm doing, classes I'm taking, and what I'll try to do." One letter from Julie thanked him for meeting with her and described how her life had improved, and Kevin says, "That made me feel real good to know that I helped her in that sense." Kevin told Julie that he is willing to participate with her in a presentation for MADD or a similar group when he is released, although doing so concerns him: "I'm not much of a people person or want to get in front of people. Maybe someday I can do a talk with her."

Kevin is proud of his work "planting seeds" inside the prison: "There are a lot of guys in here with DUIs. [They got out, and] I haven't seen them lately. So hopefully what I said, what I did, gave them something to think about—whether they quit drinking or not—stops them from drinking and driving." Kevin believes that some of his fellow inmates are intrigued by the VVH program and might be interested in participating if their victim contacted them. He talks about some of the men who knew he was working on the program with Kim. They asked him how they could get involved since they felt they wanted to apologize to their victims, but Kevin would have to tell them that it was wholly up to the victim to initiate the process. He also warned them, "Well, it's no joke, this program. If you feel no remorse and you think you are just going to get something out of it for you, don't even think about it." Kevin acknowledges that though there may be a lot of people who feel badly for what they did, they are afraid to show it in the prison environment.

Long-Term Effects

Kevin says that the consequence of his actions is something with which he has to live for the rest of his life and that he will keep his promises to himself and to Julie when he gets out. He is glad that his mother has told him that she is proud of him for not getting into trouble in prison and for doing the right thing by his victims, no matter how hard it was.

Kevin desires forgiveness from Julie but fully recognizes he may never receive that: "Well, she didn't forgive me exactly. I said I hope someday that she can forgive me. She said, 'Well, I can't forgive you right now, but I don't hate you anymore.' And that right there made me feel good—at least she doesn't hate me. Forgiveness is kind of hard for people to do." He has kept his promise to keep her apprised of his progress every six months.

Kevin was released from prison in 2010 (and is currently on probation). Throughout his incarceration, his friends and family have been solidly behind him, supporting him, visiting him, and thinking about how to help when he is released. Although he had a steady stream of visitors the first three years he was incarcerated, the stream has dwindled, which is something Kevin understands: "People have their own lives. I don't blame them. I'll see them when I get home. I know they still care about me, think about me, love me." Prior to the crime, Kevin had worked at an industrial company for fourteen years, but it has since relocated out of state. Kevin is not worried about finding employment; his friends own various construction, painting, and landscaping businesses and have offered him jobs. One friend has offered an apartment for him until he gets back on his feet. Kevin is still debating about what he wants to do and where he wants to live. He would like to live close to his mother, who will need his help more and more as her health deteriorates.

The Ripple Effect

Kevin sees the consequences of his actions as far-reaching: "It's hard. It's harder on the family than me—my family, Julie's family. Like Julie said herself, it's a big circle. It doesn't just end with us two. . . . It's like a ripple effect. You just don't know how far them waves and ripples go out. You think it's just immediate family, but it's friends, family, her work—it was everybody." During the face-to-face dialogue, Kevin told Julie that when his sister came to visit from Georgia, she and their mother went to the gravesite where Julie's brother and mother are buried. Julie asked him why they did that. Kevin replied, "That's just my family. That's the way we were brought up. We take responsibility. They just wanted to pay their respects and treat them well." And he says, "That's why she [Julie] wanted to meet my mother." When Kevin is released from prison, as he promised Julie, he intends to visit the gravesite also. "We have an agreement that when I get out, I'm gonna visit and say I'm sorry. That's one thing I will keep. I will do that. That's gonna be hard too, but

I'm gonna do it." He told Kim that doing so would give him an opportunity to tell Julie's mother and brother how sorry he is for the crash. He is also very touched that Julie wants to accompany him.

When Kevin is pressed about his plans after he is released from prison, he says he believes he will stay in the area, rather than move upstate, as was his original intention. He credits this decision to Julie. Kevin is willing, even desirous, of continuing to help Julie heal if she needs something from him. Kim has cautioned him to figure out what he might be comfortable or uncomfortable doing, such as speaking to a large audience. Kim has said to Kevin, "You don't have to do anything we ask, or anytime we ask you to do something doesn't mean you have to jump up and do it." But he says, "I would. I'd do anything if I could help someone else."

Overall, Kevin believes that the VVH program offered him a way to help his victim/survivor and express his sincere grief about his actions, and he feels that "a little bit of the weight's been lifted": "I feel peace about knowing I helped her and myself in some way. . . . I still come down on myself, still beating myself up. I can't forget about it." At the same time, however, Kevin realizes that Julie's father "is still pretty bitter and angry": "He's not ready to meet with me yet. I told her, 'That's understandable. I took his only son.' I'm sorry about this too. . . . The ripple effect is so big—I mean, on both sides of it: my family, everybody else. They are hurting too. It's both sides. But Julie said, 'At least they can still talk to you,' and I said, 'Yeah, they can. I'm sorry for that.'"

Kevin believes the VVH process is helpful for offenders. "When you did something, whether it was intentional or not, when you get out, and you still have that burden—the burden is still inside you—and if you don't get closure, you might go out there and feel so down and out, and you might do something stupid again." He appreciates Kim's role as ambassador to the program and mediator, and he expressed his gratitude several times in letters he wrote to her following the dialogue.

For both Kevin and Julie, the face-to-face dialogue was the culmination of a process that was life changing. Meeting Julie contextualized Kevin's already resolute vow never to drink and drive again, and it gave him the opportunity he longed for: to fully express his remorse and take responsibility for the crime. For Julie, by undertaking the difficult process of confronting the man who killed her mother and brother while drunk driving, she ultimately chose joy over pain, using her gaping loss as a wake-up call to find ways to embrace the living and to move beyond the grief.

11

Kathleen and Wayne

A Mother's Love

Facts of the case: In November 1983, when Wayne was almost thirty years old, he murdered Judy, forty-six, an acquaintance he met at a bar. Judy had left the bar with him but refused his sexual advances. Angry at her refusal, he murdered her with a fifty-three-pound boulder. Although he maintained his innocence at the time, he was convicted and received a life sentence. The dialogue between Wayne and Judy's daughter, Kathleen, took place in late January 2007 when Wayne was fifty-three years old. The VVH process was conducted primarily with Debbie, the volunteer facilitator. I interviewed both Kathleen and Wayne and had access to their case files, letters, and excerpts of trial transcripts. I conducted interviews with Kim and Debbie. Kathleen did not wish to have the dialogue audio- or videotaped, so my account of the face-to-face meeting is based on the recollection of those I interviewed and the case notes. I have corresponded or talked with both Kathleen and Wayne several times after our interviews for updates on their lives.

In the years following the murder of Kathleen's mother, anytime Kathleen wanted to feel close to her mother, she pulled out her crochet needles and started making another afghan. Her mother, Judy, loved creating brightly colored blankets for the people she cared about, and she taught Kathleen how to crochet when she was a young girl. Judy had old-fashioned values; she loved lilacs, dancing, and music, and she wore knee-high nylons and penny loafers. She faithfully attended school field trips, field days, parent-teacher conferences, and school functions involving any of her four children, and she organized family vacations at the beach. In those rare quiet times when she was alone, Judy wrote poetry. As Kathleen describes her, "She was a people person; she liked to talk as well as listen. If she was speaking to you, she usually would touch you in some way, whether she had her hand on your arm or put her arm around you." Judy had an infectious laugh that made every family event full of fun.

However, the idyllic times Kathleen remembers from her childhood had begun to crumble when she was about eight years old, when her parents got a divorce; her father gained custody of the children, and Judy became depressed and started drinking. Soon, depression was her constant companion, and alcohol was the only way Judy knew to ease the pain. Depression is a debilitating disease, especially if left untreated, and self-medication with alcohol is common.[1] As Judy sank deeper into depression and alcoholism, her children were baffled and hurt by her behavior; only years later did they recognize their mother's behavior as an illness.[2]

At the time of the murder, Kathleen and her mother had been estranged for a little over a year, which meant that Judy had no chance to meet her grandchildren, to be part of the special events in their lives such as weddings, birthdays, and graduations, or to reconcile with Kathleen. For Kathleen, losing her mother when they were estranged meant that Wayne, as she put it, "took away my tomorrow."

The Murder

On the day before Thanksgiving, Wayne left his house following an argument with his wife and headed out to drink. He met Judy in a bar. They were both steady customers at the bar and were casual acquaintances who had seen each other a time or two before. They drank together for a while. At the trial, the owner of the bar testified that Judy probably had eight or nine Seagram's Seven and Cokes over the course of the night and that "you could definitely say she was feeling good." She stated that Judy "tended to get quite close to people when she talked to them. . . . Judy was a little bit flirtatious," but not everyone who testified agreed that Judy seemed intoxicated. The bar owner also testified that Judy's pocketbook was open and that her money was flopping around; Judy had just got paid, and the bar owner counted about $150. Wayne was present when the money was counted, and he suggested to Judy that she leave the money with the owner for safety. But Judy did not want to do so. When the bar owner was asked during cross-examination if it was her opinion that Wayne's concern was genuine, she said, "I believe so. [Wayne] has never caused me any problems, as far as bothering anybody's money or any behavior that I felt I didn't want him as a customer."

Ultimately Judy left the bar with Wayne, and they drove to an abandoned area. When Judy refused to have sex with Wayne, he became angry with her and hit her. And when she continued to refuse, he ultimately bludgeoned her to death with a fifty-three-pound rock. What incensed Kathleen the most about that fatal night was to hear that some time elapsed between when Wayne first hit her and when he murdered her. This lag demonstrated to Kathleen that he had ample time to make other choices and that the murder was deliberate. After Wayne was arrested, he claimed that he was innocent and blamed his friend, saying he saw his friend's truck in the area. Though Wayne pled innocent to murder charges, he was ultimately sentenced to a term of natural life in prison, which in Delaware means twenty-five years.

Prior to their involvement with VVH, Kathleen and her siblings did not even have Wayne's actual sentencing information and were never told that they would have the right to go before the parole board.[3] The victim's rights movement was in its infancy in the early 1980s, and there were no victim services workers to help Judy's family members, who felt very much on their own in dealing with the murder.[4] The only bits of information they received came from newspapers or from other people. When the case came to trial, Kathleen had a brand-new baby; she was not sure she was strong enough to handle the emotional pain of hearing about her mother's murder, and so she did not attend. Kathleen had no inkling then that being present at the trial would have offered the sole opportunity she had to learn more about the circumstances of her mother's murder and about the defendant.

Because of the silence surrounding the loss among Kathleen's friends and family, she feels that no one effectively dealt with her mother's murder. It was very difficult for Kathleen to tell her own children about her mother's death, and it was not until Kathleen's participation in the VVH program that they started conversing about the crime. Her daughters grew up realizing that holidays, particularly Thanksgiving, were unhappy times for Kathleen and that she needed to be by herself. It was not until Kathleen brought one of her daughters to a victim's memorial tribute in 2006 that the daughter learned the full story on the drive home. Kathleen was relieved to finally talk about it, and she believes it helped her daughter: to "pull some pieces together about me and my behavior." Kathleen can clearly trace some of her family's emotional troubles, such as her brother Henry's heroin use and incarceration, back to the murder and the implicit instructions not to talk about it.

The Path to VVH

In the ten years prior to contacting VVH, Kathleen tried, with no success, to secure a copy of the transcript from the trial of her mother's murderer. Although the Department of Justice's victim services contact was able to send her some of the pages of the transcript, there were only bits and pieces.

Though the lay public assumes that access to transcripts is automatic for victims, the process is not that easy. Trial transcripts are recorded on microfilm, and although the state offered to make arrangements for Kathleen to read the microfilm at a state office, she found this accommodation unreasonable given the sheer length of the transcript—hundreds of pages long—and the fact that she would have to read something that intimate and traumatic in a public setting. To Kathleen, the mere suggestion seemed insensitive, as if no one had even considered how reading a trial transcript would affect a beloved victim's family member.

Kathleen was also told that Xeroxing the microfilm would be too expensive (approximately one to two thousand dollars). However, Kathleen knew that the defendant received a copy of the transcript to aid in his defense, at no personal cost to him. This imbalance infuriated her. She wants to be fully prepared with information that came out during the trial and sentencing in case her mother's murderer comes up for parole, and she especially wants to be able to counter any character attacks on her mother. Despite the gaps missing in the transcripts, Kathleen says, "The more information I get, the better I've felt. As horrible as it is to read the transcript, at least what I know now is fact, which is a lot better than the wondering, because that was torture." Kathleen feels twice victimized: first by Wayne's murder of her mother and next by the fact that the state provided no support or resources for the victim's family.

One day in 2005, after Kathleen talked to a friend who happened to see a newspaper article about VVH, she called Kim, hoping to get some answers to her questions. "That first night that I talked to Kim, we talked for what seemed like hours. I think she was the first person who could finish sentences that I couldn't even put into words yet. It was because she understood it, because of her own daughter's murder." Within three weeks of Kathleen's initial phone call, Kim was able to get the victim services representative at the Department of Justice to Xerox three of the four volumes of the trial transcripts for Kathleen at no charge, but the truncated version of the trial transcript left a lot of holes in the story of her mother's murder and raised questions that only the offender could answer.[5] From the assortment of pages Kathleen has in her possession, she is uncertain about whether her mother had been sexually assaulted or raped, as well as about the nature of her mother's acquaintance with the murderer.

When Kim first wrote to Wayne to tell him about VVH and to invite him to participate, even though he took full responsibility for the murder, he wrote, "I choose not to participate." Kim's past experience with offenders told her that they sometimes need time to think about participating, so they left the door open in case Wayne changed his mind. And about eight months later, Wayne did so and committed to the VVH process. Kathleen made sure that he knew that she was opposed to his desire to seek parole: "I wouldn't go near him till I told him that." Wayne's change of heart was prompted by the fact that one of the inmates who worked with him said that VVH was a good program, that he had done it and that Wayne should try it. This inmate was Steven, whose story appears in chapter 7.

Kathleen worked with both Kim and Debbie; Kim started the process, and then Debbie took over the preparatory sessions; they were both present at the dialogue. In the first weeks, Kathleen initially "dreaded the sessions," but in retrospect she realizes that as much as she had felt ready to confront Wayne, it was not until some time had passed and she completed the VVH process that she was truly prepared. Initially, she says, "I was so angry that meeting him would have been counterproductive."

The VVH Process

Following program protocol, Debbie worked with Kathleen and Wayne individually to prepare them for the face-to-face meeting. However, after months of preparation grew to a close and the reciprocal letter exchange was to take place, Wayne backed out again and refused to give Debbie his letter, saying that he just could not go through with the dialogue. He also refused to meet with Kim (in her role as program coordinator) to explain his change of heart. Kathleen was "beyond mad": "It was like revictimizing me again, taking all the control away." Much later, Wayne explained to Kim that he reacted to other prisoners' taunts that he was being taken advantage of, that he would not gain anything from the program and should not participate without the promise of a reduced sentence. Kim did not give up and asked Kathleen to leave the door open yet again, and with great reluctance, Kathleen agreed. Several weeks passed, and ultimately Wayne again agreed to participate.

Wayne wrote a letter to Kathleen apologizing again for quitting the program and forgetting "what this was all about": "This is not about me and what I can get out of this. This is about you and your family and the hurt and pain I caused all of you for what I did to your mother. . . . I am very sorry for what I did to your mother; she did not deserve to die like that." Kathleen's reaction to the letter was mixed. She felt he was remorseful, but she says, "I don't think I'll ever be in a place where I can ever forgive him." She was relieved, albeit cautious, about continuing the process and meeting him face to face.

The Dialogue

Kathleen was determined not to cry in front of Wayne during the dialogue: "I didn't think he was worthy of sharing my grief." She knew that talking about how her mother's murder affected the family would be emotional, so to keep herself focused, she prepared a letter to read to Wayne. Kathleen feels it was a relief to finally meet him face to face, but she feels that Wayne did not answer most of her questions. And during the dialogue she decided to stop asking Wayne to answer her list of prepared questions; she simply lost faith that he could be honest. "I told him that 'I was not there to argue with you. I'm here to tell you what you did, how it made me feel.'" Kathleen remains convinced that although Wayne felt he was being truthful, there were some things that she knew as facts, and they did not "wash" with what he said. Kathleen and Wayne did not develop an affirmation agreement because there was nothing that Kathleen wanted from him after their dialogue. She did want him to see a family photo album she had put together: "to open his eyes that what he did affected a whole lot of people; most of those people my mom never got to meet."

Wayne had also prepared a couple things to share with Kathleen, such as his rosary beads that he had blessed for her and a thick stack of certificates to show her that he had been diligent in bettering himself by completing work and therapeutic programs in prison. He also tried to give her a picture of the tattoo on his back, one he believes honors Judy, but the tattoo incensed Kathleen, as she "didn't think he had the right to have her name on his back" and feared that he was "wearing it like a trophy." Kathleen was unmoved by Wayne's attempts to convey his remorse and efforts at rehabilitation, and she fully intends to be at his parole board hearing.

Postdialogue

Despite Kathleen's decision to stop asking Wayne questions during the dialogue, she felt much better after meeting with him. Explaining the relief is hard for her: "The actual act of confronting him, looking at him in the eye and telling him, was a relief. But when I walked out of there that night, it was like, 'That's it, it's gone.' I don't know if it's because I carried all that anger inside."

Kathleen did not forgive Wayne, and she told him that though she thinks her mom would expect her to forgive, she just could not do it, a feeling that was reinforced when she witnessed her granddaughter being born: "The only thing I could think of is—here's this happy moment, and the only thing I can think of—'My mom didn't get to do that.'"

Since the dialogue on January 29, 2007, Kathleen feels "more relaxed talking about it than before": "I talk more to my family about it, to my father and all that." Wayne asked Kathleen for a copy of the letter that she read to him at the dialogue so that he could share it in group sessions with other prisoners. She provided him with a copy and wrote to him at the end that although she appreciated her participation in the program, she will never be able to forgive him for what he has done and that she feels that he should have to serve his full sentence. She also wrote, "You may be behind bars, but we have all been in our own prison, ours is just grief," and she wrote that ultimately she hopes he will "do positive things with this letter."

Kathleen is surprised about how freeing the VVH process was: "I can see a change in myself. I'm more relaxed. This year it didn't bother me at all. It's different because I faced him. . . . I vented my frustration and anger to him." Kathleen's life seems richer now; she can enjoy her grandchildren and children more because her anger has dissipated. It no longer gnaws at her: "That night I walked out of the prison, I left it all behind. I never understood what Kim referred to as peace. I finally did understand it that night. . . . Once we did the dialogue, I can't explain it other than I left it there. . . . It seems so simple, but it worked."

Wayne's Story

I interviewed Wayne at the prison in March 2007, when he was fifty-three years old. At the time of the murder, Wayne was thirty years old, working as a roofer, married with three children (ages two, five, and six), and a serious alcoholic; he describes his crime as related to drinking.

Wayne was already angry when he arrived at the bar because he had got into a huge argument with his wife, and he had stormed out of the house, already with some alcohol in him. After traveling to a few bars with friends, he ended up at his regular bar, where he met Judy. He had met her one time before but only knew her first name. Both Wayne and Judy had been drinking steadily that night; according to the testimony from the medical examiner, Judy had about a 0.26 blood-alcohol content, which is "between two and a half and three times as much as one is considered under the influence of alcohol for purposes of operating a motor vehicle."[6]

Wayne's version of the murder differed in some ways from Kathleen's telling. Wayne did not want to dwell on Judy's flirtatious behavior at the bar that night because he thought that hearing it at the dialogue would hurt Kathleen, but he described Judy as flirting with everyone, going around to all the men and taking a sip of their drinks. Wayne said that she came willingly with him to the deserted junkyard, which he had already planned to go to in order to retrieve items that he had previously stolen and hidden there. Wayne assumed that Judy wanted to "fool around" when they got to the junkyard, but when he started to make sexual advances, she pushed him away, making it clear that she did not want a sexual relationship that night. Her rejection—and what seemed to Wayne a mixed message—angered him, and when she continued to argue with him, he picked up a heavy rock and heaved it at her, then dragged her out of the car and hit her again. He later said that he was "amazed that it hit her" and that he "didn't know what else to do but escape."

Wayne stated that he left Judy fully clothed and with her money, but when a man walking his dog in the early-morning hours found her, her shirt was off, her pants were pulled down and around one ankle, and her money was missing. Wayne told Debbie that there was no sexual contact between him and Judy, a fact that was confirmed by the autopsy. He also claimed that he had not robbed her, but the prosecutor and Kathleen believed that Wayne had robbed Judy while she was still alive and then had beat her and crushed her skull with the rock. The defense attorney, on the other hand, argued that Judy was too intoxicated to tell Wayne where she lived so he could take her home, that she was the one who was insistent on having sex with Wayne, and that he did not kill her; he left her alive and intoxicated and bleeding).[7] Although Wayne's original charges included two counts of murder, with the second count included because the murder occurred during the commission of a felony (robbery), he was later acquitted of the robbery. Through the VVH process, Wayne wanted Kathleen to know that he did not rob her mother and that he did not have sexual contact with her.

Once the police identified Judy, they tracked her back to the bar, and the owner said that Wayne and Judy left together that night. It took a few days before Wayne was apprehended, and he vehemently denied everything at the time, because the possibility of receiving a death sentence haunted him. He recalls that he worried so much about it that he had migraines and stomach problems for years, even after he received a life sentence.

For the first five or so years in prison, Wayne continued to deny his crime, even to himself. He describes having an epiphany as he was preparing to pour out a drink of "prison wine": "I had a flashback to my life. I just didn't like what I saw. Since then I haven't drank. I said, 'I'm not gonna lie about this crime no more.' I haven't lied about it since that time." After acknowledging his guilt, Wayne began attending groups to deal with his alcoholism, finding a twelve-step program modeled after Alcoholics Anonymous. In fact, over the years, Wayne has completed over thirty-five programs in prison, including anger-management and domestic-violence counseling (serving as a leader for some of these groups), and he received his GED.[8] He also became involved with the prison's garden project; their vegetables have won ribbons at the state fair.[9] During this time, he thought about Judy a lot: "During the whole month of November I say the rosary in honor of my victim." And he chooses not to celebrate any holidays: "because my victim can't."[10]

Wayne was initially wary of VVH. He did not want to meet Kathleen and worried that she would only be angry and attack him. After Kim reassured him, he began the process. But then, Wayne says, "we got like halfway through, and I got to talking to some of my friends that are like, 'Why do you want to do this, Wayne? It is supposed to be for her. What are *you* going to get out of it? What are you going to get out of it?' And, I thought, 'They're right. What am I gonna get out of this?' So I wrote her back and told her that I changed my mind [again]. I don't want to do it." Kim offered some alternative ways that Wayne could participate without meeting Kathleen face to face, such as videotaping something each wanted to say to the other or having Kathleen put her questions in a letter for Wayne to answer.

Despite Wayne's changing his mind a few times throughout the process, he persevered with the preparation without any support from his family. Following his conviction, Wayne encouraged his wife to get a divorce; she has since remarried, but they maintain a distant friendship. Wayne maintained contact with his daughter and one of his sons, and after participating in VVH he told his daughter the truth: "I called her up, and I told her, 'Look, I'm going to do this. I'm going to tell this girl that, yes, I am guilty.' My daughter's always thought I was innocent and believed in me. She hung up on me; I haven't heard from her since."[11] Meanwhile, Wayne continues to send money earned from his prison job to his children to buy presents for his grandchildren at Christmas and on birthdays.

Wayne's Account of the Dialogue

Wayne was nervous about the dialogue, but he focused on his role at the face-to-face meeting: his intention was to answer Kathleen's questions truthfully, with the hope that she would get the answers she sought.

Although both the victim and the offender may bring a support person to the dialogue, neither Kathleen nor Wayne brought anyone. Wayne felt relieved when he knew that both of them would not have support people; he thought if she had one but he did not, the situation would seem as though he was meeting with two victims who were against him, with one not having participated in the lengthy preparation process. This prospect was very intimidating to Wayne. Kim's last letter to him prior to the dialogue also provided reassurances: "I know I have stated this before, but I find it never hurts to repeat it: it will be okay, Wayne. You can trust Debbie and I and that we are making this a safe place for you and Kathleen to talk. We are there for *both of you* and will do everything in our power to support you and make this a positive meeting for you and Kathleen" (original emphasis). Thinking back to the dialogue, Wayne describes his sense of it this way: "It went a lot better than what I thought it was going to." Wayne was surprised by the civility of the meeting and recalls that Kathleen was shaking a lot during the dialogue and seemed very nervous. Also, Kathleen resembles her mother very strongly, which was unnerving to Wayne.

Though Wayne promised to answer Kathleen's questions truthfully, Wayne was surprised by how very few questions Kathleen asked him. He thought he would be in the "hot seat" and that she would grill him about the circumstances of the murder. Kathleen brought a photo album of her family and showed Wayne pictures of her children, her grandchildren, her siblings, and her mother. Wayne admits that the photographs of Judy's family continued to upset and haunt him after the dialogue, especially the ones of Judy's grandchildren, because Judy would never get to see them. He was surprised that Kathleen came and stood next to him while she was showing him who was who in the family photographs: "She comes around and stands right next to me. I'm the one who killed her mother twenty-three years ago. I'm thinking, 'Man, she is strong willed.'"

Wayne told Kathleen about the rosary and the tattoo, and since he felt that it was inappropriate to take off his shirt at their meeting, he had an artist friend draw a picture of the tattoo. It was important to Wayne to show Kathleen how sincere he was about his remorse, and it shocked him when Kathleen asked him if he got the tattoo as a "badge of honor." Wayne told her that the tattoo also had his own mother's name on it and that he would never dishonor either woman.

Wayne feels that Kathleen heard what he had to say but clearly did not want to show any emotions to him. "You could see her a couple times where she wanted to cry and stuff, but she was fighting it back." Wayne says he knows in his heart that he was totally honest with her and that he is under no illusion that Kathleen forgave him. Wayne felt depressed following the mediation, as it made him realize even more deeply how much harm he did to Kathleen's life, but about three months after the dialogue, Wayne says he felt normal again. Wayne knows that a sentence of natural life opens up the possibility of parole, and he wavers about what he will do: "I was going to go up [for parole] in about eighteen months, but I'm going to wait until I have over twenty-five years in. Then I'm going to try to get a commutation of a sentence, to try to make parole."

When I asked Wayne if he is glad that he participated in the program, Wayne replied, "I am now, since I found out that Kathleen's doing a lot better." He has already recommended VVH to other inmates. He uses the letter from Kathleen to show "how alcohol and anger affects people and how victims suffer": "There were a couple of them that it really got to them. They were like, 'Man, I would really like to do this.' 'Well, I can give you the address and stuff, and you can write Kim, and maybe she can make contact and find out if they want to do this.'"[12]

Wayne sees changes in his own demeanor, although he believes these positive changes began prior to his participation in the VVH program. "I'm not as angry as I used to be. I learned patience. I've learned how to walk away from fights. The most important change is, if I have a problem, that there's people that I can go talk to and not try to handle it myself." His faith and his religious conviction have deepened in prison. Initially, Wayne believed that God must have thought he abandoned him because of the murder, but he believes that over the years he has made sure God knows that he is sorry for what he did and that now God is back in his life. For the most part, however, Wayne is a loner. In fact, he avoids visits with people from the outside, except for twice-yearly visits with his daughter. Wayne says, "I feel better about myself because I finally let the victims know exactly what happened. It took some weight off my shoulders. Except my daughter's response then put a lot of weight back on my shoulders."

Wayne believes VVH is a "real good program." He knows a few other inmates who participated and were glad that they did. He also mentioned one inmate's disappointment when a victim backed out of the program.[13] "One of the things that Kathleen put in her letter was the weight was lifted off her shoulders. I wrote back and said to her, 'The weight that was lifted off your shoulders I now carry on my shoulders, knowing that I killed your mother and now knowing what I did to you and your family and all the suffering that you suffered all these years.'"

Kathleen: The Final Word

In many ways, going through the VVH program has been life changing for Kathleen. She described this feeling in a thank-you email to Kim after the dialogue, in which she wrote that she was glad that she participated in the program because it helped her to "talk and express" herself: "I've talked more with my family in the last six or eight months than in the twenty-three years I've lived with it." She also wrote, "Mom would be pleased with what I've done." And she feels her guilt about not going to trial has been relieved: "I wasn't strong enough then, but I am now."

Much good came out of this process. For Kathleen, the preparation, letter writing, and dialogue all helped her to fully explore the consequences of her mother's murder and its ramifications. She gained invaluable knowledge about how the criminal justice system works, particularly with regard to her rights as a victim/survivor for parole hearings. That Kathleen was able to face Wayne and speak her mind, vent frustration and anger, and show him the family photographs to reinforce the consequences of his violence gave her much relief, and she feels that she was finally able to move on. The program also helped open up more intimate conversation between Kathleen and her brother and her daughters, showing the powerful ripple effect on the family. Wayne finally faced up to the truth with his own family, fully understanding the consequences, and he feels he was able to give Kathleen some information she desired. Regardless of these developments, Kathleen pledges to show up at every parole hearing to ensure that Wayne remains incarcerated. Although both the victim and offender in this case feel that the VVH program was beneficial in a number of ways, it is important to note that victims and offenders do not necessarily come out of this process as friends, nor are all offenders forgiven. VVH and similar RJ programs do not mandate such an outcome. As this chapter shows, healing may take many forms.

12

Chris and Brett

Misguided Chivalry

Facts of the case: Twenty-nine years ago, Chris and two codefendants plotted to murder Greg, who they believed was abusing his second wife and their disabled child. Chris committed the actual act of murder. The victim's son, Brett, requested a dialogue with his father's murderer but started and stopped the VVH process many times over several years. Chris and Brett finally met face to face in the prison where Chris was serving time. Although Brett was initially intrigued about participating in my research for this book, he eventually declined to be interviewed. This chapter is based on an interview conducted with Chris in prison, his case note files from VVH, and a discussion with the VVH facilitator who worked with both Chris and Brett in preparation for their face-to-face meeting. The dialogue was not videotaped, at Brett's request.

Five months after an honorable discharge from the navy, at the age of twenty-three, Chris brutally stabbed a man to death. Chris has spent the bulk of the twenty-nine years since then behind bars trying to figure out how he was capable of committing such an atrocity.

Chris believes that his two codefendants, John and Andrea, manipulated him into carrying out the murder of Greg. Andrea, Greg's estranged second wife, convinced Chris that she had been severely emotionally, sexually, and physically abused by Greg and that he also was sexually molesting her children. Chris believed at the time that the murder was justified to protect them from further harm, although today he states forcefully, "After having all these years to think about it, I realize that still doesn't justify murder." At the time of the murder in 1980, however, Chris felt that he was Andrea's hero: "I pictured Andrea's daughter calling me 'Uncle Chris' and telling me how much good I had done for the family." Viewing his violence through that lens is the only way Chris can make sense of his acts during a time when he describes himself as having been "naive, gullible, stupid, adventurous, with a warped sense of honor." Given the social prominence of the victim and the horrific nature of the planned murder, the case was contentious from the start.[1]

Background

Chris was born and raised in the Midwest. He initially described his childhood to me as "normal," yet as our interview progressed, Chris confided that emotional and physical abuse were common in his family.[2] After graduating from high school, Chris joined the navy. Military service was not his first choice, but after he failed the vision test for a state trooper position, his dream of being a police officer ended. Chris experienced some minor trouble while in the navy, going absent without leave a few times and getting busted once for possession of an ounce of marijuana. These infractions did not prevent an honorable discharge, however, and he was even recommended for reenlistment. In fact, Chris was in the process of joining the air force reserves in Delaware at the time of the murder. Nothing in Chris's juvenile or military background foreshadowed the violence he was to commit.

Chris was restless after his discharge from the navy, and after a brief move to Florida, where he had trouble finding work, he and one of his codefendants, John, decided to move to Delaware, where employment prospects seemed rosier than in Florida. Once they arrived in Delaware, John introduced Chris to Andrea, and they began to spend a lot of time together. When Chris needed housing, Andrea let him stay in her basement. Chris was drawn to Andrea. She was flirtatious, although he maintains that they did not have a sexual relationship. Andrea was maternal and seemed genuinely interested in Chris's well-being; she and her circle of friends became his new family. Both Andrea and John were twelve years older than Chris, and he looked up to them. Chris had felt like he was a misfit all his life, and Andrea made him feel as though he fit in. "I had self-esteem around her. . . . I felt grown-up finally. . . . I really thought I found family and acceptance among Andrea and her friends, and I wanted to meet their expectations of me." Challenging Greg's cruelty tapped directly into Chris's desire to be needed and to feel as though he was a protector, especially to women and children.

There was a lot of drinking involved when the friends got together, and it was during these times when Andrea confided in the men about her abusive husband. Many of the stories were accounts of how Greg raped Andrea, how he beat her up so badly once that he almost killed her, and even that "her four-year-old son had only one functioning leg and arm" because Greg beat Andrea when she was pregnant.[3] Chris never saw Greg's abuse with his own eyes; he says only once did he see Andrea's face looking very red, and she claimed it got that way when Greg slapped her.[4] Andrea's daughter (from a previous marriage) was only thirteen at the time but asked Chris to buy her a gun, saying that "she was going to shoot Greg with it." To Chris, the teenager's desire to shoot Greg reinforced Andrea's stories of living in fear of Greg's violence.

Chris is not sure today if John was also taken in by what he sees now as "Andrea's lies." In retrospect, Chris thinks that Andrea and John sent him in to commit the actual act of murder because they could not do it themselves, and he also maintains that a number of people, including the police, knew about Andrea's plans to kill Greg and that they should have intervened. However, by the end of the VVH process, Chris better understood that he needed to accept what he did and to stop blaming other people for failing to stop him.

Greg and Andrea's family ties are complicated: Greg had been in a long marriage with his first wife, and they had five children together. Greg left her for a younger woman, Andrea. Andrea had also been married before and had two children from that marriage. Andrea and Greg had one child together, a son who was four years old at the time of the murder. By the time John and Chris moved to Delaware, Greg was legally separated from Andrea, but they still saw each other frequently. At the time of the murder, however, Chris contends that he did not know about Greg's first wife and family. Today, Chris confesses his sadness over "how many children were involved and affected by the murder."

The Murder

On the night of the murder, Chris says, "I drank a little bit just to calm my nerves, like a country-western song I heard about a cowboy needing to drink a little courage before killing his wife's lover. I was calm, but not drunk." Retrospectively, Chris has two versions of the story about Andrea and the planned killing, and he vacillates between seeming to believe that Andrea was abused by Greg and trying to please his victim's son by agreeing that Greg was not really abusive and that Andrea was lying.

Prior to that April night, there had been two abortive attempts by Chris, John, and Andrea to kill Greg. Andrea seemed to be getting desperate and was adamant that the murder "had to happen that night." Chris recalls, "She suddenly decided she wanted it to look like an accident, even though every time we discussed it before, we were going to use a knife. The plan was—she said she was going to drug him. She wanted me to come into the apartment and hit him in the head, knock him out completely, and drown him in the bathtub. But she wanted me to bring the knife along just in case." Chris was an avid knife collector, especially knives designed to kill people. In fact, he stated that Andrea paid to have the knife he was to use to kill Greg shipped to Delaware.

Before the murder, Andrea and Greg had sex in his apartment. He fell asleep, unconscious from drugs Andrea slipped into his drink to knock him out. Once Greg fell asleep, Andrea called Chris, who was waiting for her call at her house, and told him to come over. John gave Chris a ride to the apartment, where Andrea was waiting for him. Andrea showed Chris where Greg was sleeping, but both she and John quickly backed out: "She said he was the father of her baby, so she didn't want to be there when he was killed. And I accepted that as a legitimate answer, and I committed the crime by myself."[5]

Early on, something in the plan went terribly off course. Chris was supposed to use a whiskey bottle to knock Greg into a deeper unconsciousness so that he would easily drown in the bathtub without a struggle, making his death look like an accident. But that did not happen. Chris says the knife that Andrea had arranged to have shipped to him ended up playing a key role: "If I had forgotten the knife, he would have probably lived through it, 'cause when I hit him with the bottle, all it did was wake him up, and he rolled out of bed." There was a moment of hesitation as their eyes locked, and then, Chris says, "I just remember pinning him against the wall with one hand while I continually stabbed him with the other hand until he stopped moving." Chris then put the body into the bathtub and left.

In Chris's VVH paperwork, he stated that he remembers stabbing Greg, but after striking the final blow, he experienced no satisfaction. He thought he would have felt more relief in killing a "bad guy." "I was just disappointed that I did not feel joy, excitement, relief—none of the things I thought I would feel after killing this bad man." Ultimately he left Greg naked and in the tub, stabbed twenty-seven times. Apparently, the photographs of the crime screen were so gruesome that the judge would only let one juror see them. When Chris left the apartment, he says, "Andrea was out there with the car waiting on me and offered me a ride. I told her I still had blood on me, and I would walk back." She asked him if Greg was dead, and Chris assured her that he was. He told Kim (and later me) that he remembers feeling confused about why he killed Greg since Greg was scheduled to leave the state the next day to move out west and would presumably no longer be a threat to Andrea.

In retrospect, Chris realizes that the murder hinged on his feeling like the protector for Andrea—a woman victimized—and was more about achieving revenge than eliminating a direct threat.

In the days that followed, Chris does not recall feeling scared about getting caught or feeling any misgivings about the crime. He started to feel like the avenger of a great wrong. Chris continued to live in the basement of Andrea's house. The reality of what he had done did not really hit him until he remembered how "the water in the bathtub turned bright red." But he tried to put it all out of his mind, thinking he would get away with it.

The police figured things out very quickly. They told Chris after they arrested him that "once Greg turned up dead, they knew she [Andrea] was behind it, and it was just a matter of figuring out who she got to do it for her." The police traced Chris through his motorcycle registration and a computer check on the address, locating him in his home state, where he had gone to visit his family. John also told them that Chris had gone home for a family visit. Chris was arrested and stayed in the county jail for about a week before confessing to the crime, at which point he was extradited to Delaware. Chris contends, "One of the reasons I confessed was because my mom begged me to."

The case went to trial, despite Chris's confession, because of confusion over the three codefendants' conflicting stories.[6] Chris's parents attended the trial. Chris believes that the trial was unfair from the beginning, and he has based his appeals on this contention. For instance, Greg was a professional coach/trainer and well known around the state, and "even the judge himself had mentioned during the trial—admitted that he had played golf with him one time before."

Chris knows that it was very difficult for his mother to be in court, especially after the jury came back with a guilty verdict and next deliberated to determine whether Chris would receive the death penalty or a sentence of natural life. In the early 1980s, in Delaware and elsewhere, it was not possible for victims or their supporters to present verbal or written statements that described the impact (psychological, physical, and financial) of the crime to the court, but the prosecutor conveyed these sentiments. Chris feels that the prosecutor lied to him about seeking the death penalty, although Chris ultimately received life imprisonment rather than the death penalty.

At the time of the murder, Chris was convinced that Greg was every bit the cunning molester and batterer whom Andrea described. Today, he remains confused about whether that portrayal was false, since journalists told him that there exist police records that show that Andrea sought help.[7] Chris now seizes any opportunity to protect the family that he hurt so irrevocably. For

instance, when he read a story in *True Detective* magazine that sensational-
ized his trial and provided lurid details about Andrea's sexual abuse, he wrote
the editors a letter disputing their account. But when asked why he thought
Andrea had so much power over him at the time of the murder, he compared
her to a "damsel in distress" in a novel, who "used her petite size to make
herself seem really weak and made people feel sorry for her." Moreover, in
Chris's VVH paperwork, he wrote the following in answer to the question "If
you hadn't been turned in, what would you be doing?": "If I had not gotten
caught I like to think I would be living a normal life, but who knows. Andrea
had more murders in mind."

Chris is proud that his mother always supported him, even in spite of his
crimes, and he stayed in close contact with her until she had her first stroke;
she died at age sixty-seven.[8] His relationship with his father is nonexistent.[9]
Although his brother does not visit him, they remain in fairly close contact
through letters and phone calls.

While in prison, Chris has participated in a variety of rehabilitation
programs, including anger management, the Alternatives to Violence Project (AVP), character development, domestic violence, stress management,
violent offenders, and victim sensitivity. Through a Pell grant, Chris finished a year of college through Delaware Tech.[10] In his twenty-eight years
behind bars, Chris has never been in a fight.[11] Chris believes his conversion
to Catholicism and involvement for the past seventeen years in the Church
has helped him become a better person, and although, he says, "it's not easy
to be a good person in jail, . . . being a Catholic, wanting to be a good Catholic, is one of the reasons I get involved in programs like the Alternatives to
Violence Project."

During another prison program, called Positive Healing, Chris was
invited to talk to the group about the subject of charity and justice. "I basically said my experience with the judicial system told me there is no charity
in justice. But then I went on and talked about how as inmates we can put
charity back in justice by reaching out to the victims. We need to figure out
how to do that without breaking the law or without offending the victims."

The Path to VVH

Offenders' remorse and responsibility are cornerstone requirements for
participation in VVH. Chris contends that he has felt remorse for twenty-
eight years, the entire time he had been incarcerated. In fact, he says some
of the other inmates have ridiculed his efforts to figure how he was able to

kill a man and have urged him to get rid of the psychology books he pored through looking for explanations and to stop beating himself up.

Chris was already eager to pursue a dialogue with any member of his victim's family. Chris constantly thought about forgiveness and wanted his victim's family to know about his deep remorse. He was surprised to receive a letter from Kim inviting him to participate in the VVH program, though he had become aware of VVH three years earlier. In fact, he had written to Greg's first wife, asking for her forgiveness and suggesting that she pursue the VVH program. Chris hoped that she would be willing to participate in VVH, but, he says, "One of her sons called Kim to complain about my continued attempts to contact them, so I was told not to contact the victims no more, so I didn't." The family had not appreciated hearing from Chris and contacted the attorney general's office to prevent any further correspondence from him. About two years later, however, Greg's oldest son from his first marriage, Brett, contacted the VVH program. Chris was glad because he believed that meeting his victim's son was the right thing to do, and he hoped that it would be healing for Brett to know the truth.

By the time I interviewed Chris in prison in 2007, he was in his early fifties, a slight balding man with glasses. His eyes tear up easily. He has an unassuming demeanor and does not assert his views forcefully, yet he was eager to meet with me. Chris had been before the pardon board four times, but, he says, "they kept shooting me down. . . . My lawyer told me I would never get out because my case was so political. I've just been trying to accept that, deal with that."[12]

The preparation process for VVH was rocky. It took well over a year due to several false starts by Brett and was complicated by the fact that Brett resided out of state. At one point, Brett wanted to bring in a video recorder and make a documentary, which Kim would not permit. The delays were frustrating; Chris was aware of another inmate (Wayne, whose story appears in the chapter 11) who began the VVH program after he did and but finished his dialogue first. This was one of those serendipitous circumstances in which inmates who participated in the VVH were friendly before their involvement in the program and encouraged each other's participation. Despite the frustrating delays, Chris valued Kim's role as facilitator. Years earlier, he had read about Kim's daughter's murder in the book *Chicken Soup for the Prisoner's Soul*. In the time leading up to the meeting, he says, "I was a little more stressed out than normal," but despite the emotional upheaval, he was determined to see the process through and meet with his victim's son. He had resigned himself that he would not be released from prison and realized, "I was doing it because I needed to put all of the dirty things behind me and get on with my life." Kim validated his feelings, agreeing that both Chris and Brett needed to move forward with their lives.

Part of the preparation process requires offenders to write a hypothetical letter to victims/survivors, even if it is never sent. Although Brett and Chris never exchanged letters, Chris wrote a letter full of apologies, saying, "I know I am not deserving, or worthy, for a meeting with you, but I hope to be allowed to meet with you, face to face, so I may tell you how guilty I feel and how ashamed I am of the fact that I took your father's life, of the way I took his life and the way I disrespected him and your family when I did so." Chris also wrote a hypothetical letter to his direct victim, Greg, apologizing for his actions.

The Face-to-Face Meeting

As a way to give back some control to the victims/survivors, the VVH process allows him or her to make the decisions about the sequence and organization of the dialogue. Brett wanted Chris seated in the room before he came in.[13] Chris describes the mediation in this way: "Brett conducted it much like a newspaper interview. . . . Basically he brought a list of questions. He asked me one, and I answered, and he then asked me another one. Kim said he was doing that for his own safety, not physical safety but just emotional safety; that was his way of keeping it impersonal." Chris thinks that this method decreased the emotional intensity, since Brett seemed removed from the dialogue in his role as "journalist," and that Brett might have conducted it that way to avoid breaking down.

Chris thinks it seemed as though Brett was still struggling with his father's murder, especially since he had been only seventeen years old at the time. Chris found it very disconcerting to be in the same room, talking with his victim's son. He found it difficult to look directly at Brett during the dialogue, although he tried his best. There were times when Brett seemed to doubt what Chris was saying, such as his assertion that he moved his father's body from the bedroom to the bathroom by himself. During the dialogue, Brett talked a little bit about the disruption his family went through after Greg was murdered.

Chris says, "I answered everything he asked as honest as possible during the time," and "I was trying to keep my ears open so I knew exactly what it was he was looking for." Brett did not want to talk about the actual murder or whether his father was abusive, and Chris did not mention these things except when he finally got to tell Brett face to face about his remorse: "I told him I was sorry I killed his father. I told him that I didn't believe his father was a wife beater or a child molester, even though Andrea said he was. But even if they were true, it wasn't my place to try to punish him."

The most emotional aspect of the dialogue for Chris came at the end of the meeting: "Brett told me that he forgave me for killing his father, and his aunt, my victim's sister, was there—she's a retired nun. She forgave me too." This was very powerful for Chris. Chris asked Brett why he wanted to meet with him rather than with Andrea, and Chris says that Brett said it was because he "had expressed remorse and Andrea still justifies the crime." Unlike most of the other participants in the VVH program, however, Chris and Brett did not pursue an affirmation agreement. This omission reflects the tailoring of VVH to individual needs; Kim was not sure that continued contact would be beneficial for either party and dissuaded them from completing an agreement.[14]

Postdialogue

Chris felt a considerable degree of relief after the dialogue: "I actually felt pretty good, more at peace." And that sense of peace has persisted. He experienced a number of emotions—relief and happiness at being able to meet the expectations of his victim's son were the chief ones. Before the dialogue began, Chris felt scared, nervous, and ashamed. He worried most that Brett would not get what he wanted or what he was looking for. Brett wanted Chris to understand the long-term consequences of his actions. As Brett told Chris about the impact the murder had on his family, Brett's words "drove it home" to Chris what he had done. Chris maintains that the most important thing he experienced was forgiveness. He has no regrets about participating in the VVH program; that Brett and his aunt forgave him went beyond his expectations. When Chris thinks back to the ways that he punished himself in the past and wallowed in self-hatred, he realizes that now he can move forward. His hope is that much good came out of the dialogue, with the best outcome being peace of mind for both him and Brett.

Chris has not really talked to anyone else about the dialogue: "I'm not really a person who shares too much with others. Our AVP counselor wants me to share with the other facilitators. . . . I talked to Wayne [see chapter 11] about it more than I talked to anybody else. It's hard." Kim believes Chris needs to feel needed—as in his belief that the counselor "needs" him to tell his story. Chris offered some insight about Wayne: "He actually experienced the hardship that I never experienced, 'cause he's been telling his family all these years that he was innocent. He finally admitted guilt. They cut him off; they haven't made contact with him since he told them." In contrast, Chris said, "My family I told from the beginning, and they've always had contact with me." These different responses from family members highlight the pivotal role they may play in an inmate's rehabilitative progress. Being cut off from contact with the outside world is difficult. As Chris stated, "Prison is a place where you are always lonely and never alone" and never with the people with whom you would freely choose companionship.

Since the dialogue, Chris has had no continued contact with Kim because, he says, "I have to deal with the fact that I'll be in here forever. I've been cutting off the outside world. I don't even have an address book no more." Despite this self-imposed isolation, Chris enjoys corresponding with people and meeting them so that he can psychoanalyze himself and his case. Participating in the dialogue process meant that Chris had a regular visitor with someone from outside the prison walls and a valid reason to go over his own behavior with a microscope.

The following incident—which Chris related both to me and to Kim—indicates just how much Chris wants to convey his personal transformation. Chris says that a student journalist interviewed him a few years ago and asked him what he would do if he were on the street now and saw somebody being abused. "I told her, basically, that I wouldn't want to look the other way, but you wouldn't want to go and do violence to the offender either, that you would want to get the person help even if you'd have to pack her up and drive to a shelter." Chris's answer is revelatory, demonstrating that he still feels like a protector of women, even though he would now try to handle the situation without violence.

Today

At the time I met with Chris in August 2007, he still felt the peace he experienced since meeting with Brett. He had wanted to finally put it all behind him and move on. Despite this wish, Chris continued to provide new details to Kim during their final meetings and teared up when talking about how Brett and his family were affected by the murder. It is no surprise that the crime will stay with him forever. He wrote to Kim about the pain that his own family has gone through: "My family and friends did not suffer the way Brett's family and friends did, but some of the same shock, grief, pain, guilt, and anger had to be there. They too lost someone they loved and they had to live with the idea that someone they knew could commit such a hor[ri]ble murder."

Chris hopes for a future that could allow him to accomplish some good for other people. For instance, he would like an opportunity to "give blood, help build homes for the poor, help train or care for medical alert animals." Or, he says, "I could tithe to a victims' group." He says that he still prays for the soul of Greg almost every night. Chris describes his full understanding of the effects of his crime:

> My crime ruined my life and destroyed my dreams. I have no future now. I was an honorably discharged vet with my whole life ahead of me. . . . What happened to me as a result of my crime is I ruined my life and destroyed my hopes and dreams. I have to live with the guilt of knowing my life sucks because of *me*. Not to mention the guilt I feel behind murdering a man and how much I hurt my family and his. I will never know what it is like to love, be loved, and be in love, and I have no one to blame but myself.

Chris also worries that his future plans to continue pursuing release or a new trial will produce unintended consequences for his victims: "An inmate controls victims just by being alive. Parole, pardon, media allows him to control victims somewhat even if he doesn't mean to or even knows it." Chris realizes that his own actions will constantly remind his victims of the crime. In some ways, this realization captures the enigmatic nature of Chris: On the one hand, he clearly enjoys talking about his crime, craving the attention it brings through interviews with journalists and college students, since without these things, prison time moves slowly. On the other hand, Chris embraces a victim identity, believing he was duped by Andrea and manipulated by her and John. Although meeting with his victim's son helped to assuage some of Chris's guilt in that he was able to express remorse and help Brett, one is left with the sense that he is a lost soul who has not moved much beyond the maturity level of the twenty-three-year-old who committed a murder almost thirty years ago.

Analysis

The Importance of Storytelling for Restorative Justice

It has become common for advocates of restorative justice programs to highlight emotionally gripping stories of transformation to demonstrate its qualitatively distinctive approach to healing and justice.[1] Like the pairings provided in this book, the stories are compelling. They are powerful and evoke fascination and curiosity. They also reassure us that the justice system is not inherently flawed but that justice can be cause for celebration when healing and growth occur for victims and offenders. To fully explore the potential of RJ programs for responding to crimes of severe violence, however, one must move beyond the powerful storylines toward an analysis of what they mean in a larger sense. This chapter draws on the themes and patterns that emerged in the multiple data-collection sites—the interviews with participants, the case files, the interviews with the facilitator(s), and the dialogue videos—to offer insights into the potential successes and limits of postconviction therapeutic RJ programs in general.

Reconciling Retributive and Restorative Justice

Often restorative justice approaches are described as alternatives to a retributive criminal justice: the claim is that that RJ programs will offer a kinder, gentler approach for victims and also for offenders. Advocates also argue that the community will benefit from more benevolent treatment of offenders, most of whom will return to society after prison, and that the victims will benefit too, because they deserve a voice in the process. At the same time, RJ proponents describe the criminal justice system as overly punitive, as discriminatory, and as prioritizing offenders' rights at the expense of victims' rights. In this comparative context, RJ is presented as a way to correct all these problems inherent in the formal justice system. RJ's focus is on correcting a harm, whereas retributive justice strives for proportionate punishment to teach an offender a lesson through some kind of suffering. Instead of a focus on adversarial relations—as in a retributive justice model—restorative justice favors dialogue and negotiation.[2] But is it really correct—or even helpful—to set up this contrast as a zero-sum game?

Postconviction therapeutic restorative justice programs combine elements of both retributive and restorative justice. All the victims/survivors discussed in this book (and friends and family members closest to them) fully desired the offenders to receive punishment. Many were frustrated, disappointed, or flabbergasted at sentencing hearings that yielded light sentences for offenders. The victims were united in favoring an initial punitive response, conveying their unqualified support for punishment. Those victims/survivors who were unable to or were not asked to or did not know they could participate in their cases harbored similar feelings of vengeance and a need for retribution. Many victims saw offenders as animals who committed unspeakable, inhumane acts of aggression. Severe and certain punishment seemed the least that could be done to restore the balance disrupted by their cruelty. The victims' retributive feelings are consistent with Kathleen Daly's belief that "fundamentally, victims want a sense of vindication for the wrong done to them, and they want the offender to stop harming and hurting them or other people" and that, as Cretney and Davis note in their research on violence, a "victim has an interest in punishment" because it "can reassure the victim that he or she has public recognition and support."[3] Yet ultimately, these victims' quest for vengeance did not fulfill them. Although punishment for the sake of punishment conveyed that the individual committed a terrible wrong, it did not allay victims' fears, their bewilderment, or their struggles with memories about the incidents themselves. Healing was elusive for the victims described in this book, regardless of whether they participated in the trials of their offenders or spoke out at the sentencing hearings.

The passage of time changed victims' feelings about punitiveness, tempering their initial support for severe penalties. Victims did not believe punishment was any less deserved; however, many felt hollow, as though the satisfaction they were supposed to feel by participating in the formal criminal justice process or knowing their offenders were behind bars was not enough. Over time, victims' desires for retribution were eclipsed, but not completely replaced, by the need to find answers and be heard. The case notes taken by the dialogue facilitators during the VVH processes followed in this book indicate that even as the victims' understandings of their own feelings and about the crimes and the offenders became more complete, they still would *not* have favored a diversionary RJ program. These victims experienced very severe, often life-threatening violence themselves or lost a loved one to violence or drunk driving. These experiences put the crimes in a very different context from the nonviolent property and juvenile cases typically negotiated through diversionary RJ programs.

At the same time, however, the VVH process exposed the victims to an understanding of the individual offender's background and mindset and the kind of person they were at the time of the crime. Victims integrated information about the offender's history with the information they received about the current situation of the offender through their letter exchanges and at the face-to-face dialogues. Although victims continued to feel that the original punishments imposed were justified, this belief was tempered by their hope that prison time could be a catalyst for positive change for offenders. Victims' views about punishment for offenders became more complex: they believed that incarceration was deserved for the crime—it offered protection for other potential victims (who would not be harmed if offenders were locked up), and it offered offenders the time to contemplate and develop empathy for the victims—but they also realized that offenders' incarceration did very little to help victims themselves cope in the later stages of recovery. Even after the dialogues, the bottom line for the victims was simple: despite how meaningful the exchanges with the offenders were, remorse did not substitute for punishment—they wanted both. It was only after offenders had completed some of the punishment imposed and were able (and willing) to engage in such a difficult process that the victims' feelings about punishment tempered. Victims moved from the purely retributive, punitive orientation they exhibited at the time of incident and its aftermath to a more restorative orientation—precisely because offenders demonstrated they were "doing time" constructively, asserted responsibility for their behavior and a desire to help victims and to help themselves change, and engaged sincerely in the VVH process. During the VVH process, many victims and offenders came to articulate a critique of the prison system and the ways it infantilizes and marginalizes offenders.

The victims' initial embrace of punishment was challenged by the fact that it did not help them recover from the crime. For many victims, the loss of dignity, trust, often embarrassment or shame, and—if the offender is known—betrayal are constant companions. Similarly, when a person loses a cherished family member, the gaping hole where that person fit into the daily rhythms of family life is an ever-present reminder. Time passes, and victims/survivors are expected to move through stages of grief to the other side, achieving closure of some sort so that the future can be reconstructed in a new and more positive way. But some victims remain stuck, no matter how desperately they try to resolve or bury the past. Some keep their frozen emotions to themselves, others express their continued sense of injustice or fear or bewilderment by raging at other people, and still others blame themselves for actions they should or should not have taken.

Victims often keep silent about their unresolved feelings, finding it hard to admit that they have not moved on in the manner others think they should or at a faster pace. This silence reinforces a feeling that may already exist from their own victimization—that they are not "good" victims. A "good" victim would have processed the pain, handled it better, reconciled with their new reality, and reached some closure. But the participants who sought out the Victims' Voices Heard program found that they could not move on and that the path to healing was not linear. In retrospect, all of them realized that they were stuck because of things unsaid and unclear. Some were fearful that they could again be targets of random violence; for others, the fear that had accompanied them since their victimization never abated. Although therapists can work wonders, and positive social and emotional support of family and friends is integral to victims' healing, the victims/survivors featured in this book felt that they had received their limit of compassion and understanding from others and/or from therapy and yet had not been able to forge ahead in a way that reconciled their victimization experiences with their futures.

What I learned from the conversations with most of the offenders is that they, too, believed they deserved the prison sentences imposed on them, in light of the violent crimes they committed. The majority of the offenders credit their time behind bars with helping them to develop the ability to shed their "street façade" and develop empathy for their victims. With three exceptions, the offenders I interviewed accepted their punishment and even thought it was the "wake-up call" they needed. One offender even told his victim how, in retrospect, he was thankful that he got caught, telling her, "You saved my life."

The exceptions were the men sentenced for child sexual abuse and an additional man sentenced for marital rape at knifepoint who admitted during the dialogue that he had done some kind of "harm" to his nine-year-old daughter. Although the three men expressed remorse and took responsibility for their acts, they minimized their behavior by comparing themselves to other inmates (not part of VVH) who had committed, in their assessment, far worse sexual abuses. Their denials were further underlined by their belief that they had received excessively long sentences compared to others whom they considered more egregious sexual offenders. These men seemed more concerned about repairing their own reputations than about repairing the harm to their victims or making good on the promises reached at the dialogues. For example, one of the men (Paul) promised to send a monthly financial contribution to his children from his prison pay but made only one payment. Another (Steven) agreed never to contact his daughter again (although this was redundant at the time since a no-contact order was to remain in place indefinitely) but manipulated her brother into conveying a false message to her that he was dying from an illness so she would contact him to say good-bye. The letters, dialogues, and case notes demonstrate the sincerity of these offenders' apologies; they did not appear to be staged or disingenuous performances. At the same time, however, the research literature suggests it is very difficult for sexual offenders who know their victims to change enduring behavioral patterns that are emotionally manipulative and coercive.

Evaluating whether apologies are sincere is subjective; an offender may offer a very sincere apology, yet the victim may hear it as disingenuous (as did one of the VVH victims whose mother was murdered). Ultimately, for the victims with whom I spoke, receiving an apology was not the crucial dénouement. Rather, what mattered most were the offenders' actual words of remorse and accountability that conveyed their commitment to *do* something with their remorse—by not harming anyone again, by honoring the dead or the victim's wishes, and so forth.

The VVH program was a lifeline for the victims portrayed in this book. In every interview or further conversation I had with the victims, not one had a shred of hesitation about contacting the VVH program. They knew that it was exactly what they were searching for, even if they had not explicitly realized or acknowledged that the opportunity to talk with their offender face to face was what they sought. They persevered in the VVH process, despite (in many cases) lukewarm enthusiasm or support from significant others in their lives.

Motivations for Participation

The Victims' Voices Heard program is aptly named since all the victims emphasized that having a voice and being heard were key motivators for and the most satisfying aspects of their participation. It is interesting that even those who were given the opportunity to participate in their criminal cases felt as though they did not really have a voice. Several victims described it succinctly: after carrying the weight of the crime for so long, the VVH program gave them the opportunity to load it onto the offenders' shoulders. Getting answers to questions or achieving a sense of clarity were their paramount desires. It is clear from the victims' words that the VVH program—the extensive preparation, the letter exchange, and the face-to-face dialogue—was transformative, empowering, and cathartic and brought them a sense of peace. It did not necessarily provide "closure," but it facilitated forward movement.

Although some victims had extremely positive experiences with individual prosecutors or victim services workers, overall they remained frustrated with a system that often does little to balance victims' needs and offenders' rights. Victims spoke with one voice about the capriciousness of the steps in the process of the criminal justice system, the mystery surrounding decision-making, their relative lack of input, and even the physical structures of courtrooms in which they had to stand near or even sit beside offenders or offenders' family members and friends. Many of the victims also expressed frustration with no-contact policies. Although they understood the intent of the law, victims felt stymied in their desire to find out information about the person and act that had so profoundly affected their lives. Many of the victims interviewed for this book mentioned that prior to VVH they had tried to send letters to the offenders through the judges or prosecutors or the courts with no success.

Despite protections offered by no-contact policies, victims continued to fear that offenders would harm them again when released or that offenders might commit new crimes and harm new victims. One often hears about how prisons breed antisocial feelings and violence, and since the offenders had already committed violent crimes, victims were understandably worried about what to expect when they were released. Victims did not want prison time to be counterproductive; they wanted some information about programs that offenders completed, how the offenders changed while incarcerated, and whether they needed to be afraid of the offenders' rage or vengefulness when the prison sentence ended.

Victims had already begun to wonder about their offenders before their involvement with VVH; the VVH program simply gave them a space to voice their concerns without recrimination. They shared a frustration with receiving incorrect information or no information at all—its absence or invalidity meant that they filled in the missing pieces themselves, often in very damaging assessments of their own actions or inactions. Their false assumptions led to strong feelings of self-blame and guilt. Victims were doggedly determined to go through the dialogue process no matter how emotionally overwhelmed or pained they felt reliving the experiences by talking about them over many months.

Receiving answers was particularly important for the victims of rape who participated in the program. These women sought information about the attacks they had either completely erased from their memories or just could not seem to recall with any clarity. In particular, they wanted to know if they had fought back and whether the rapist knew them or had been stalking them. These questions from victims indicate that they blamed themselves for their actions or inactions, feelings of inadequacy that may be reinforced by insensitive questions or statements posed by others. In fact, the victims recalled questions or comments such as "Did you try to fight him off? I would have killed anyone who tried to do that to me"; "Why did you open the door that night?"; "Did you know him? I would be afraid it was someone I had angered who followed me home or something."

Victims who sought the help of the VVH program struggled with these victim-blaming messages received from both strangers and their loved ones. Getting answers relieved victims of these heavy burdens and began a healing process that restored their self-respect. In fact, both the rape victims interviewed for this book discovered that they fought back incredibly hard against their rapists, accounts that not only surprised the women but also empowered them. Although they remembered some of the things they had said to deflect or defuse the rapists' anger, the additional knowledge the women gleaned during the face-to-face dialogues with the rapists reinforced a sense of courage and competence in saving their own lives. Moreover, learning that the rapists did not know them prior to the rapes also served to erase the lingering feelings the victims had that something they might have done unknowingly contributed to being a target.

Being relieved of blame through genuine apologies and remorse expressed by offenders was especially crucial for the two victims/survivors of child sexual abuse committed by family members. Children are blameless, and these victims needed to hear the offenders fully and genuinely apologize, without a shred of self-pity, victim blaming, trivialization of the abuse, or denial of the harm. An affirmation of responsibility for the atrocious betrayal of trust is only part of what the incest victims wanted to hear. These victims also wanted to demonstrate to the offenders that they were no longer passive or helpless victims; rather, they were in control of their lives and were not going to permit the offenders to (figuratively) overpower them again during the dialogue process and beyond.

Several of the victims expressed a need to "forgive" their offender or chose to express forgiveness when they met with the offender. I deliberately place "forgive" in quotation marks to signify that this word often has very different meanings for victims. For some victims, forgiving someone who has harmed them so much is necessary to move beyond their anger or feelings of revenge.

Forgiveness becomes one of the steps they take to reclaim control over lives once so colored by rage. By giving up the anger and forgiving, they are able to savor life once again. Forgiveness does not mean reconciliation with the offender or a pardoning of the crime. Forgiveness does not mean releasing offenders from responsibility of the choices they made and actions they took. and it does not mean a victim will ever forget what happened. But, as Kathleen O'Hara says, "To forgive is to put an end to that futile form of anger that we have turned without mercy upon ourselves."[4] Victims who seek peace and balance in their lives may find that forgiveness helps to restore that equilibrium. It may also be the case that when many victims get to the point of releasing the trauma through an emotional process, they might define it as "forgiveness," since the trauma moves from being the central burning and consuming injury at the center stage of their lives to an important part of their lives on the side stage or backstage. When this shift occurs, they can then experience more fully other emotional realities that may have nothing to do with the trauma, such as the joy of a new baby or an educational accomplishment or going on vacation.

Most victims also want the offenders to be cognizant of the harm and long-term effects of their crimes. They want offenders not only to know how their own lives were affected by the offenders' violence but also to understand how their loved ones were harmed. In cases of family members killed by drunk drivers or murdered, the victims wanted to tell the offenders about the lives that were lost and make their family members real to the offenders, to recount their despair and longing for their treasured and missed loved ones.

Ultimately, victims and survivors need to feel they can accept the horror of what happened and also achieve a sense of peace so they can move forward in their lives. None of them saw this as "closure," a concept that many victims reject. Howard Zehr (2002) suggests that the word *closure* is often offensive to victims (especially those who experience severe crimes) because it implies that "all can be put behind and the book closed, and that is not possible. However, the word does imply a sense of being able to move forward, which restorative justice aims to make possible."[5] From countless hours listening to the victims who participated in the VVH program, it became abundantly clear to me that they felt a profound sense of empowerment as well as a greater ability—and even desire—to move forward. Their words resonate with scholars' discussions about how victims' empowerment involves restoring a sense of self-control and autonomy that was lost as a result of their traumatic experience.[6]

That the victims shared an ability to look beyond the specific crimes committed against them and toward a larger curiosity about whether the punishment imposed had any positive effects on offenders suggests a broader understanding of the complexity of crime and punishment. Why would these victims—who experienced such severe violence—harbor any curiosity about their offenders' lives? This interest could reflect the structure of the VVH preparation process, one that encourages victims and offenders to think about how crime may affect everyone's lives. Alternatively, it suggests perhaps that most people are not inherently vengeful and that they strive to see the good or the potential for good in others.[7] Although it is not a surprise that four of the offenders admitted they committed other prior offenses or knew about offenses committed by close relatives, at least six of the nine victims also had family members who had been arrested and processed by the criminal justice system. This familiarity with the criminal justice system within their own families could lend support to victims' softening of their punitive feelings for the offenders and allow them to wonder about the impact of punishment.

When victims talked about their experiences with the criminal justice system, a pattern emerged. For the victims in whose cases the victims and offenders were strangers to one another and the offenders were quickly apprehended and admitted guilt, outcomes were more positive. These were also the kinds of cases in which victims were more likely to receive unconditional support from others because of the social distance between the victims and offenders, the violent nature of the act, the presence of weapons, and race or age differences between the victim and offender. Police and prosecutors treated the "good victims" with respect and believed their stories.[8] Experiences with the criminal justice system were negative for victims who did not conform to "good victim" stereotypes. For example, Laurie's domestic-violence case typified a situation in which police have not always treated victims seriously or granted victims credibility, and the biracial aspect of their relationship may exacerbate a negative response.

Features of the Victims' Voices Heard Program

Victims stressed the importance of the way Kim and the program were able to get them the information or tangible items they needed to allay their fears or curiosity about offenders. For some victims, Kim was able to get photographs of the offenders. Without a photograph, many victims had no memory of what their offenders looked like, so the "unknown" translated into fear of *any* man. Since many years had passed since the crimes, victims wanted to have a sense of who the offender was today. One offender explained this need of his victim: "The more she knows, the less she fears." Victims were also able to get records of programs the offenders completed in prison, access to original police reports, and other pieces of information. In one case, Kim used her contacts with the attorney general's office so that for the first time in over twenty years a victim was able to read a good deal more of the court transcript from her mother's murder trial.

Another key feature was the aspect of VVH as a form of "talk therapy." Victims and offenders greatly benefited from the opportunity to talk, talk, and talk. The facilitators listened. They validated feelings, challenged stories if needed, offered alternative ways of looking at things, and helped with making sense out of tragedy. The extensive preparation process is designed to further encourage introspection, to process feelings and conflict, and to develop a more complete understanding of what had happened and its aftermath. Victims who had participated in some form of counseling after the crime believed they never got as much out of it as they did from their meetings with the facilitators.

The commitment to the VVH program is time consuming and emotionally draining. The participants met with their dialogue facilitator for at least six months. Kim believes this is necessary, although other states often require only a few meetings with the facilitators before the parties have their dialogue. The longer time is beneficial: by all the victims' accounts, talking helps healing.

A disadvantage to such a lengthy and intensive process is that victims and offenders may grow to rely on Kim; for some offenders, Kim (or Debbie) was their only visitor. She provides a sounding board for things offenders might not express to prison personnel or to other inmates, and she holds them accountable. When the program ends, some victims or offenders may feel abandoned. Although formal sessions with victims and offenders do not take place after the completion of the face-to-face dialogue and the two-week and two-month follow-ups, VVH maintains some connection to the participants. Offenders often mail progress reports as part of the affirmation agreements, and victims check in through email or with a phone call when something happens that they want to share (good or bad). But most victims find that their need to see Kim becomes less acute after they complete the program; their earlier, all-consuming need to go over and over the details of their experiences diminishes.

Offenders' Motivations and Experiences

Although VVH is first and foremost a victim-centered program, offenders also benefit. The program states up front that there are three stipulations necessary for offenders: to accept responsibility for their crimes, to have remorse for their actions, and to understand that they receive no tangible reward for their involvement.[9] One of the advantages of a therapeutic RJ program that operates in addition to the criminal justice system rather than in lieu of it is that offenders typically have been incarcerated for quite some time before victims try to contact them. This time factor can serve as a cooling-off period in which victims might move beyond thoughts of revenge and better channel their anger; offenders, too, might find some degree of understanding about the harm they caused as well as experience heartfelt remorse. Although complete solitude might elude inmates in facilities housing thousands of prisoners, they still face many empty hours, giving them plenty of time to think about the paths their lives have taken.

Most of the offenders portrayed in this book had fleeting thoughts about contacting their victims even before the VVH program's initial query about their willingness to participate. The offenders understood why they were not permitted to contact the victims, but several wanted to express their remorse. For most of the offenders, remorse and empathy for their victims were already present prior to hearing about the VVH program. Research demonstrates that empathy for victims takes time to develop.[10] Over time, most of the offenders became very cognizant of the pain they caused their own families and close friends by committing their crimes, a clear example of the "ripple effect": offenders came to understand that violent acts do not just harm the victim but affect everyone connected to both the victim's and offender's lives.

All the offenders portrayed in this book welcomed the opportunity to express their apologies and remorse to the victims. Although some of them had attempted to offer these sentiments at their sentencing hearings, they felt much better prepared to express their genuine remorse after having had the time to reflect on their actions and the harms they caused. Both Jenny and Kevin, who killed people in drunk-driving crashes, believed their verbal statements to the victims in court were insufficient—at the time, they were too overcome with their own emotions to effectively convey their sincere apologies. Jenny was battling with her parents in their attempt to influence the judge, and Kevin had difficulty with publicly expressing his deep regrets. VVH provided them with the venue to convey their heartfelt apologies. The letters they wrote and the face-to-face conversations in which they discussed their recognition of the harm they caused the victims (and their families) were very well received, particularly since their victims had felt the most insulted by the offenders' demeanor or the content of their statements to them in court.

Offenders who had no prior relationship with or knowledge of their victims described the process of reconciling the horrific trauma they inflicted out of their own rage or insecurities onto someone who was not a real person to them but merely a target or recipient of their anger. They expressed profound remorse about the senselessness of their crimes and the inexcusability of their acts. Both the offenders who committed stranger rape and those who killed people while driving drunk were more sincere and active in their efforts to try to make things better, writing even to many extended family members of their victims. Through their paperwork and assignments required by VVH, they were able to put themselves into the shoes of their victims, to more fully understand victims' feelings of fear, pain, and anger. These offenders who had committed crimes against strangers were the most astounded that their victims had any desire to talk with them or see them.

Despite the offenders' eagerness to participate, most of them were worried about how angry the victims would be and the verbal abuse to which they might be subjected during the dialogue. A number of the offenders were also concerned about retaliation from victims or victims' family members upon their release from prison. This concern surfaced even though Kim assured them that angry victims were not ready to face their offenders and that she would not tolerate any offender bashing. Following the dialogues, without exception, the offenders remarked about how civil the tone of the discussions was and how respectfully the very people they had harmed treated them. The victims' ability to treat offenders with dignity amazed them; many offenders believed they were not worthy of such respect. The civility of the dialogues also served as a motivator for them to continue to earn the respect of their victims. The offenders also commented on the letters written to them by the victims, which almost uniformly demonstrated humanity and mutual respect. The victims were less mystified by this tenor of their letters, feeling that further anger was counterproductive. Consistent with the research on offenders' backgrounds and childhood histories, most of the offenders interviewed came from very difficult home lives, with absent or physically and sexually abusive or neglectful parents.[11] With few exceptions, the offenders talked about their backgrounds (to the facilitators, in their paperwork, to their victims, and with me) without a trace of self-pity. They stated facts and did not use their situations as excuses or rationalizations for their crimes. On the one hand, the manner in which the offenders discussed their backgrounds might demonstrate the success of prison therapy in confronting their attempts to minimize or excuse harmful behavior. On the other hand, it could be that the over time offenders developed empathy for their victims, which supplanted evasion of responsibility. Offenders stressed to victims that their crimes were the result of choices they alone made and that other people who had similar backgrounds of parental abuse or indifference did not make the same hurtful choices.

The empathy for victims expressed by nonstranger sexual offenders conveyed a slightly different tone. Although the sexual offenders who knew their victims took responsibility for their crimes and apologized to their victims, their contrition rang a little hollow. This does not suggest that their participation was insincere—these offenders revealed important things to their victims and urged the victims not to blame themselves. Their victims emerged from the VVH program empowered. But clearly their comparisons to "worse" sexual offenders did not entirely disappear. We know that sex offenders use many techniques to neutralize their crimes. Sex offenders who manipulate children with emotional threats and bribes may find it easier to hide behind rationalizations than do sex offenders who use violence with strangers. In addition, their posturing—similar to the offenders who refused to blame the past for their criminal activity—could highlight the enduring costs of maintaining a masculine front in prison, a persona in which self-pity or weakness are not desirable traits.

When most offenders arrive in prison, they are often hostile about getting caught and punished, blaming everyone but themselves and unable or unwilling to look beyond their immediate situation. Over time, however, this scapegoating disappeared for most of these offenders. Without being asked a direct question regarding incarceration, almost all the offenders emphasized that prison was a good thing for them. Jamel said it saved his life since his behavior was spiraling out of control. Both Jamel and James believed that if they had not been apprehended for rape, their next crime might have been murder. Incarceration woke them up. It matured them; it gave them the time-out from the streets to figure out who they are and what direction they want their lives to follow. As the months and years progressed, the group of offenders featured in this book took great responsibility for their actions and endeavored to be better people.

The offenders acknowledged that they were insensitive to their victims when they were first incarcerated. Anger had been a constant defining force in the lives of the violent offenders in particular (except for the cases involving child sexual abuse and DUI). The trigger for the anger expressed in their crimes was often a totally separate and unrelated incident or altercation with other people, but their anger was displaced onto the victims. Following this insight, dealing more effectively with anger became a strong commitment for these offenders. It was only after time that their empathy developed—with initial seeds planted in requisite victim-sensitivity classes—and then grew under the tutelage of VVH. Offenders also began to understand better how their actions affected others once they realized the impact of their crimes on their own family members. Their relatives communicated the shame, disappointment, and disapproval they experienced, which facilitated offenders' better understanding of how victims and their family members felt. Without the time to reflect on these things in prison, offenders doubted that they would have fully understood the far-reaching consequences of their criminal behavior.

All the offenders, whether they knew their victims or not, impressed me with their commitment to do whatever they could do to help the victims heal. They pledged that they would answer any questions the victims asked, no matter how uncomfortable they felt, and my interviews with the victims indicated that this commitment was amply fulfilled. Offenders often have key pieces of information about the incidents that victims want or need to know about, and these kinds of details are things that the offenders would usually rather forget. However, they cooperated fully, freely providing answers and doing their best to fill in the blanks of missing details.

Process versus Outcome

Findings from the broader criminological literature reveal that individuals who perceive that they have been treated fairly, even if they do not like the outcome, will have a more positive opinion about the justice process.[12] This concept of procedural justice is important in understanding the experiences of the victims who participated in the VVH program. For most, meeting with their offender was the apex of an emotionally intense journey; they derived a great deal of solace from having the chance to ask their questions and have them answered at the dialogue, as well as having the opportunity to describe fully the short- and long-term consequences of the crime. Not all the victims, however, attributed their feelings of satisfaction, peace, or empowerment to the face-to-face dialogue. About half of them spoke of having derived the greatest understanding and satisfaction from the preparation process itself. All that emerged on the way to the face-to-face meeting was "transformative" for many victims; the dialogue, as one survivor put it, was just "icing on the cake."

It is important to understand why the process itself was so powerful, at least in part because this understanding can offer some general guidelines for other RJ programs. One factor that was raised frequently by both victims and offenders was the role of the facilitator. From the totality of the responses from participants, it is clear that Kim was equally comfortable working with both victims and offenders. All of them, without prompting, talked at length about her ability to be nonjudgmental, even when she was presented with horrific details about the crime or facts about childhood experiences or feelings that were uncomfortable and unsettling for the participants themselves to talk about. Both victims and offenders felt she treated them with dignity, respect, and fairness. The comfort Kim provides is reflected in her evenhanded approach during the taped dialogues (in addition to unsolicited comments from the victims and offenders about her fairness).

These comments lead to obvious questions: Is the considerable success of VVH due to qualities of Kim herself? Or are her abilities and methods transferable to other coordinators and to other programs? The admiration and respect and closeness that victims and offenders have for Kim speak volumes. They identify with her because she has experienced a similar, horrible tragedy and because she fully understands the range of emotions they feel. The victims also see Kim as a beacon of hope—if she could get through to the other side, maybe they can too.[13] Most of the victims and offenders talked about their ease in connecting and opening up to Kim because of their shared traumas. Justine expressed it best when she talked about how conventional therapy failed her because the therapist she went to did not seem to truly "get it," because she had not experienced sexual abuse herself when she was a child.

So could a facilitator who did not have a horrible crime befall her or him be as effective? The answer probably rests on the qualities that Kim and all skillful facilitators possess. The qualities mentioned by victims and offenders include an ability to listen, to nudge and challenge them, to provide them with a safe space to vent, question, confront, and dissect, and to *really* feel their feelings about the crime. While Kim's empathy and understanding are genuine and strong, she also knows how to set boundaries—what she is able to take on and what stays part of the program and not part of her own private life. This is a formidable task, given how close the process brings a facilitator to the participants. But this healthy separation is crucial for facilitators, who would otherwise be emotionally burned out over time. Part of the program's goal is to empower victims to have a voice, which includes facilitating their efforts to stake a claim for what they want and need and to develop the confidence and support to go after it.

Kim found her own path to recovery through her strong faith and forgiveness of her daughter's murderer, but she does not believe there is only one path to follow; each victim has to find what works best, and Kim supports any decision or road she or he takes on the journey. Striving to find a facilitator with these qualities (and having remarkable facilitators like Kim to train them) will increase the potential for success in other restorative justice programs. Not all survivors will make great facilitators and have the skills, insight, and intuitive understanding that Kim possesses, and not all facilitators need to have been victims. Kim's personal experience gives her initial credibility with the victims and offenders in her program. At a minimum it seems that a facilitator with victimization experiences and a deep understanding of victims' needs would be better able to connect with participants.

Flexibility is built into the VVH program. There is no set time for a victim to finish the preparatory process and meet the offender; facilitators recognize that every victim has different needs and follows a different timetable and path to get to the point of meeting the offender face to face. In fact, some victims initially resist the extensive preparatory process—they do not want to dig through their past; they do not understand the need to be emotionally ready to face someone who severely harmed them or their loved ones—and the preparation itself is daunting. Offenders, too, initially express alarm when they learn what their agreement to meet with their victim entails. The process is emotionally arduous; it is not easy for either victims or offenders to go back to their darkest days. Yet even the most recalcitrant participants acknowledged how enormously helpful the preparation process was to them. They realized that no matter how ready they thought they were to meet their offender or victim, they were not as prepared as they thought. Facilitators do not want any surprises at the dialogue that could undo months of very hard work should something be revealed that derails the victim's recovery or adversely affects the victim or offender. As indicated by the RJ literature on what makes a successful dialogue, the best scenario is when the facilitator says little or nothing because all the hard work to get both parties that far has already been accomplished.[14]

Since the VVH program is an independent, nonprofit program that exists separately from the state criminal justice apparatus, its flexibility and time-consuming nature is not threatened by bureaucratic pressures to resolve cases more quickly or to expand the number of individuals it serves. By not being under the auspices of the state, the program is free of any quota constraints or other exigencies of government-funded programs. A more formalized program might lose the open-ended structure of the preparation process and sacrifice the depth of the process for breadth.[15]

For victims, the factors that motivated them to make the initial call to the VVH program and commit to the emotionally strenuous program requirements have a great deal to do with their evaluations of the process and the outcome of the program. The victims' initial goals, unanimously, were to meet their offender in order to get some questions answered or points clarified and to convince themselves that the offenders truly understood the profound sense of violation and harm created by their actions. Whereas one victim wanted the offender to know that she forgave him, another victim wanted to be sure the offender knew that her forgiveness would *never* be given to him. Regardless, the victims felt that the offender held the keys to resolving the questions that haunted them, often shadowing them for years, making it impossible for them to move on or find a sense of peace.

Over time, it is clear that victims also received other benefits from the process. Most spoke of their friends and family having what is known in the victimology literature as "compassion fatigue." They do not understand why a victim remains troubled, especially if a lot of time has passed since the crime and if the outward appearances give the impression that the victim has moved on to succeed in other realms (completed an education, achieved success in employment, married, had children, and so forth). What was so affirming for victims was to be able to go over the entire incident—its antecedents and aftermath—with Kim. At least half the victims told me that they had never shared some of the details, or some of their emotions, about the crime to anyone else. Kim made the environment safe for them to feel free to dig around in the most unpleasant of memories. She provided insight and made connections between things the victims were talking about, and the victims responded without fear of being censored.

In many ways, what the victims gained during the preparation process was the very thing that eluded them in the criminal justice system: a voice. They were heard without judgment. Gaining this voice empowered them, giving them the strength they needed to meet their offender. Having a voice was relevant and important for even the two victims who had made lengthy victim impact statements to the court (Julie and Leigh). They found they had different things to say since those public statements made years ago in court.

Compartmentalizing versus Integrating

The victims/survivors emphasized how personally empowered they were by the VVH program. The victims talked about the trauma and violence they experienced as a shadow or a dark cloud that hovered over their daily lives. Yet they had long learned to keep the lingering impact of the crimes to themselves. Following their involvement with the VVH program, they felt their victimization no longer had to be compartmentalized. They had control over it, and by regaining a sense of personal efficacy, victims were able to put it aside or take it out when they wanted to, rather than having it permeate every second of their lives. This allowed a full and healthy integration of the crime/victimization into their lives that was healing and brought them relief.

All the victims said over and over again how glad they were to find and participate in the VVH program. As a tribute to the program, they credited it (and Kim's capable stewardship) as the missing piece they needed to be able to better integrate their victimization into their lives and move forward with a greater sense of strength. Although many victims mentioned that there are triggers still—sounds or smells or circumstances that remind them too vividly of the crime—more importantly, there is also a sense of acceptance, an ability to integrate the change into their lives. Their victimization has become a factual statement they make about their lives, rather than something amorphous that exerts control over them. These were not just superficial feelings for the victims; following their participation in VVH, many have moved on, engaging in activities that they would never have considered before.

Offenders' Experience with Integration

The offenders expressed similar feelings of satisfaction; they were able to make some amends for their behavior—actions that brought them shame and regret when they thought about their victims and the larger circle of people affected by their crimes. But ultimately, they were still locked up following the VVH meetings during the preparation process and after the dialogue. The emotional catharsis that many of the offenders experienced and about which they spoke to me (and others) with so much emotion was not as fully integrated into their daily lives as was the case for the victims. Part of this difficulty may reflect cultural expectations of masculinity—which include not wearing one's emotions on one's sleeve or appearing "soft"—constraints exacerbated in men's prisons, in which there is the constant need to confirm one's masculinity. Another factor may simply be the reality of their situation: no matter how personally and deeply satisfied they felt in facing their victims, expressing remorse and responsibility and helping victims in the best way they could to heal (by answering questions, providing missing information, and so forth), the offenders still had to face that they were not free; their actions put them in prison. No matter how deplorable they now assess their criminal behavior as being, every day in prison works to test their resolve to do better. Only time will tell if the lessons learned by offenders about the futility of anger, the responsibility to make better choices, and the utility of expressing emotions and empathy will exert an effect on their prison behavior in light of the oppositional pull of traditional masculinity. These challenges are exacerbated by the fact that upon their release, most offenders return to "their same disenfranchised neighborhoods and difficult conditions without having received any services to address their underlying problems," as noted unequivocally by researchers examining the collateral consequences of prison reentry.[16]

Face-to-Face Dialogues

Of the nine dialogues discussed in this book, I watched six (the two cases involving intentional murders were not videotaped, and Kim reviewed Melissa's tape for me, taking extensive notes with the victim's full permission). The dialogues were impressive in their scope, in their intensity, and in the emotional effort it took for both sides to face each other and confront very painful memories. Despite the trauma that brought victims and offenders together, the dialogues powerfully revealed the emotional reconciliations and healing that occurred. Clearly, the preparation undertaken by victims and offenders prior to the face-to-face meeting was crucial—for the most part, there were no real surprises in the dialogues. The strength, courage, and emotional fortitude the victims demonstrated went beyond my expectations. The dialogues were the culmination of so much hard work that the entire process was transformative and empowering, not just the actual dialogue.

What else accounts for why the dialogues work so well? First, the victims had already moved beyond their anger.[17] It was not that they wanted to pretend they were not angry (or that they had not been extremely angry), but they knew it would be counterproductive to face their offender with a conversation shaped by hostility. Second, as victims approached the dialogue, their fear became the background, while their desire for something positive to emerge from the awful experience moved to the foreground. Victims wanted the VVH process to be meaningful, not just for their own peace of mind and healing but also to be a catalyst for (or reinforce) an offender's motivation for positive change. Consistently, victims mentioned that they wanted the offenders to learn something and to use their knowledge to motivate them after they reentered society. In some ways, this wish reflects an assertion of power—that a victim could facilitate transformation of something previously purely negative. Meeting their offenders face to face and conversing with them about emotionally difficult and private things not only honored the victims' rights and desires to be heard; it also gave victims back their power. The asymmetry of power that was present during the crime and the case processing was reconfigured.

Finally, victims wanted offenders visibly and publicly to acknowledge the consequences of their actions, particularly if the offenders' behavior had been callous during the trials or if there had been no statement from the offender to the victim. This acknowledgment was crucial because it validated victims' memories of the actual incident and their subsequent fear in the aftermath of the crime, regardless of whether the offender was a stranger or known to victim. For victims who lost a beloved family member or members in the two murder cases or the two DUI cases, it was especially important for them to bring photographs of their families with and without their loved ones in the frames. This visual display reinforced the reality of the untimely deaths of family members and demonstrated how much they were loved and missed. The offenders were humbled and incredibly respectful of such personal displays, despite their own horror (which they shared in talking with Kim, in their letters to victims, and later in their interviews with me) in knowing that they caused the deaths.

The Role of Forgiveness

There is no expectation or requirement in VVH that the victims forgive their offenders. Although Kim has forgiven the young man who murdered her daughter, she does not presume to think that all victims will feel as she does. Kim explains what forgiving him means to her: "He no longer has the power to hurt me, even when he messes up." Some victims feel ambivalent about forgiveness, although they say they could see themselves forgiving the offender once he has been released and proves himself by not reoffending (Julie, Donna). Melissa does not forgive her father, and Kathleen does not forgive the man who murdered her mother. Two victims, Allison and Scott, entered the VVH program with the intention of achieving forgiveness because of their strong religious faith. Laurie struggles with forgiving her ex-husband. Chris's victim (the son of the man he murdered) said he forgave Chris at the end of their dialogue. This surprised and amazed Chris, even though his accounting of it seemed as though it was not the cathartic moment for which he had hoped. Leigh forgave Jenny for killing her son during a DUI crash, urging her in a secular sense to "be better." Given the severely violent and damaging nature of the crimes, the offenders who heard their victims forgive them were delighted and full of gratitude. Not all offenders sought forgiveness, however, as some thought they did not deserve such a gift from the person they hurt so badly.

Gendered Violence

The cases of gendered violence presented in this book shed important light on the debate over the appropriateness of using RJ models for these crimes. Since the VVH program is a victim-centered, postconviction, therapeutic RJ effort that offers no incentive for offenders to participate beyond a desire to help their victims heal, it avoids most of the criticism aimed at diversionary RJ. Five of the nine cases explored in this book involve gendered violence (sexual and domestic). Two were stranger rapes, one was a marital rape and attempted murder that also included child sexual assault (incest), and the remaining two cases involved incest committed by a father against a daughter and child sexual assault perpetrated by a grandfather against his granddaughter (although the VVH victim who participated in this latter case was the girl's father).

What propelled victims of gendered violence to meet with the source of their trauma and pain? Consistent with the motivations stated by all victims who participated in VVH, the women said that it was time to give the offenders the emotional baggage they had been carrying all these years. They wanted answers. They wanted to fill in pieces of the puzzle. They wanted their misplaced guilt erased. They wanted reassurances of no further harm or contact. Most important, they sought empowerment over people and situations over which they had previously no power. And, indeed, as the victims processed details of their lived experiences, they became stronger and more emotionally confident and, in turn, resolved in moving beyond the crime.

The accounts of victims of gendered violence exhibit common themes: at the onset of the VVH program, they blamed themselves. This is understandable, especially for the younger victims of child sexual abuse, because it reflects the manipulation by child sexual offenders who use children's naïveté and hunger for affection to suggest that the victims somehow initiated, wanted, or caused the abuse. Victims of stranger rape also engaged in self-blame, having been affected by social stereotypes that question a rape victim's credibility and second-guess what she could or should have done to prevent the rape. The survivor of marital rape and battering voiced similar victim blaming. There were some differences between victims of gendered violence who were related to their offenders and victims whose offenders were strangers to them. When offenders were strangers to their victims, fear of the unknown was magnified. For victims who were related to their abusers, the sense of betrayal was amplified, as was the conflict involved in hating what happened at the hands of someone whom one is expected to respect and love.

Benefits in Cases of Gendered Violence

To attest to the success of using this kind of therapeutic, postconviction RJ model, victims of gendered violence in the cases presented in this book described their achievements best: first, victims received immense satisfaction when offenders told them that nothing about the crime was their fault (Melissa, Laurie, Donna). The offenders' acknowledgment alleviated the self-doubt and blame the victims had carried with them for many years. The stranger rapists were able to explain to their victims that they were selected randomly and that the acts had little to do with them but, rather, were the result of displaced anger and an inability to channel aggression or frustration in an acceptable way. The stranger rapists reminded the women that they fought back, a fact the victims had not remembered, and this information became a crucial source of pride.

Regardless of the victim-offender combination (i.e., stranger or nonstranger), victims wanted the chance to tell the offenders about the consequences of their crimes. Donna appreciated the symmetry in the fact that Jamel was also in prison, given that she felt locked up herself by her unrelenting fear since the rape. She wanted him to know that and fully understand how his actions affected her life. Through the intense conversations and introspection that were part of the VVH preparation process, Donna realized that she was in a prison of her own making, and it was during her involvement with VVH that she began taking steps to regain her power. If she had not had the opportunity to exchange letters with Jamel and meet him to ask him about the rape, she would still be mired in guilt and making choices, such as her self-imposed house imprisonment, on the basis of misinformation. In fact, today Donna is proud to reveal her real name and discuss the personal effects of the rape in her life because she no longer feels any stigma or shame about it.

For the two direct victims of familial abuse, both physical and sexual, the sense of betrayal was perhaps the deepest. Melissa wanted answers from her father regarding his behavior. She also wanted to show him that despite his abuse, she was successful. When her father wrote and also told Melissa face to face that all the blame was his and his alone, she felt empowered. When a parent sexually abuses a child, the violation of trust is very deep. Melissa wanted him to tell her how he was able to commit such an atrocious violation and to explain the last words he said to her when he was arrested ("I didn't think of you as my daughter"). Because five years had gone by since his arrest, Melissa felt better able both to formulate the questions she wanted answered and to hear from the man who had hurt her so deeply. She was in control and no longer too terrified of his anger and its repercussions to say no.

One of the most interesting tests of postconviction therapeutic RJ will be its handling of domestic-violence cases. What Laurie gained from the VVH program epitomizes the potential for success in these cases. In many ways, Laurie's story is typical of battered women: she was married to an abusive husband who was jealous and controlling, easily attacked her low self-esteem, and was manipulative, striking out at her with emotional, sexual, and physical abuse to intimidate her into submission. He also sexually abused at least one of their children. Laurie confronted him eight years after he raped and tried to kill her. Her primary motivation was to verify her suspicion of his sexual abuse of their oldest daughter, but she also wanted to address his years of abusive behavior toward her. Laurie wanted to express her fear of him and her anger, but she also saw the forum as a way to highlight where she is now and that he no longer controls her. The most important aspect was the shift in power; Laurie was in full control of her situation, reversing the asymmetry of power that characterizes domestic violence.

As an indirect or secondary victim, Scott entered the VVH program with a different motivation. Rather than directly addressing the sexual-molestation charges, Scott wanted a chance to talk to his father-in-law about forgiveness. Talking about his daughter's victimization might have been too "real" for a father, but dealing with issues of forgiveness in the context of religion—which is very important to Scott—was safer. Scott himself was a paragon of support for his daughter; he believed her and would have done anything to protect her from future harm. The criminal justice and the medical system (through the SANE program) also validated and soothed his daughter, as SANE did for Donna following her rape and also Laurie's nine-year-old daughter. Although Scott's initial response was rage, he sought forgiveness because of hateful thoughts and statements he made about Bruce.

Offenders' Perspectives on Crimes of Gendered Violence

How did the offenders who committed crimes of gendered violence cope with their victims and the process of RJ? They maintained that the process reinforced their empathy for their victims and helped them to better recognize their triggers for anger. In particular, the offenders who committed rape and were strangers to their victims exhibited the deepest remorse and the strongest desire to make things right. In contrast, the offenders who were intimately connected to their victims through family ties were more likely to minimize their actions and the effects, and they often even wanted praise for recognizing that what they did was wrong. At the same time, however, despite the sex offenders' rationalizations and minimizing, ultimately, and when it mattered the most, they at least said the right things to assuage their victims of any guilt or self-doubt.

In my own conversations with the sex offenders who knew their victims, the men offered personal evaluations of how their victims looked or handled themselves during the dialogue. They admitted that they were eager to see their victims—not for the motives that the other sex offenders offered (in order to apologize)—but because they missed them or missed being part of the family. Like many child sexual offenders, Steven and Bruce minimized and rationalized their behavior. Bruce, Paul, and Steven were eager to disclose good things about themselves (to Kim and to me) and also about what they did for their families (such as taking them on vacations or opting to waive a trial to avoid dragging their family through a battle). This positive spin they wished to convey reinforces their interest in reconciling with their families. Although they wrote and said all the right things to their victims, they still waffled about taking complete responsibility for their actions. In contrast, the offenders who raped strangers did *not* minimize their acts in any way, nor did they rationalize away their crimes. Nor did the offenders who raped strangers raise anything positive about their own behavior during the crime.

Nonstranger sexual offenders joined the stranger offenders in evaluating their experience with VVH positively. They were proud to help the victims they had hurt so severely, they answered any questions the victims asked, they took away any blame the victims still carried, and, perhaps most important, they listened to what the victims said, giving them back their voice.

Murder Cases, Intentional and Unintentional

Both Chris and Wayne received life sentences for the murders they committed, although they were originally candidates for the death penalty. Both have been incarcerated for a long time and have participated in many programs. Neither has received more than one disciplinary infraction in their twenty-plus years of time in prison. For various reasons—probably because their crimes were so violent and disturbing to confront—both of these dialogues had several starts and stops, either because of cold feet on the part of the victim (the son of the man Chris killed) or because of the offender's struggle with coming to terms with his crime (Wayne).

Although I am treating these homicides separately from the gendered violence in cases of rape, incest, and domestic violence, in some ways they are gendered as well. They follow traditional homicide patterns in that the offenders are male and the victim and offender are acquaintances or known to each other in some way. In these cases, one could argue persuasively that both men killed because of gendered issues: Chris believed that he was avenging a wrong and that by getting Greg out of the picture, he could rescue Greg's wife and her children. Wayne killed Judith after she refused to do what he wanted her to do (have sex with him, get out of his car after she refused).

In these two murder cases, the offenders may have received more benefits from the program than the victims/surviving family members, although the victims still believed the program was worthwhile. The victims used prepared statements during the dialogue, so the meetings were not spontaneous in design. Both victims left the dialogue unsettled—perhaps the violent nature of the crimes sabotaged a more cathartic response. For Kathleen, though she was ultimately unmoved by Wayne's apology and remorse, she felt immeasurably better by being able to confront him. Her feeling of relief continues to this day, freeing her up to confide more in her daughters and other family members and even to speak publicly about how crime affects victims and their families. Since I did not have the opportunity to meet with Greg's son face to face, I do not know his motivations for being a part of the VVH program. Chris wanted the opportunity to apologize to Brett and his family, particularly because he now doubts that Greg abused his wife and children.

In contrast, both the victims and the offenders of the unintentional murders caused by drunk drivers gained a lot more from the program. The surviving family members who met with the offenders in the two cases both viewed the deaths as resulting from terribly tragic choices, but they did not condemn the offenders as bad people. Although they wrote extremely harsh victim impact statements for the sentencing judges, over time their anger dissipated, leaving them with the means to make sense of the tragedy, feeling that losing *another* person's life (or chance) over the crime would only compound their loss. Similar to what Donna said to her rapist, both Julie and Leigh told the offenders that they needed to move forward, without guilt, and find a way to make their lives better because of what happened. All three women told their offenders, "I believe in you; I want you to do better." The selflessness of this gift cannot be understated, and its magnitude was not lost on the offenders. In the time since the dialogues, both the victims and offenders have kept this sense of hope and optimism alive, and all expressed feeling lighter for it.

After the Formal Program

Following the victims' participation in VVH, their responses ran the gamut: some said they no longer opposed early release for their offenders, some reaffirmed their intention to show up at every pardon board or parole hearing to add their voices against release, and at least one became invested in helping pragmatically with her offender's continued rehabilitation and reentry into society. Most of the victims, however, wanted nothing further to do with their offender (regardless of whether the offender was a stranger to them), although they did express their hope for the offender's continued commitment to law-abiding behavior.

Since VVH is not a diversionary RJ program, no tangible benefit was offered to the offenders for participation. Affirmation agreements developed between victims and offenders are voluntary and not legally binding, nor are they subject to any punitive response if the offenders fail to carry through on their promises. By not having VVH participation tied to coercive control, victims felt more free and creative in their admonitions or requests to the offenders, such as asking an offender not to give up hope or to be more respectful to his grandmother or asking an offender to take advantage of every program offered in the prison so that she could contribute something positive to the world since the victim's son no longer could—or even the cases in which two different victims asked their offenders to study Christian teachings so they might follow a stronger moral compass upon release. Victims' recovery, however, did not hinge on following up to ensure the promises were kept; time and time again, victims told me that their ability to move on after the dialogue rested on a feeling that they no longer had to fear that the offender would hurt them or others and that the offender would make a better choice in the future. In this way, the VVH program achieved restorative success for victims. In addition, all that transpired through the intensive RJ program planted a seed for offenders' aspirations to change. Ultimately, it will be up to the offenders to integrate these experiences fully into their lives upon release.

14

Conclusion

Restorative justice means many different things. Its position in the cultural lexicon demonstrates its versatility, with restorative justice practices operating under many different models as part of conflict-resolution strategies in schools, workplaces, and juvenile and adult criminal proceedings. On the larger political stage, restorative justice methods played a central role in South Africa's postapartheid Truth and Reconciliation Commission, in negotiations in postgenocide Rwanda, and in postsectarian Northern Ireland.[1] The popularity of such programs demonstrates a widespread interest in more fully incorporating the needs and voices of victims into justice-system processes as well as fostering greater accountability by offenders. Restorative justice has also been bolstered by a movement to shrink government involvement in social problems and the hope that movement away from a retributive, punitive response to crime will yield more long-term positive effects for communities.[2] Restorative justice practices have made significant inroads in providing alternative ways to address crime and victimization.

Criticisms voiced by victims about their minimal inclusion in their own cases paved the way for a reexamination of how victims could be better served. The victims' rights movement, from its inception in the 1970s, has created a space for victims to play a larger role in the formal criminal justice system by inviting their input, if not also their presence, at various points in case decision-making processes. Victims' forays into this terrain reflected their growing and vociferous dissatisfaction with their limited involvement in cases addressing crimes that created such disruption and trauma in their lives; victims harshly criticized a system that seemed inherently unjust and imbalanced in favor of offenders' rights. Study after study documented victims' frustration, marginalization, and exclusion from the criminal justice system.

In response to this pressure by victims, states and other jurisdictions implemented various reforms, most of which involved welcoming victims' input at various stages of the court decision-making process. However, despite reform efforts, including the addition of victims' rights amendments to most state constitutions, research reveals that the level of victims' involvement in criminal cases is much lower than anticipated. Researchers and advocates attribute victims' absence to a lack of information about policies that facilitate their involvement.[3] Some research has also found that victim impact statements, one of the signature reforms of the victims' rights movement, have little effect on rigid sentences often already set by determinate sentencing guidelines.[4] One well-known study compared two states with strong victim protections to two states where victims' rights were more limited; the researchers found that although victims fared better overall in the states with provictim legislation, more than 60 percent of interviewed victims in those states were not notified when the defendant in their case was released on bail, almost 40 percent were not informed about their right to file an impact statement at the parole hearing (72 percent of those who were told in time did participate at hearings),[5] and approximately 40 percent of local officials surveyed were unaware of the new victims' rights laws.[6] These disappointing findings and victims' frustrations reveal that rhetoric fails to match reality, a disconnect that has spurred activists to move away from reform efforts and toward more informal venues for dispute resolution.

Some victims of severe violence seize the opportunity to play a significant part in their cases from their earliest points, whereas for others a reluctance to participate often reflects the fact that they are simply not ready to tackle an emotionally draining and often public presentation in the relatively close aftermath of a serious crime. Their wounds may be too fresh, or they are unaware that their right to offer input is guaranteed. When victims do make initial statements, they are emotional and usually extreme, reflecting the immediate horror of the crime. At that point in their lives victims are still reeling from pain and loss, and they may not have had the opportunity for therapy or enough time to reflect and have space to heal. Of the victims/survivors of severe violence followed in this book, only two presented information in the form of a victim impact statement at sentencing hearings, and both of these were the family members of loved ones killed by drunk drivers. These victims/survivors requested the maximum punishment and found it impossible to accord the offenders any humanity during the processing of their cases. Over time, however, their retributiveness diminished as other concerns rose to prominence—a shift experienced by the other victims portrayed in this book as well.

This is where postconviction restorative justice comes in. These programs provide an opportunity to meet the needs articulated by victims: getting information, participating in the process, receiving respectful and fair treatment, gaining material restoration from the offender (which often serves mostly a symbolic function), and fostering their emotional healing.[7] Victims play a major role in educating offenders so they better understand the consequences of their actions and take responsibility for the harm they caused. This victim-centered focus is a huge departure from offender-centered, court-based formal justice models. It also differs in meaningful ways from diversionary restorative justice programs.

It is often said that a crime is an offense committed against *people*, rather than solely a violation of a law. Restorative justice practices attempt to repair the harm caused to people and relationships, promoting victims' empowerment through direct input and facilitating offenders' remorse. While some scholars express the hope that restorative justice practices will *heal* relationships, others maintain that this is not a necessary goal, particularly since some victims and offenders have no "relationship" they seek to repair (e.g., in a stranger rape case). The key principle of restorative justice is that a person is responsible for how his or her behavior affects others.[8] The VVH program addresses the inability of formal justice processes to meet victims' needs by creating a different path that victims may follow.

Updates and Lessons Learned

In 2008, I reconnected with every victim/survivor and offender I could find. I had not formally talked with many of them in two years, although I still received brief updates from Kim, and occasionally some victims emailed or called me. I was eager to find out how they were doing. Happily, most were interested in telling me what was going on in their lives, and they emailed, phoned, or wrote back quickly.[9] The victims/survivors' comments clearly displayed how buoyant they still felt; the victims continued to define their participation as a watershed moment, seeing VVH as essential in breaking the silence and mystery surrounding their victimization and providing a mechanism to combat feelings of being trivialized, condescended to, and disempowered by the criminal justice process. The offenders, too, believed that the program helped them to better understand the consequences of their choices and actions, as well as provided the opportunity to help their victims heal by answering their questions, listening to their experiences, and allowing them to express their remorse and also their plans for conducting themselves differently in prison and upon release.

On the basis of my several years of exploring the effects of VVH, the restorative success for victims is crystal clear. It fulfills its promise as a victim-centered program in that participation is initiated by victims and victims control the terms of interaction with their offenders. Simultaneously, this restorative justice model benefits offenders. Although their initial motivation may spring from a wish to assuage a guilty conscience, they ultimately gain more long-lasting benefits from their participation in the program. Even as time went on after the formal program ended—for more than two years in most cases—the offenders persevered with their resolve to change and become law-abiding citizens who contribute to society. This growth seemed especially powerful in the conversations with the offenders who committed crimes against strangers, no doubt because they had not been enmeshed in prior intimate relationships with their victims.

One of the key findings is the persistence of victims' self-described sense of peace and their positive evaluations of the program. My follow-up material reveals that the participants' satisfaction was not fleeting. These feelings are captured in victims' comments:

I'm more relaxed and at ease than I used to be. The constant fear and chronic anger that plagued my life for years is gone. . . . I gained a great deal of confidence and a new sense of self-worth through the successful completion of the program. (Laurie)

I can honestly go a day without dwelling on what could have been. I have learned to live with their memories for the time I had them in my life, rather than for the time I don't. . . . Without this program, I couldn't have closed that chapter in my life. VVH allowed me the freedom to live again. (Julie)

There is no longer the constant haunting, nightmares, and invasions into my daily thoughts. I'm not as fearful. . . . I feel greater comfort in talking about what happened; VVH took the burden and guilt off of me. I don't feel shameful anymore. (Melissa)

Beyond noting the changes they observed in the larger picture, the victims were very cognizant of more personal changes; several talked about their ability to better communicate with family members, co-workers, or even strangers. Laurie explained that whereas she used to be extremely shy and quiet, she is now able to talk to the customers at the retail store where she works. And she described how her male manager now sees her: "A part of his team, hardworking, intelligent, with the ability to run my department successfully. That's a far cry from the woman who met with Kim to talk about possibly meeting her offender, frightened to death just thinking about it."

Giving victims the opportunity to secure the things they needed—and were unable to obtain earlier in the formal justice setting—was crucial: input, a voice, answers to questions, the ability to tell the offenders about the consequences of the crimes and to hear what offenders had to say about their actions.

The only offender who expressed ambivalence about the program did so because of his depression about the prospect of dying of old age behind bars. Except for the two lifers who committed murder, the offenders felt they were doing well after their participation in VVH. For the lifers, this positive feeling was tempered by the reality of being incarcerated for many more years with little hope of parole. Overwhelmingly, offenders acknowledged the importance of the entire process (and not just the face-to-face meeting), noting that they acquired "tools" to negotiate other problems in their lives. Several offenders noted how important it was to them to have been able to help their victims and how the program had changed their own lives. Jamel explained that he not only feels better about himself, but he has also "become more understanding of other people's feelings." He now realizes, "It is not all about me all the time."

Creating empathy for victims was a powerful consequence of the VVH program for offenders. Empathy develops over time, with several years often passing before incarcerated offenders truly understand the ramifications of their harmful behavior. For the most part, the offenders who participated in VVH acknowledged that when they were sent to prison they initially thought very little about the effects of their crime on their victims. Over time, however, this changed. The offenders were all relieved to hear that following the dialogues the victims were doing better and that all the hard emotional work and time was worthwhile in helping to repair the damage they caused. Kevin's words convey many of the offenders' sentiments: "I just hope and pray that her life has gotten a lot better since I saw her last. I really wish her the best in life and that someday she can forgive me for what I did to her family." Offenders felt they had made sincere pledges to victims about their future behavior and, even several years after the dialogues, saw their promises as motivators. As Jamel put it, "My victim remains on my conscience heavily. To the point of if I fail, it feels like I've let my victim down."

One of the key reforms touted by the victims' rights movement has been the requirement to notify victims about the status of their case. This notification is particularly significant given that many victims confess to living in fear, terrified about what might happen when their offender is released on bail or after incarceration or following parole decisions. Participation in the VVH program wiped away this fear for most victims, who repeatedly told me that they had moved forward, living their lives without worrying that offenders will physically harm them again. The effect was slightly less pronounced for the victims whose offenders were family members, who remained concerned that their offenders might try to contact them in the future. This feeling might be common for any victims with known offenders, particularly family members, since the crime generally manifests itself as part of ongoing family or intimate-partner dynamics.

For instance, in the fall of 2008, Melissa discovered that her father's three sentences of ten, one, and one year were to be served concurrently, and he would be released in ten years and not the twelve she had anticipated, a fact that causes her some concern.[10] This issue of public safety is particularly salient for victims of interpersonal violence and is often cited as a reason to oppose restorative justice programs for victims of gendered violence. Yet Laurie defied expectations by overcoming her fear that her batterer will track her down: "He was recently released from prison, and the idea honestly doesn't frighten me. I thought I would be petrified, but I'm not. I have my life, and he has his."

Most victims express no hatred for the offenders—the offenders have essentially disappeared from the victims' radar screens until someone asks them about the incident. Several expressed pity for the offenders, and others expressed hope that offenders would proceed with a better life and make better choices. Scott and Julie both said they "feel sorry" for their offenders, and Donna said, "I do not even think about him until someone brings up his name. And when they do, all I feel is kind of a sadness for a wasted life."

For offenders' part, often years after their participation in the program ended, they continued to talk about how much they valued the opportunity to help their victims in the only way they could. A number of the offenders mentioned that they wished people could know that there are other offenders who also regret their crimes and who wish they could apologize to their victims. In my communications with the offenders, their comments revolved around gratitude that the program exists and their appreciation that the program was concerned about offenders too, even with its primary focus on victims' healing. Jamel described what apologizing did for him: "It lifted a heavy weight off my heart." Wayne said, "It was a relief to tell the truth about what happened that night and to the person that needed to hear it the most. I am glad I was able to help my victim's daughter get on with life." And Kevin said that, despite the difficulty he had in facing his victim, he was glad for what his experience did: "It gave me a chance to show her I wasn't the animal she thought I was and that the remorse I expressed was true from my heart and not just words and that I was truly sorry."

Some offenders continued to struggle with their feelings about their crimes, believing they did not deserve to be forgiven (not that forgiveness was required in the VVH program); for instance, one of the offenders who committed incest wrote, "While I did not and will not ask for forgiveness, I was able to apologize and express my remorse." Forgiveness may be given by a victim to an offender for a variety of reasons, and whereas offering this "gift" could be healing for one victim, even the thought of forgiving an offender might be unthinkable to another. For offenders, however, being forgiven by a victim can serve as a catalyst for change or as a reinforcement of change. But offenders can also accept responsibility for their crimes and desire to reform without a victim's forgiveness.

None of the offenders who participated in the VVH program were candidates for diversionary restorative justice programs sometimes offered in lieu of formal criminal justice proceedings. Indeed, most people would align themselves with the victims in these cases, believing punishment for offenders of severe violence should communicate both the abstract societal message that what they did was wrong and also the message from the individual victim that their choices damaged others' lives. At the same time, however, to be meaningful, incarceration (or punishment) cannot just warehouse offenders—it is clear from the offenders portrayed in this book that developing programs to assist offenders in understanding the injuries they caused and to support offenders in taking responsibility for their past, current, and future actions is paramount. Although the offenders who participated in the VVH program believed that prison served as a wake-up call to change their behavior and seek rehabilitative programs, surely it is incumbent on policymakers to create opportunities to help repeat offenders desist from crime *before* they must be locked up to serve lengthy sentences.

The long-term effects of participation were noteworthy. Scott, who had religious reasons for pursuing forgiveness, believed that VVH was instrumental in moving him beyond the crime. Laurie explained what the program gave her: "a strong sense of achievement, of facing my fear, my worst nightmare, and coming through the experience stronger. It proved to me that I am capable of doing things that might seem difficult or intimidating because I have the strength and courage to face whatever comes my way." Leigh said the program provided "an ability to go on, to continue to enjoy life and not dwell on the horror, but look for the joy." Donna found self-confidence she had been missing: "I am more confident in general. I tend to be more outspoken than I ever was. I can now laugh about myself and life." For the first time since Donna's rape happened in October 1997, she gave out Halloween candy to trick-or-treaters in 2007 and felt joy in resuming this tradition. Julie summed up her long-term benefit this way: "Getting a chance to love life again."

The offenders also mentioned that they feel more at peace today. Steven said, "I am glad that I don't have to live with the regret of not being able to do something for my victim." Kevin maintained that his involvement with the VVH program made him "a better person": "It made me understand how my decisions in life affect other people."

The fact that the offenders so eagerly participated in the program—and that the victims were genuinely committed to playing a part in this research—suggests the transformative effects of this restorative justice program. In other words, the offenders' enthusiasm, alongside their victims' support for their efforts, could offer outsiders hope that violent offenders' perceptions and actions can change with meaningful interventions, programs, and, of course, the passage of time.

The Ripple Effect

Whenever a crime occurs the primary victim is not the only person affected; the repercussions of crime spread through the lives of partners, spouses, family members, and friends of the victim—and of the offender—who are engulfed in the experience. Not only might they experience similar reactions, such as fear, confusion, rage, or frustration, but in cases of severe violence, the people in the victim's and offender's familial and social circles confront the vicissitudes of violence that often bring them too into uncharted and unwelcome territory. The paths of many of the victims and offenders introduced in this book led to using their tragedy to help others. As I listened to them talk about the effects of their participation in the Victims' Voices Heard program, I noticed an abundance of ways that the horror of victims' experiences—or the violence of the offenders' acts—facilitated growth, such as an ability to touch other people's lives in a positive way. Listening to their voices also revealed that the ripples extended beyond their immediate circle of family and friends, moving many of them to make a difference in the lives of strangers as well.

Prior to the crimes the victims experienced, none of them sought the public eye. In the immediate aftermath of their victimization, the last thing the victims wanted was to expose themselves to public scrutiny. They were simply surviving, feeling unsettled because of the trauma they experienced yet nonetheless persevering with their family and intimate relationships, work, and education—in other words, functioning as best they could. How far they have come from that point astonishes them. If one were to have suggested to them that their victimization experiences would have propelled them to speak out in public forums or to be activists in the quest for victims' rights, they would have dismissed such notions as fantasy. Participation in VVH, and the opportunity it provided to reclaim their voices, turned their grief into courage and transformed them into people they would not have recognized. This change occurred not only in some victims' involvement in public speaking or talking with inmates in prison about victim impact but also in the emergence of a new set of personality traits, the roots of which these victims trace to their participation in VVH: bravery, assertiveness, extroversion, and leadership.

Integrating the knowledge that the crime was not their fault and that any stigma, shame, or embarrassment from the crime was not their burden to carry was profoundly life changing. What was once a secret told to only a select few became a catalyst for most of the victims. They believed that more good than harm could come out of sharing their stories and reaching out to other victims walking the same dark path they had and that doing so could help to educate victims' loved ones and the larger community about how they could play a more positive role in victims' recovery. The fact that most of the victims wished that their full names, rather than pseudonyms, could be used in this book shows how far they have traveled.

Although the victims affirmed the importance of the VVH program in giving them the space and support they needed to go over every tiny and large detail of their victimizations, ultimately they believed that at the end of the program they no longer needed to broach their victimization or to talk endlessly about it to anyone in their circle of family and friends who would listen. Instead, the victims talked about incorporating their experience within the larger fabric of their lives, giving it less prominence and letting it empower them but not define them. They have become captains of their own ships, authors of their own stories, and their violent violation has become one of many, many chapters in their life. Kim describes it eloquently, when she is asked if she still thinks about her daughter:

> I have gone through different stages in dealing with Nicole's murder. I like
> to explain it as if it were a box on a book case with many shelves. For the

first few years, the box was on the shelf right at eye level. As the years went on the box moved higher up, and I had to stand on my tippy toes to reach it and take it off the shelf. Today the box is so far up on the bookcase that I have to get a step ladder to reach it.

Today, Melissa feels as though her parenting skills are stronger and she is better informed about the potential dangers of child sexual abuse. She shared the draft of her chapter in this book with her mother-in-law, who in turn revealed her own victimization experience, a revelation that brought them even closer. Melissa's voice radiated joy when I spoke with her in September 2008. With both her children now in school, she has found a job she loves at an animal shelter (and has even adopted a few stray dogs). Not surprisingly, Melissa continues to struggle with feelings about her father—hating what he did but sad because he is the only father she has. Her husband has noticed changes in her and has commented on how much more at peace she is. An example of a ripple effect in Melissa's life occurred when she was able to help some relatives who were going through a similar crisis: a daughter was abused, and her mother did not understand why her daughter did not initially tell her and, once she did, why she had waited so long. Melissa was able to answer the mother's questions and explain why a daughter might delay confiding and how difficult it was to tell even one's mother. Melissa felt she really helped the mother understand her daughter better since she could provide a victim's perspective on the situation. It felt right to her—being able to counsel another person about child sexual abuse—and she has a dream to someday have a job where she uses her own experiences and insight to help children understand that the abuse is not their fault and interrupt their feelings of guilt and self-doubt.[11]

Donna attached a column she wrote about her rape and subsequent experiences for the VVH newsletter to a listserv to which she subscribes and has heard from her friends about their own victimization experiences; they tell her how much her frankness and lack of shame have inspired them to grapple more successfully with their own inner demons. Donna also met with her offender's grandmother, has talked to prison groups, and has twice spoken to my students. Perhaps most surprising, given her past shyness, Donna spoke publicly in April 2007, using her full name, at a statewide event to raise awareness about rape and sexual violence, called "Walk in My Shoes." She continues to participate in public forums using her full name.

Scott and his wife volunteer to help other parents in their church who are going through similar family tragedies, and Justine (Scott's daughter) hopes to become a counselor for teens who have experienced child sexual abuse. Scott has moved on and seems to have developed more pity and compassion for Bruce. Justine has no interest at this time in having her own dialogue with her grandfather, but the door to VVH is open if she changes her mind.

Laurie writes eloquently about the long-term effects on her children. Not only are they growing up in a house no longer dominated by marital strife, but they have also seen their mother emerge from the violence as a stronger, more empowered person. She credits these changes to the VVH process and the dialogue and reflects, "All of my kids see me today, handling my job and other aspects of my life in ways I never could have prior to VVH. VVH is one of the best things that ever happened to me. It helped me to get my life back and helped me grow in confidence and courage as well as self-respect." She is eager to talk to other women who find themselves trapped in abusive relationships and need inspiration to get out, believing her own experience gives her a better understanding of their situation. Today, Laurie is the manager of a store for a national coffee-shop chain.

Leigh finished her doctorate in education, is happy with her life and work, and spends time with her children and friends. She maintains close ties with Cam's friends. She speaks at various university classes and public forums about the effects of DUI on families. She says, "I really think that the program made it better for me to go on. My attitude is so much better. I have gotten past thinking about Jenny, I don't reflect on that night so much. Though I still have some really rough days, overall I am very happy with my life." As discussed in chapter 9, several months after Leigh completed her follow-up, Jenny died in an automobile accident. Leigh believes this is another tragedy in an already awful story in which the lives of two young people were cut short.

Kathleen continues her quest to enhance rights for victims, drawing on her own frustration with her inability to obtain a copy of the court transcript from the trial of her mother's murderer. She is a prolific letter writer, peppering state and local politicians with her pleas for victims' rights. Instead of keeping silent about the effects of her mother's murder as she had in the past, Kathleen is now able to talk more about how this horrific event shaped her life, especially to her daughters—she brought one of them to a statewide Victims' Rights Tribute and told her about her mother in great detail on the way home—and to inmates when she has accompanied Kim to speak with them about the effects of crime on victims.[12] Kathleen also feels much closer to her brother and better able to understand—and help him understand—how their mother's murder affected their lives. Kathleen says, "I believe that the VVH program gave me the opportunity to share my story in a positive way to my daughters. I believe it brought my brother and I closer together."

Julie found that reading the rough draft of her chapter to one of her brother's close friends, a woman who has never really grieved about losing him, gave her friend a sense of peace. Her marriage and her family are thriving. After a stretch of time volunteering to help police at drunk-driving checkpoints, Julie has stopped participating in these events because she feels her anger has dissipated and she no longer has to channel her energies in this way. Although she will always miss her mother and brother, she is able to live in the present, which means focusing on her family and other aspects of her life.

Kim continues as the lead coordinator and facilitator of VVH. Influenced by a similar program in Minnesota, Kim has recognized the need to create an Apology Letter Bank in Delaware. Over the years, Kim has received many letters written by offenders offering apologies to their victims. She has kept these letters on file in case their victims should ever contact her.[13] Kim formalized this process in 2007, and the bank receives letters of apology on a weekly basis. Victims can find out by word of mouth or on the VVH website about the Apology Letter Bank. They are then able to contact VVH and ask whether their offender has deposited a letter, and they can choose whether to receive it. Offenders will never know if the victim receives the letter they have placed in the bank unless the victim chooses for them to know. If no letter has yet been deposited, the victim's information remains on file so that they can be contacted should a letter become available. Kim continues to gain publicity for the VVH program and participates frequently in statewide victim tributes and memorials in addition to her ongoing volunteer work in fellowship groups in men's prisons.

For the offenders who participated in the VVH program, some of whom had never before talked about their responsibility for the crime outside of mandatory prison groups or to family members, their clarity in understanding how their actions severely hurt their victims started them on paths to educate others—to describe their work with VVH to other inmates, in anger-management groups, and in conversations and letters to their own family members (as well as to the family members of their victims). Offenders told me about speaking to individual inmates who they believe are struggling with guilt, shame, or remorse about their crimes. Chris found that some of the other lifers he knew were interested in hearing about the VVH program. Paul wrote that VVH helped him to know himself better: "I know that I love me more now than I did in my [w]hole life." Kevin knows that his friends and family members think the program is great and recommend it to others: "They have seen the change in me and the things I have told them through the process I have gone through. Also other inmates wanted to know how to get into the program after they found out I was doing it." Most of the offenders mentioned that, upon release, they hope to be involved in programs in which they could mentor young men or teenagers so that they would not follow a path of crime. They feel that their personal experience with prison, in addition to a deeper understanding of how their choices negatively affected both their own family members and also their victims, gives them the "authenticity" needed to demonstrate that crime is not a good choice.

Final Thoughts

The catharsis and empowerment ultimately felt by the victims whose stories appear in this book are truly remarkable, yet we cannot forget how dear a cost they paid to achieve this peace. The VVH program extended a lifeline to victims who for so many years struggled, searched for answers, internalized blame, and shaped their days out of caution and fear. Timing is a crucially important factor in several ways: by the time the victims connect with VVH, often many years have elapsed since the original criminal incident occurred. Victims are well aware of what is and is not working for them, and their embrace of the program illustrates not only their readiness to do hard emotional work but also their potential for restorative success.

Victims must be aware that the program exists, however. Nonprofits such as VVH are sparsely staffed and funded and do not have the luxury of vast dissemination of information about their services. However, if providing information or a pamphlet or website address at the time the case is assigned to a prosecutor became routine practices, victims could have the necessary information in case they wanted to participate at a later point. A potential benefit of having a program such as this under the auspices of the justice system (at the prosecutorial or correctional level) could be that the dissemination of information becomes more common and that more victims hear about VVH as an option. However, access to information depends on buy-in from the agencies asked to support and promote such programs. The victims interviewed for this book often learned about VVH in a random or serendipitous way; getting the word out earlier in the recovery process could accommodate each victim's personal time frame for seeking help. As the stories told here reveal, victims move at their own pace in the preparation process, and there is often a great deal of time that elapses from the time of program entry to the face-to-face dialogue. Both victims and offenders mentioned the preparation process (without prompting from me) as an arduous necessity.

Although many victims (and offenders) would not be emotionally prepared for a face-to-face confrontation closer to the criminal incident, some of the needs victims articulate that facilitate their healing *can* be met earlier in the process: answers, input, and an open-door policy that would create a way to get questions answered in the future—questions to which victims might not even realize they need answers. Establishing a method for getting information from offenders at earlier stages would still entail coordination and oversight between a program such as VVH and the criminal justice system. Victims who desire to meet with their offenders should have this opportunity through programs similar to VVH, with all the protections and procedural safeguards necessary to provide support.

In so many ways, VVH achieves more of what victims had in mind when they (and their advocates) so resoundingly criticized the criminal justice system for failing to provide the things they valued most. The formal justice system and the diversionary restorative justice programs that occur early in the criminal justice process continue to fail many victims, and most are offender oriented.[14] VVH is truly victim centered, as are most postconviction therapeutic restorative justice programs.

Precisely because of VVH's format as a postconviction therapeutic program, the potential for restorative efficacy for victims of gendered violence is vast. Since the process begins after guilt is established and punishment imposed, victims have the upper hand in their dealings with the offenders, just because of the simple fact that the offenders are locked up or under the control of the correctional system. Although the psychological manipulation that is part and parcel of intimate-partner and familial crimes, committed overwhelmingly by men against women and girls, could still rear its ugly head, the VVH program includes so many checks and balances that the victims who knew their offenders felt safe and strong in "dealing with the devil they know" (as one victim phrased it). Moreover, the victims—perhaps for the first time since the abuse and violence began—felt empowered by the process. They were no longer terrorized into compliance and silence; rather, they found their voices and expressed the anger, bewilderment, hurt, and betrayal that characterized their daily lives with their abusers. No longer were they without control. They were able to face their offenders head-on, challenge what they did to them, explain the effects of their abuse, and turn the tables on the debilitating loss of power and self they experienced as victims.

For victims/survivors of violent rapes perpetrated by strangers, the process was no less empowering. Not only were they able to discover details about the crime either that they had blocked or of which they had been unaware—such as their efforts to fight off the attacks—but they also shook off the self-blame (and the internalized victim blaming from others) that had pervaded their daily existence. Victims could instead draw on their courage in knowing that they now controlled their own fates and were in no way to blame for their victimization. This piece of their recovery was crucial and had escaped them until they participated in VVH. Moreover, all the victims of crimes of gendered violence cast off the shame they felt about the crimes, redefining themselves as proud survivors. If they had not had access to their offenders' accounts of the incidents and confronted them from a place of strength, the victims contend they would still be stuck in their fears and doubts. Postconviction dialogues between victims and offenders offer the potential for profound self-realizations that can propel victims of gendered violence forward in their recovery. Erasing fears, self-doubt, and debilitating self-blame is vital for victims' recovery, and programs such as VVH offer a beacon of hope in achieving these goals.

The benefits of VVH for the offenders, an important side effect, must be acknowledged. The opportunity to offer their accounts of the crime to the victims reinforced offenders' acceptance of personal responsibility. Hearing what their victims had to say to them exerted a long-lasting effect on their remorse and their determination to become better people. Things will undoubtedly become more difficult as many of them are released from prison. For all ex-inmates, and particularly for sex offenders, reentry into society is difficult. Recidivism rates are high, even for the most determined individuals. To shore up offenders' own efforts to become contributing, law-abiding members of society, correctional and social-service programs must provide a continuum of care for newly released inmates. Good intentions and a list of rehabilitative programs completed in prison do not necessarily translate into finding housing, employment, and support for a crimefree life. Although VVH, along with other prison programs, may address offenders' anger and facilitate their empathy for victims, ex-inmates' commitment to rehabilitation will be tested frequently on the outside. Alcohol and anger played such big roles in many of the offenders' lives at the time of their crimes that the pulls toward these familiar feelings and coping styles need to be addressed in meaningful programs for all released inmates. It will be interesting to follow the offenders who participated in the VVH program to see if they fare any better than similarly situated offenders who were not involved in the program.

Thus far, VVH has served a largely white population. Although there was some racial variation among victims and offenders, the cases explored in this book generally reflect the experiences of white victims and white offenders (there were two African American offenders). This is curious, given what we know about the very high victimization and incarceration rates of people of color in our country. How can a program such as VVH reach out to communities of color? It is imperative to be culturally sensitive to the needs of different communities. If the victims in this book had negative experiences with the formal criminal justice system, imagine the layers of distrust and disappointment that are added for members of minority communities, who may also experience racism at the hands of the justice system. Although there is a small but growing body of research literature that explores informal justice programs specifically tailored to meet the needs of people of color,[15] more attention is needed to attract and to garner the trust of diverse communities.[16] Kim is spreading the word through faith communities by speaking at diverse congregations about VVH, forgiveness, victims' recovery, and offenders' rehabilitation. In the past year, she has also responded to more inquiries from people of color about her program, by attending community events (such as the Homicide Survivors Tribute in Wilmington, Delaware, a city that is majority African American). Word of mouth has begun to spread after a successful 2008 dialogue between an African American victim and offender. Kim recently trained an African American woman as a volunteer cofacilitator in the hope of furthering her outreach efforts.

This issue leads to a bigger discussion about the role of community. Advocates of restorative justice consistently claim that programs benefit victims, offenders, and the community. There is not always agreement about how *community* should be defined, however, and how exactly a community benefits. The ripple effect created by the VVH program extends far beyond the original primary victim and offender to their familial and social support networks. People who hear Kim or any survivor speak about the program often find their previous ambivalence or even punitiveness toward offenders challenged. Victims' Voices Heard and other restorative justice programs remind us of the possibility of rehabilitative success for offenders and empowerment for victims, both of which promise a better future in the social justice realm as well as for all individuals affected by crime and victimization.

Whereas some victims' journeys include forgiving their offenders, others see no reason to contemplate such an act. Forgiveness is a complicated issue in that it can be viewed as a gift given by a victim to an offender, a release of a burden by a victim so that the anger and other negative emotions no longer have to be carried, or in a multitude of other ways. Social psychologist Sharon Lamb's work on blame, responsibility, and forgiveness cautions victims not to prematurely forgive: "to forgive too easily shows a lack of self-respect. . . . If we do not resent the violations of our rights, then we do not take our rights very seriously."[17] It is vitally important to guard against the use of forgiveness as a criterion for assessing the "recovery success" of a victim or to characterize a victim as "good" or "bad" based on her or his willingness to forgive. For victims already burdened with the aftermath of crime, classifying their reactions as either good or bad adds an unfair judgment to their recovery process. Forgiveness should not be seen as the standard of a higher moral evolution; rather, if it is given, it must be given freely, unconditionally, and for reasons that make sense to the person offering the forgiveness. It should not be given to satisfy any external agenda or to fulfill any social expectation of altruism. For victims who have already survived the initial attack and its aftermath, it is cruel and unfair to place expectations on them that they do not otherwise seek independently.[18]

Victims and survivors must be given the opportunity to tell their stories, to make sense of the chaos caused by crime, and to fully express their needs and emotions. Despite the best intentions of the victims' rights movement, the formal criminal justice system fails to respond adequately to the needs of many victims. Victims who have survived particularly violent or severe crimes or surviving family members of loved ones lost to violence might find better support for their healing if their needs were fulfilled earlier in the process. Some of these needs cannot be met in the immediate aftermath of the crime; many offenders will not hear descriptions of victims' harm in a meaningful or rehabilitative way until some time has passed. But a simple recognition of the path victims take—full of starts and stops—can go a long way in reorganizing and creating more meaningful responses to victimization. When the formal justice process does not accommodate victims' needs, or when victims or survivors are out of step with the expected timetable of recovery, VVH—and the programs like it that now exist in twenty-five states—can play a crucial role.

I end this book with the voices of the victims and survivors, the people who have reclaimed their lives as a result of their participation in the restorative justice program Victims' Voices Heard. The program was life changing and personally affirming, despite the fact that the initial catalyst, the crime, was horrifying and violent. VVH gave these victims the feeling of finally being at peace, something that had once seemed impossible. Two victims sum it up best:

Even as time goes on, I become more thankful for this program. Who would I be? Where would I be? My life had come to an end before VVH—it saved my life and my marriage. (Julie)

I am at peace with the way my life has gone. We can't go back and change anything, so we can only look at it in a more positive way. What happened in my life can't be what defines me, but what I do with what has happened to me does. (Donna)

Appendix A

Restorative Justice: Theoretical
and Empirical Studies

This appendix provides a fuller overview and discussion of the theoretical issues that pertain to restorative justice, as well as a brief summary of research findings.

The formal, retributive justice system represents the state against the offender such that the victim serves as a component of the evidence but not as an equal partner. The victim is not a key stakeholder in the adversarial justice system. In contrast, RJ programs share common assumptions: victims and offenders should be personally and integrally involved in the process; crimes happen within particular social contexts which necessitate different kinds of responses, depending on the crime and parties involved; and problem-solving should be the goal, not just punishment.[1] Many people believe RJ offers great potential for addressing victims' needs and facilitating offenders' responsibility because of its more relational approach to resolving conflict and responding to crime.[2]

RJ programs encompass a wide range of forms, with the four most common being victim-offender mediation (VOM) or dialogue (VOD), community reparative boards, family group conferencing, and circle sentencing.[3] All share the goal of involving victims, offenders, and the community in a process in which the impact of crimes is communicated differently to offenders so that they can better understand the harm their actions caused, giving victims the chance to participate more fully in the process and to receive answers to their questions and shaping appropriate responses to crimes.

Programs that fall under the umbrella of restorative justice have a long history and can be found around the globe. In North America, the first victim-offender mediation program began in 1974 in the Mennonite community in Kitchener, Ontario, Canada, with the first U.S.-based program established in 1978 in Elkhart County, Indiana.[4] Conservative estimates suggest that VOM programs number at least seven hundred in Europe, three hundred in the United States, and twenty-six in Canada.

The first large-scale American RJ effort, launched in the 1980s, involved victim-offender mediation programs, sometimes known as alternative dispute mediation or resolution programs (typically referred to today as dialogues). These mediation programs are diversionary—they circumvent the formal justice process. They are outcome driven, with criminal cases diverted to mediation proceedings in lieu of processing in the formal criminal justice system. They often result in offenders apologizing to and achieving reconciliation with victims in addition to other possible outcomes such as restitution or community service. Geared to handle minor offenses (such as school-related offenses and general property crimes) that mostly involve juvenile offenders, VOM and VOD rarely address more serious felony cases.[5] Though these programs were initially conceived as a way to better handle *offenders,* more recent restorative justice efforts aim to give *victims* a greater voice in the criminal justice process while preventing further miscarriages of justice against them, offenders, and the community.

Most diversionary RJ programs rely on practices such as victim-offender mediation or conferences and sentencing circles that bring together stakeholders such as family and community members.[6] In the United States, most RJ programs are run by private nonprofit organizations (about 40 percent) or religious organizations (about 25 percent) outside the purview of the criminal justice system.[7] Offenders often have to meet stringent criteria to participate: in about 20 percent of the programs reviewed in a 1999 survey, offenders *had* to participate if so desired by their victims; in 65 percent of the programs offenders had to admit guilt before they could participate;[8] and about 33 percent of offenders participated as a condition of diversion before a determination of guilt or innocence.[9]

Empirical evaluations of diversionary RJ dialogue-based programs reveal some evidence of success. For instance, one early study, conducted by Mark Umbreit in 1984, found that juveniles who participated in mediation, rather than going through the formal justice system, committed fewer and less serious offenses than a control group of their peers during a one-year follow-up period.[10] Umbreit published another study in the same year that examined four juvenile mediation programs; findings revealed high levels of satisfaction: almost 80 percent of victims and almost 90 percent of offenders felt the process was fair, and victims' fear for their safety markedly decreased after mediation. About 80 percent of juveniles fulfilled restitution obligations, compared to 58 percent of their peers ordered to pay restitution by juvenile court judges.[11] A few years later, a number of other studies reported high satisfaction rates for both victims and offenders who completed RJ programs.[12] Reductions in recidivism rates for juvenile offenders have also been documented.[13] Some studies have also shown positive results in programs for adults. In 2006, Umbreit and colleagues reviewed eighty-five studies conducted using four general types of RJ dialogue practices for both juvenile and adult cases—(victim-offender mediation/dialogue, group/family conferencing, circles (sentencing, peacemaking), and hybrids (reparative boards and other community-based RJ programs)—across a range of dimensions: participation rates and reasons, participant satisfaction, perceptions of fairness, restitution and repayment of harm, diversion issues such as net widening, recidivism, and costs.[14] Their comprehensive review reveals positive outcomes of RJ practices across the board for all four types of RJ dialogue programs.

RJ programs often take into account the role of community in formulating justice since crime affects communities. Community members may be involved in supporting victims and/or offenders and may become stakeholders in the sense that they pay attention to the needs of other community members and try to foster the conditions that promote healthy communities.[15] Critics have argued that notions of community may be far too homogenous, however, contending that RJ ignores structural dimensions of crime, such as gender, race/ethnicity, and class-based conflict, instead prioritizing (seemingly generic) interpersonal concerns.[16] For instance, Daly and Stubbs raise questions about the lack of attention to diversity in RJ's treatment of violence against women, since prevailing justice models (which form the backbone of typical RJ approaches) do not take into account, for example, the cultural uniqueness and variety that indigenous women may employ in interpreting violence, their lack of interest in further engagement with the criminal justice system and formally recognized justice alternatives, and their ideas about punishment. At the same time, however, women of color and indigenous women are often more amenable to trying alternatives to an established criminal justice system that has been monumentally racist.[17]

Evidence of the success of RJ in such communities is mixed, however. Goel's research on RJ processes and abused South Asian women concludes with an admonishment that RJ options are ill suited for immigrant communities because of immigrant women's reluctance to advocate for themselves or their values of community and self-sacrifice—whereas autonomy and independence are key conditions and abilities assumed by RJ practices.[18] In a similar vein, Cook, who studied RJ programs in Australia and Maine, suggests that gender, race, and social-class positions in RJ juvenile conferencing reinforce social privileges and disadvantage.[19] Social hierarchies are not always reduced by face-to-face conferencing (as some advocates had hoped) because of implicit assumptions guiding offenders' obligations that raise "invisible privileges around gender, race and class [that] are reproduced, embraced and recommended as strategies for future goals,"[20] such as military participation, following middle-class rules of proper citizenship rules, and "being white." For example, Cook found that in the Australian programs, facilitators and victims' fathers performed an accomplished middle-class masculinity in contrast to working-class Aboriginal adolescent males' (inferior) masculinity.

In contrast, Coker's research on Navajo peacemaking in domestic-violence cases offers a unique view into the shape of RJ practices designed and administered by indigenous communities themselves. Peacemaking is a process administered by the independent Navajo judiciary, and opportunities to participate are determined by Navajo tribal courts (or by self-petition) (other RJ practices that include indigenous populations are typically administered by nonindigenous authorities). A valued Navajo cultural feature is gender harmony, which provides the process "with a particularly powerful cultural resource," especially in regard to domestic violence.[21]

Contrasting Diversionary and Therapeutic Programs

In stark contrast to the *diversionary* programs discussed so far, other RJ programs focus on a *therapeutic* process that is not outcome driven and does not mandate victim-offender reconciliation or restitution (although those may occur). Instead these programs facilitate a dialogue between victims and offenders as a therapeutic tool after conviction and sentencing. Therapeutic programs do not function in lieu of formal case processing and punishment. These types of programs are increasing in popularity, and given recent reports of victims' satisfaction with RJ programs in general and lower offender recidivism rates, there is tempered enthusiasm for applying RJ principles to more complicated cases, such as those of victims who have experienced severe forms of violence. This type of program is more common abroad than in the United States; for instance, both Australia and New Zealand have experimented with RJ programs for juvenile sexual offenders or family violence in the past several years.[22] Interest in expanding programs to include violent interpersonal crimes is growing in the United States: in Pima County, Arizona, an RJ program designed to respond to victims and first-time offenders of acquaintance rape, indecent exposure, and peeping has been in operation for several years.[23] As of early 2008, twenty-four states in the United States had developed postconviction RJ programs for victims of severe violence, and about half of them include domestic-violence cases as eligible for participation.

There have been very few evaluations of mediation/dialogue programs for victims of violent crime. Only a handful of programs in the United States include violent crimes, such as homicides, and even fewer permit cases of gender violence, such as incest, child sexual abuse, rape, and domestic violence.[24] Mark Umbreit and his colleagues have conducted the sole study of victim-offender dialogue programs in violent crime cases, and thus their work warrants a closer examination.[25] In both the Texas and Ohio severe-violence dialogue programs they studied, offenders were incarcerated, and nothing was promised or received by the offenders for their participation in the program. This RJ model exemplifies a postconviction therapeutic model rather than a diversionary one. Approximately half to two-thirds of both state samples involved homicide cases. The motivations of surviving family members who met with the offenders were to gain information, to demonstrate the impact of the crime, simply to see the offender face to face, and to facilitate greater healing. These same motivations were echoed by the victims of other severe crimes such as rape or incest. For offenders, goals included being able to help the victim heal, to answer the victim's questions, and to help with their own rehabilitation and healing. The offenders sought to provide information about how they had reformed since committing their crimes, to change the victims' views of them, or to allay their fears. Based on Umbreit et al.'s sample of forty victims and thirty-nine offenders, the authors found that most (91 percent) of the participants had high levels of satisfaction with the face-to-face dialogue, with 89 percent finding the dialogue very helpful. Despite a lack of recidivism measures or long-term follow-up, the study's findings revealed that face-to-face structured encounters between offenders and victims who experienced a severe form of violence or victims' family members who lost a loved one due to homicide achieved important and positive life changes for offenders and for victims or their family members. This finding suggests that postconviction therapeutic RJ programs can empower victims and contribute to their personal growth and healing while simultaneously exerting a positive effect on offenders' outlook about their own rehabilitative efforts and personal growth.

Crimes of Sexual Violence

The expansion of restorative justice programs into crimes of gendered violence has been accompanied by great controversy. Most of these concerns and criticisms focus on *diversionary* RJ practices that occur in the beginning of the justice process and operate in lieu of involvement in the formal criminal justice system. In contrast, *therapeutic* RJ practices (such as VVH) generally avoid such concerns. For the most part, crimes involving gendered violence, such as male battering of women and other forms of family violence, child abuse, and sexual assault, have been off-limits to restorative justice practices that focus on diversion.

One notable exception involved a series of studies by Mary Koss and her colleagues,[26] who ague that using RJ models as an alternative to the formal criminal justice process could not only "increase the number of cases in which offenders are held accountable but also holds the promise of promoting rather than interfering with victim recovery, promoting community involvement in crime control, and providing for safe offender reintegration into the community"; thus, RJ could "increase the likelihood of preventing future sex offending by individual perpetrators and of enhancing prevention of sex offending generally due to increased community awareness and education."[27] The hope is that further trauma to victims could be avoided by using a RJ process.[28]

Hopkins and Koss put their beliefs into practice through the creation of a program in Arizona funded by the Centers for Disease Control (CDC). The program, called RESTORE (Responsibility and Equity for Sexual Transgressions Offering a Restorative Experience), is victim driven, and cases arrive postarrest but preconviction; it uses a community-conference approach for cases of acquaintance rape in which the use of force was minimal, as well as for cases of nonpenetration sex offenses, such as peeping and indecent exposure.[29] There are a number of program requirements, such as a psychosexual evaluation of the offender, which becomes the basis for a treatment plan that includes regular monitoring for one year. Following extensive preparation, the victim/survivor and people she has designated as her support network meet face to face with the offender and his support network (the pronoun use reflects the typical victim-offender combination for cases from RESTORE).

> The survivor is given a full opportunity to describe what the responsible person did and the resultant harm to her and to her relationships with others, after which the responsible person acknowledges the wrong committed and the harm done. The survivor's and the responsible person's support networks are then given an opportunity to describe the impact the wrong has had on their lives. The participants next develop a redress agreement that outlines what the responsible person is going to do to make right the wrong done, not just to the survivor but also to the community

support network and the broader community (with compliance overseen by review board). . . . Successful completion of the terms of the agreement results in a dismissal of charges, while the case is referred back to the prosecutor should the responsible person fail to abide by the terms of the agreement.[30]

Koss and her colleagues argue that although sexual violence occurs in many battering relationships, the nature of acquaintance sexual assault (they exclude marital rape) makes it less risky to use RJ than in cases in which the victim and offender are cohabitating. For instance, one of the chief feminist objections to using RJ in cases of battering is the possibility that the survivor is subjected to further violence, which could easily play out in the face-to-face meeting,[31] particularly since batterers are often savvy in manipulating the formal court process on their behalf. Unlike domestic battering, acquaintance sexual assault is typically not part of an established, ongoing relationship, but rather it "spells the end of whatever relationship existed between the parties, whether immediately or in the short term."[32] Thus, acquaintance sexual assault is a more isolated act that usually occurs only once between people who do not have a long relationship. Under these circumstances, a face-to-face meeting may be less compromising to the physical safety of the survivor. Similarly, there is less potential for emotional abuse from the offender to surface during an emotional contact with a battered woman; the sexual offender's conversation will more likely be framed by denial of coercive actions or by blaming the survivor of the attack. Hopkins and Koss recognize that no empirical research has been conducted to assess the postrape behavior of acquaintance rapists, so RJ programs that deal with sexual assault must be proactive in recognizing such possibilities and use clear and consistently enforced rules; indeed, the RESTORE program in Arizona screens out any case that seems to be characterized by ongoing emotional and physical violence.

Although the victim-centered approach of RESTORE and the success attributed to it in the degree of victims' satisfaction and empowerment are noteworthy, it cannot be compared to postconviction RJ programs such as the one explored in this book (VVH). RESTORE operates postarrest but preconviction, and the successful completion of the terms of agreement for redress results in a dismissal of charges. Postconviction RJ programs typically take place a number of years after the offense and offer offenders nothing in compensation, such as assistance with their sentence or future parole/pardon board hearings. Since offenders gain no reduction in sentence or lesser punishment, their reasons for participating may be vastly different from those given by offenders in diversionary RJ programs that offer offenders, at the very least, an alternative to more formal and punitive responses to their crimes.

Crime of Battering by Partners or Former Partners

The arguments against the use of diversionary victim-offender mediation for battered women are compelling and were enumerated in a remarkably influential 1991 position paper by scholar Heather Astor that excoriated the use of victim-offender mediation in these cases.[33] The hallmark of RJ is often understood as the face-to-face meeting and the reconciliation between victim and offender, complete with an apology—practices that Astor argues are wholly unsuitable to cases in which power imbalances are significant and ongoing, such as rape, child abuse, or battering.[34] The philosophical objections to using restorative justice to address crimes of gendered violence raised by Astor were followed by a legion of theoretical and ideological papers in agreement with this position.

For instance, it is common for RJ proponents to assert that RJ allows victims a voice with which they can assert their own interests, that the RJ process overcomes power differentials, and that victims move from a position of passivity to one of agency. However, these possibilities do not always resonate for battered women, whose actions are often terribly constrained by limited choices. Battered women who seek help are very likely mothers, and children—and threats to children's safety—are often the catalyst for leaving the violent relationship. The importance of children to their mothers is not lost on the batterers, who manipulate women by using threats of harming or taking the children through legal or illegal means.[35] Thus, "where women's interests do not coincide with those of their children they face difficult choices," and seeking legal help or criminal justice intervention is one of them.[36]

There are further reasons to question the efficacy of RJ in domestic-violence cases. The nature of battering is that it occurs in an established, ongoing relationship in which victims and offenders share many experiences, resources, and connections including a residence, children, vehicles, extended family networks, friends, and so forth. A violent act within a relationship in which abuse exists is not a one-time occurrence, nor is the sum total of the event only about the violence. Part and parcel of physically violent relationships are other forms of control and tactics of intimidation, including verbal and emotional abuse, fear, manipulation concerning children, sabotaging of employment, pet abuse, and financial abuse. Some of the most popular and widely used RJ models include apologies and reconciliation. But many battered women do not wish to be reconciled (although some do), which raises questions about "restoring" unequal relations and thus reaffirming inequality.[37] RJ efforts may not be as successful in these cases as they are with minor or juvenile crimes because the process may not adequately take into account the social context of men's violence against women.[38]

The general emphasis of restorative justice on apology may also be unworkable for battered women. This good intention fails to take into account the totality of a battered woman's layered experiences, with all their complexities and ambiguities. Most battered women have heard too many apologies that are empty, insincere, and routine, whereas male abusers have routinely denied and minimized their violence, typically blaming their victims. It is difficult to envision how an apology could change men's understandings and rationalizations of their use of violence. As a result of this dilemma, many scholars continue to wonder whether the focus on apology offers a false sense of hope for victims of domestic violence that could jeopardize their future safety by potentially drawing them back into an unsafe situation.[39]

Active participation in the RJ process as a way to achieve empowerment for victims may be also be unrealistic for battered women, who have learned to swallow their needs, desires, and demands. It is common for battered women to be silenced out of fear and retaliation or to accede to a batterer's wishes, a situation that could arise in face-to-face meetings. Unlike the formal courtroom, an informal meeting between a battered woman and her abuser may be wholly unappealing for the victim, yet she may participate out of a sense of guilt or obligation.[40] There also may be subtle gestures or phrases used by the offender that carry much meaning for the victim, but the implied threat or emotional abuse will be undetectable to others present at the meeting. Psychological and emotional coercion that has been used in past situations to exert or maintain control over a victim will likely continue long after the physical violence—or RJ practice—ends. A battered woman who has children with her abusive partner, and who may desire to stay in the relationship (although she wishes the violence would stop), might agree to RJ practices that are not in her best interest because she wants to be persuaded about his remorse and sincerity.

Though all these critiques are important—and they reflect the many complexities of battering relationships—it is important to note that they apply to diversionary programs. As the cases in this book suggest, many concerns are circumvented with postconviction therapeutic RJ programs, which typically occur years after the original offense: offenders are under the control of the correctional system, and victims control the restorative justice process. Feminist concerns about crimes of gendered violence, safety, and revictimization, however, should always be at the forefront of any victim-offender program, regardless of whether it is a diversionary or postconviction one.[41]

The few studies of programs that employ diversionary RJ practices in dealing with men's violence against their female partners are exploratory, with no measures of the effectiveness of the interventions. Even so, findings are contradictory, with research on aboriginal[42] and indigenous[43] battered women finding that these women perceive that offenders receive more support than victims and that RJ processes used in their cases suffered from a lack of accountability and a victim-blaming mentality. Research examining how abused women fare in child-custody mediation finds that both courts and mediators failed to identify many cases of domestic violence and that physical custody to fathers or joint custody was recommended in more cases in which violence had occurred than in traditional family courts.[44] Abused women reported less power and greater disagreement over financial and visitation issues in mediation than nonabused women in mediated cases.[45] After conducting an extensive review about the use of RJ for domestic violence and its ability to address the concerns raised in the literature thus far, Cheon and Regehr conclude that there is insufficient evidence to support its use in these cases.[46] Further, research conducted on batterers and their ability to take responsibility for their abuse in confrontational treatment approaches have not shown effectiveness or lasting behavioral changes, which suggests that RJ practices that promote offenders' acceptance of responsibility for their behavior may also fail.[47]

There is some evidence, however, that victims of child sexual abuse, sexual assault, and intimate-partner violence may benefit from victim-centered RJ programs that stress victims' participation and empowerment.[48] In New Zealand, Julich interviewed adult survivors of child sexual abuse by a family member, a close family friend, or a neighbor.[49] Of the eighteen women and three men interviewed, four women and three men had reported the abuse to the police. Julich was most interested in hearing survivors' suggestions regarding how the criminal justice system might better serve them. Although the survivors did not participate in an RJ program, what they indicated that they wanted contained elements of restorative justice. For instance, regardless of whether survivors had relied on the police or went through a trial, they all wanted the opportunity to tell their story. Most also wanted to hear offenders take responsibility for their actions and see them held accountable in front of others as a way to validate their own victimization and its impact. Another common theme was that survivors wanted to address the offenders' motivations, believing that addressing underlying causes of offending could offer some sense of justice in a more helpful way than relying solely on imprisonment. Particularly since the offenders were known to these victims and resided in the same community, the survivors wanted to renegotiate the relationship between themselves and the offenders so they could coexist. At the same time, however, the survivors recognized the limits of trusting communities for support and the potential that responsibility for ensuring safety or providing oversight would be transferred to female community advocates.

Final Thoughts

Despite all of these concerns, many scholars and practitioners remain optimistic about the role that RJ can play in challenging and changing social norms about gendered violence.[50] The hope is that victim-centered responses could reduce victims' trauma and honor their expressed preferences—all of which could ultimately increase reporting of sexual violence and other forms of violence committed against women. However, RJ's success may depend on its ability to address underlying systemic oppressions and norms that shore up violence against women. The potential is promising: RJ could offer more significant consequences for offenders, since the criminal justice system (in the unlikely event that cases are even prosecuted) fails to treat these crimes seriously. RJ could reduce emotional trauma to victims, respond to their preferences, and craft redress according to their wishes, which adds their voices and context to the justice process.[51] Also, the RJ model stresses victims' empowerment, in contrast to the formal criminal justice system, which often characterizes battered women as powerless and passive and male batterers as empowered and stable. Ultimately, RJ programs could increase reporting and increase understanding about the prevalence of these crimes and increase community awareness of them, which might decrease incidence rates and create more educated jurors.[52] The host of legitimate concerns about the use of restorative justice programs for crimes of gendered violence, as well as the outcomes of the cases explored in this book, suggest that RJ programs may be most efficacious and beneficial for victims if they are therapeutic programs rather than diversionary ones.

Appendix B

Methodology

The research presented in this book follows a three-year intensive project featuring multiple data-collection sites across people and sources. Participants were part of Victims' Voices Heard (VVH), a restorative justice program intended to provide victims of severe violence with the opportunity to prepare for and to have a face-to-face conversation with offenders about their crime and its effects. Since the program began in 2002 through the end date of data collection in 2007, ten victim-offender dialogues occurred (although the VVH program is ongoing). This project explores the experiences and perceptions of the victims and offenders in nine cases—all but one of the total cases completed during the time frame. Qualitative research often focuses on small samples that are selected purposefully in order to understand a phenomenon in greater depth.[1] Employing a purposive sample from one specific program allows for very "thick" or "information rich" case studies about the subject of interest, without attempting to generalize empirically from the sample to a population.[2]

I treat some of the standard methodological issues in the beginning chapters of the book. For instance, chapter 2 covers my interest in restorative justice and my connection to the VVH program. Background information regarding victims' characteristics, with a particular focus on the VVH program's founder, Kim Book, and the story of her daughter's murder—the catalyst for the creation of VVH—are covered in chapter 3.

Despite my lengthy experience with interviewing people who have experienced abuse and violence in their lives, this project presented a number of challenges. My guiding compass was to listen to participants, to do no further harm, and to facilitate reciprocity between myself and the participants in the interests of empowering them to engage actively in the research process. The victims and survivors endured either very severe forms of violent victimization or loss of their loved one to murder or drunk-driving fatalities. Kim Book, the VVH coordinator, was often the first person to whom they had confided their deeply private thoughts and experiences, and often their trust in her required months of meetings to develop. As a researcher, my development of rapport with the victims and survivors was complicated by my plan to interview the offenders, whose stories might challenge their versions of the crimes. Or so I thought. Surprisingly, refreshingly, the victims were almost without exception eager to speak to me and encouraged me not only to contact and interview their offenders but also to watch the videotapes of the face-to-face dialogues of their meetings with offenders.

The victims shared a compelling need to be heard—to find their voices and to be able to speak about what had happened to them and its consequences and also to reclaim a sense of control over their own choices and destinies. They sought, with great urgency, to break the silence surrounding the crimes and their victimizations and to emerge on the other side as resilient and strong, as survivors. Their determination was apparent in the hard work they did with the VVH program (meeting biweekly with Kim for six months at a minimum, completing extensive paperwork) and in their ability to confront the offenders who had caused them so much pain. In fact, their courage is a lesson in how being persistent is an act of bravery. In following this spirit, my intention during the interviews was to validate their courage and recognize the importance for victims of finally finding their voice about things that happened to them over which they had no control.

I made a number of strategic choices as I conducted the research, some of which are atypical for social science research endeavors. First, I deliberately kept participants in control of the process. I left it up to them to decide to how much information—in the form of case files, videotapes, and other records—I had access to. Second, I honored their voice in their stories. It is standard in qualitative research to gain permission (after IRB[3] approval) from individual participants to tape-record their stories, with the assurance of protecting confidentiality by not revealing real names or using any identifying information.[4] A small number of qualitative researchers take this one step further, allowing participants to review interviews in writing after they are transcribed verbatim.[5] I did so, but I went beyond this with an additional step, inviting respondents (victims only, not offenders) to read the chapter drafts I wrote. My paramount concern was to ensure that the victims did not feel as though they lost control over their stories.

My decision to share chapter drafts with victims was unanimously welcomed and enormously productive, with one exception (as noted in chapter 5). This interaction reflects my commitment to research that honors the collaborative process between researcher and respondent,[6] one that allows participants to tell their own stories. Having the opportunity to see their words in print, with the ability to elaborate on what they said (or clarify or even ask for a deletion) empowered the victims and reinforced their trust in the research process and in me. I refined and improved chapters with their input—and nothing factual or central was deleted. These deletions usually reflected how the victims felt about something superfluous to the main story; nothing central to the restorative justice dialogue or process or victims' perceptions was lost. Accuracy was improved, and by having a chapter draft, victims felt that they had tangible evidence that affirmed the value and meaning of their lived experience. As one participant exclaimed after reading her chapter, "It's awesome! I can't thank you enough." Most victims shared the chapter drafts with significant others, which they told me was important for receiving support from family members, who expressed greater pride in and a better understanding of the victims' active participation in the VVH dialogue process. Validity is also achieved when participants agree with the analysis when they read it.[7]

In addition, other central components to the qualitative research design gave victims control over the process: we negotiated where to meet for the interviews, with the victims taking the lead in selecting a place that offered comfort, safety, and privacy. Most often, we used an office of the agency that sponsors the VVH program, although on occasion I met victims at coffee shops. Although I had an open-ended schedule of research questions, the interview format was flexible enough to invite victims to elaborate or raise issues or situations that extended well beyond the constructed questions.[8] Ultimately, this fluidity accomplished two things: first, it let victims set the pace and direction, controlling when to talk about difficult or uncomfortable topics; and second, it facilitated the emergence of themes I had not considered or realized might be significant. This allowed me to understand more fully what pieces were most important to the victims themselves.

Initial contact with the program participants was orchestrated through two letters of introduction to the project. The first was from Kim. It provided a broad description of the project and, more important, vouched for me, emphasizing that the victims (and offenders) had a choice to participate or not. The second letter was from me and offered more details about the project and their participation.

I interviewed victims first, and their stories begin each of the chapters. The research protocol approved by the university's IRB stipulated that interviews with victims and offenders were separate entities neither contingent nor dependent on respective or reciprocal permissions. The victims themselves became a driving force behind my contacts with offenders, a fact that reflected their positive experiences with the VVH program. I followed no particular chronology in choosing whom to interview first, although the nonstranger murder cases were the last interviews I conducted. This was as much a function of the order of the individuals who pursued the VVH program (the nonstranger murder cases occurred last) as anything else. I use the word "case" here not to objectify or reduce the participants' stories to a "psychological" case-study approach but to use the nomenclature that Kim developed in designing VVH. In total, nine cases are covered in this book, reflecting six complete victim-offender pairings, two victim-only cases (chapters 8 and 9), and one offender-only case (chapter 12). Of these, five involved nonstranger crimes, and four involved crimes that occurred between strangers. Another way to describe these cases is that five reflect crimes of gendered violence, meaning that men are overrepresented as offenders and women and girls are overwhelmingly the victims in cases of sexual violence (rape, incest, child sexual abuse) and intimate-partner battering. The debate about whether restorative justice programs are appropriate forums for handling crimes of this nature is further discussed in chapter 1 and in appendix A.

I conducted interviews using open-ended questions, a standard feature of qualitative research; such questioning offers greater depth of inquiry so that detail, context, and nuance are unconstrained by forced choice or predetermined answer categories.[9] This approach takes a lot more time, given that the mission of "thick" description is to "take the reader into the setting being described"[10] to really help the reader experience and understand the complexity of being a victim of a severe crime or an offender of the same and how the VVH program facilitates healing so that the reader can better understand the subject studied.[11] I followed Denzin's admonishment to go beyond mere record keeping, since thick description "goes beyond mere fact and surface appearances. It presents detail, context, emotion, and the webs of social relationships that join persons to one another. Thick description evokes emotionality and self-feelings. It inserts history into experience. It establishes the significance of an experience, or the sequence of events, for the person or persons in question. In thick description, the voices, feelings, actions, and meanings of interacting individuals are heard."[12] All told, the interviews lasted between one and a half hours and slightly over three hours; I spent twenty-five hours interviewing victims and thirteen and half hours interviewing offenders. The transcribed interview material alone amounted to almost five hundred pages of single-spaced text.

In addition to the interviews with direct participants, I conducted an additional twelve hours of interviews with some key supporting players, such as victim services workers, Kim, Kim's supervisor, the then-coordinator of public outreach for MADD, and professionals associated with the state's Coalition Against Domestic Violence. Kim's path to the position of coordination of VVH was shaped by her own experience with severe violence, the murder of her seventeen-year-old daughter in 1995. I conducted a formal interview with Kim about Nicole's murder and her own trajectory of healing and creating VVH. Moreover, I had constant access to Kim as a sounding board to cross-check and explore questions that emerged in the research process.

Similar to other research projects I have led, when conducting the interviews I followed Lofland and Lofland's interview preparation guidelines: I initially explained who I was and gave a broad outline of the project; I adopted the language of the respondents and tried to be sensitive to what made sense to them; I structured the questions around general clusters and topics, beginning with less sensitive material in order to build trust and rapport; and I developed probes that took into account both what the respondents mentioned and what they did not mention.[13] Although for consistency I followed an overall checklist with each interview, I also used a flexible format and stayed open to pursuing other issues of merit. This is a benefit of qualitative methodology: the inherent flexibility in the interview format allowed unexpected tangents to emerge.[14] Respondents were free to interrupt, clarify my questions or their responses, and challenge my questions (e.g., on the grounds of style or content). They were also free to turn off the tape recorder at any point or to ask me to erase any of their comments. By the end of each interview, the participants uniformly thanked me for letting them tell their own stories, despite any discomfort they experienced while talking about the actual crimes or loss of their loved ones.

The presentation of the data and analysis follows in the tradition of a comparative case-study approach using "thick" description. Comparative case studies allow for "(1) high-quality, detailed descriptions of each case, which are useful for documenting uniqueness, and (2) important shared patterns that cut across cases and derive their significance from having emerged out of heterogeneity."[15] Thus, it is appropriate to write first about each individual's experience, prior to an analysis of core consistencies and meanings, and I follow this convention.[16]

I used a triangulated methodological design, collecting information from multiple sites of inquiry. Multiple methods are less vulnerable to errors linked to one particular method (such as a loaded or biased interview question or respondents' social-desirability bias), and they allow for cross-data validity checks.[17] The beauty of a triangulated approach is its ability to examine a social phenomenon from different perspectives, as it is reflected in interviews, archival records, and so forth. This permits validity checks, which I also achieved by contrasting the participants' perceptions and narratives to additional documentation.[18] Besides the rich detail contained in the in-depth interviews conducted with victims and offenders, I gained their permission to read their case files. "Records, documents, artifacts, and archives—what has traditionally been called 'material culture' in anthropology—constitute a particularly rich source of information about many organizations and programs. Thus archival strategies and techniques constitute part of the repertoire of field research and evaluation."[19] These case files offered descriptive accounts of the time participants spent with Kim in preparation for their face-to-face dialogues. As described in chapter 2 and in appendix C, the paperwork was extensive, covering exercises about feelings, remorse, childhood background, criminal history, victim empathy, and so forth. Since each victim and offender complete open-ended questions in "homework" packets that total 29 and 35 pages, respectively, I read over 240 pages of victims' material and 260 of offenders' material. Victims and offenders had to be clear about the reasons why they wanted to meet and had to write letters (as an exercise) to explain these reasons to each other. The letters were included in the case files, as were the facilitator's summary and case notes; I had access to this material as well. Finally, I watched the videotapes of meetings available for all but one pair[20] and took extensive notes during the viewings that I later transcribed (totaling over twenty hours of viewing and close to one hundred pages of single-spaced transcribed pages).

Table 1: Summary by Crime Type

Dialogue Session, By Crime	Both Victim And Offender	Victim Only	Offender Only	Total
Murder (stranger)	1		1	2
Vehicular homicide (DUI)	1	1		2
Rape (stranger)	1		1	2
Incest/child sexual abuse	1	1		2
Attempted murder/marital rape/IPV	1			1
Total	5	2	2	9

Table 2: Summary by Crime type—Relationship

Case #	Crime	Victim Died in Crime	Relationship of Dialogue Participant to Offender	Interview With Victim or Victims' Family Member	Interview With Offender
1	Rape	No	Self	Withdrew	Yes
2	Rape	No	Self	Yes	Yes
3	Child sexual abuse	No	Victim's father	Yes	No
4	Incest	No	Self	Yes	Yes
5	Attempted murder/Marital rape/IPV	No	Self	Yes	Yes
6	DUI murder	Yes – mother and brother	Sister/Daughter	Yes	Yes
7	DUI murder	Yes – son	Mother	Yes	No (deceased, unrelated to VVH)
8	Murder	Yes	Son	Yes	Yes
9	Murder	Yes	Daughter	Yes	Yes

Table 3: Summary by Crime Type—Race and gender of victims/offenders

Case #	Crime	Race Of Victim Or Victims' Family Member	Race Of Offender	Gender Of Victim	Gender Of Offender
1	Rape	White	White	F	M
2	Rape	White	Black	F	M
3	Child sexual abuse	White	White	F	M
4	Incest	White	White	F	M
5	Attempted murder/ Marital rape/IPV	White	Black	F	M
6	DUI murder	White (both)	White	F and M	M
7	DUI murder	White	White	M	F
8	Murder	White	White	F	M
9	Murder	White	White	F	M

Through my firsthand experience of viewing the videotaped dialogues (I would not have been allowed in the actual room in real time), I could observe things that might be taken for granted by participants but gave me the opportunity to notice important nuances and the context and manner in which people relate and interact, forming a holistic perspective that included body language, words used by participants to each other, what happened during breaks or before a formal dialogue began—essentially letting me absorb the setting as well as the intensity of feelings that occurred during the dialogues.[21]

Interviews with offenders took place in two prisons in Delaware. The state of Delaware has only three counties, and most of the population lives in the more developed and urban northern county. The prison in the northern county, opened in 1971, is the largest adult male correctional facility, housing approximately twenty-five hundred inmates in minimum-, medium-, and maximum-security units; it also houses inmates sentenced to death. The southern prison is one of Delaware's oldest correctional facilities, opened in 1931, and houses approximately twelve hundred minimum-, medium-, and maximum-security inmates. Although the southern prison houses an all-male population, it is also the site of the only boot camp in Delaware, which accommodates ninety men and ten women. This prison is located in the most rural part of the state, an area rich with farmland and chicken factories—a fact made more salient for me on one research visit when I followed a chicken truck, and my car was pelted with feathers for miles.

Two offenders were incarcerated in the southern prison, and the other offenders were housed at the northern prison. I gained approval from the commissioner of corrections to conduct the inmate component of the project, reflecting the Department of Corrections' tacit approval of the VVH program and its positive ramifications. I was always greeted courteously by the corrections officers and permitted to have total privacy in my conversations with the inmates and the freedom to tape-record our conversations.

For the two interviews conducted at the southern facility, the pace was relaxed—for instance, when officers escorted me across the compound, they gave me a minitour of the prison grounds and key buildings, pointing out some of their "model" inmates and offering me rich descriptions of various programs and regulations. I interviewed the inmates in comfortable settings; I met with James in the general-purpose room where programs such as twelve-steps or Alternatives to Violence had their meetings. For Kevin's interview, we were ensconced in a prison counselor's office. This interview was interrupted at midpoint when, with no explanation, an officer came through the closed door and took Kevin away. I had no idea what was happening or if I had somehow played a part in his departure. I left the room, hoping to locate a guard who could tell me what was going on and was stopped quickly at the door and told that if I crossed the threshold into the next room, I would see fifty men with their pants down, bending over half naked as officers performed a visual cavity search for a correctional officer's missing keys. When Kevin reappeared to continue the interview, he looked a little chagrined, and I commented on the indignity of the situation. He told me that strip searches were so routine that he hardly noticed—and in fact, he is searched every time he has a visitor, including me. Without losing his composure or enthusiasm, he delved right back into our conversation where we had left off.

The interviews at the northern prison were different. Correctional officers were also accommodating though brisk and more cynical about the inmates in their conversations with me as we walked across the compound. There was often some confusion when I first arrived, as officers at the front gate seemed to have no inkling of how to process me, despite the scheduled meetings. Except for one inmate, Jamel, who was housed in a maximum-security unit[22] where we had to talk with a wall of glass between us, with him shackled at his wrists and ankles, the interviews were conducted in tiny rooms, similar to police interrogation rooms. The rooms were bare except for a small table with a chair on either side, and they were painted the common institutional gray with no adornment. The sterile environment reinforced the inmates' powerlessness, so their eagerness to talk with me about something with great passion was a marked contrast to the barren physical and emotional ambiance of the setting.

During the initial few minutes upon meeting the offenders, I explained the project and how I (and their victims) welcomed their perceptions and reflections about the VVH program. The enthusiasm the offenders felt for the program was apparent; most saw their interview with me as an extension of something they wanted to do to honor their victim(s). Although I talked with the inmates about their perceptions and ideas related to their choices and the consequences of these choices, along with the VVH program, I deliberately refrained from asking them questions about why they committed their crimes. Some told me many details regardless, whereas others focused on other particular aspects of their story, choosing what they believed were the important components to share.

Whenever research participants have committed deviant or criminal acts that are judged pejoratively by society, researchers have to be aware of social-desirability bias. This refers to the common inclination to present oneself in the best possible light so that others view one favorably, a strategy used (even subconsciously) to achieve social acceptance. Offenders who commit serious and heinous crimes such as incest, rape, and murder may be even more likely to answer questions in a socially desirable manner because of the stigma and contempt associated with such crimes. In my many hours working with the inmates' own words—during the in-depth interview time I spent with them, reading their paperwork and letters to their victims, and watching the face-to-face dialogues with the victims—I am convinced that their characterizations of situations and their feelings associated with them rang true.[23] Through the process of triangulation, I was able to confirm what they told me, often with additional details, by using different points of data. Since I reconnected with all the offenders whom I interviewed in the year following our time together, I had an additional point of comparison to use in gauging their sincerity and veracity; what they told me fit well with other indicators.

Most of the victims were women (there was one case in which a father participated on behalf of his daughter, who had been sexually abused by her maternal grandfather). I was comfortable sharing some of my past activism and research on behalf of victims, a fact that might have helped develop their trust in me. We established an easy rapport in our time together, and with some frequency victims contacted me later by email or phone to check in on the progress of the book as well as to offer me updates on their lives and their thinking about the crimes and the VVH program.

I also believe that the fact that I am a woman greatly facilitated the research process for both the victims and offenders, despite the nature of the crimes the offenders committed. All the offenders I interviewed were male, and although five had been convicted of committing crimes of sexual violence against women and girls, my gender posed no real barrier to open communication.[24] In fact, my gender might have encouraged the men to talk more openly about gender or violence issues. As a woman, I did not challenge their masculinity as a man might have; I was a safer confidante. Other women who have researched men's violence committed against women have experienced similar ease—and attribute it to the removal of a masculine posture that might be elicited if a man asked another man about his violence.[25] Similar to the victims, when the offenders communicated with Kim, they continued to ask about the book long after our interviews were completed (and they quickly responded to my short, open-ended questionnaire "Where Are You Now?" which they received about a year following the initial interviews).

My commitment to honor victims' voices and empower their decision-making and their need to feel safe surfaced at a later point in the data-collection process, as I was finishing the chapters of this book. One of the victims ultimately withdrew her consent for her interview and other materials to be a part of the book. She believed that having such a detailed published account of her story would preclude her writing about it, and writing a book about her experiences is a goal that she has for herself. Of course, I honored her request to withdraw the interview material. My intention has always been to give victims a voice and empower them to be in control of their stories and lives. Since my interview with her offender was not contingent on her participation, his story remains a part of the book. In reading his story—in addition to three pieces the victim has since written in public forums—it is clear that the VVH program provided an enormous transformative effect on her life as well. Today, she plays an integral part in conducting faith-based groups inside prison as a volunteer for a Bible-studies class, and she is tireless in working on reentry challenges faced by her own offender and other sexual offenders.

Chapters 13 and 14 reflect my analysis of the themes that emerged from the multiple data-collection sites—the interviews with participants, the case files, the interviews with the facilitator(s), and the viewing of the dialogue videos. I read each transcript multiple times and analyzed the words, coding them into emergent conceptual categories using grounded-theory methods. I followed an "open coding" inductive strategy that facilitates the discovery of patterns, themes, and categories in the data.[26] Following grounded-theory methods, I used themes if they were discussed at length or if they evoked powerful meaning from participants.[27] The challenge then was to move beyond the powerful storylines from the participants' narratives and toward an analysis of what it all means. It is absolutely necessary to separate description from interpretation, the latter of which should include "explaining the findings, answering the 'why' questions, attaching significance to particular results, and putting patterns into an analytic framework."[28] Grounded-theory analytical strategies emphasize becoming immersed in the data so that embedded meanings and relationships can emerge.[29] It involves "the interplay of making inductions (deriving concepts, their properties, and dimensions from data) and deductions (hypothesizing about the relationships between concepts)."[30]

Once no new conceptual categories emerged from the interviews, I had achieved saturation and had confidence that these themes were an accurate representation of the most prominent elements of meaning in these stories.

My intention has been to explore the potential successes (and pitfalls) for postconviction therapeutic restorative justice programs in general and for the VVH program in particular. I have made every effort to conduct thorough, rigorous, and sensitive research. I hope that my attention to these concerns is apparent in the pages of this book and that the findings inform our understanding of how some harms can be repaired through victim-centered programs that include offender participation. Although the sample size is small in this study, what is achieved here is "thick description" and "thick interpretation" using a comparative case-study approach in which individual cases are connected to larger social issues and to programs that provide the link between individual circumstances and public concerns.[31] As work advances and continues with other RJ studies, empirical comparisons can be made in regard to the effect of RJ on various types of crimes, such as gendered violence, and types of RJ programs, such as conferences and court-affiliated programs, to further explore victims' empowerment and recovery and offenders' change and recidivism.

Appendix C

Victims' Voices Heard Program Structure

This appendix provides a detailed description of the steps followed by participants in the Victims' Voices Heard program. The entire preparatory process that unfolds prior to the face-to-face meeting between the victim and offender typically consists of a minimum of four to six months of biweekly (separate) meetings with a facilitator, but there is no set expectation of how long each component of the preparation takes. Victims' journeys are unique and not necessarily linear, and often feelings that victims had long thought reconciled are resurrected during this stage, prolonging the process. The VVH facilitators work with victims and offenders at their own pace. The preparation process entails responding to a series of questions, both in writing and orally. In Kim Book's experience, victims face greater difficulty with the preparation process than offenders do—some victims complete the paperwork in a timely fashion, whereas others are unable to progress with answering questions about the crime and its aftermath. When participants are stuck, Kim uses these opportunities as starting points for their in-person discussions. Some victims write responses with a great deal of detail, finding it cleansing or reassuring to catalog their early emotions and marvel at how far they have come. Offenders, on the other hand, typically complete the paperwork quickly and with no questions asked. Kim believes the offenders' ability to do this is because of the institutionalization effect of prison, where inmates are used to being told by correctional staff what to do and complying with orders.

Completion of the initial bureaucratic paperwork clears the way for the emotional work to begin, as victims and offenders receive a fourteen- or twenty-page handout, respectively, labeled "Preparation Packet." Much of it is adapted or modified, with permission, from the Victim Offender Mediation/ Dialogue Program housed in victim services as part of the Texas Department of Criminal Justice—the program after which VVH is modeled. The questions posed are written to encourage self-reflection, and the responses are open-ended, leaving participants room to write out their thoughts rather than simply asking them to check off different choices in a self-inventory or to provide numerical responses (e.g., "How do you feel on a scale of one to ten?"). Facilitators find participants' responses more useful when they use their own words to describe their thoughts and concerns rather than using preset response checklists. Even responses left blank offer opportunities to probe why a question remains unanswered.[1] Although this is true for both offenders and victims, it is especially useful to hear how offenders talk about their crime and characterize their actions, so that facilitators can discern what needs to be addressed regarding offenders' accountability. Of paramount importance is the need not to revictimize the victim by using a careless phrase that might sound victim blaming or through a misunderstood expression of an offender's remorse. For instance, early in the preparation process offenders often vacillate between expressing apologies and sorrow for the crime they committed and mitigating their responsibility with explanations for their behavior, similar to what Daly found in her research with youth offenders in a diversionary RJ program in Australia.[2] It is only after considerable work and reflection that offenders integrate their background experiences with their understanding of motivations in order to take full responsibility for their actions.

For victims, the preparation packet begins with an opening that encourages them to get in touch with their feelings and reflect on the questions as they work through them. Participants are reassured that none of the questions is meant to be offensive or insensitive to their needs, but they should realize that in responding, "troublesome unaddressed wounds and issues" may be uncovered that "evoke raw, painful responses." Participants are urged to take their time, to involve supportive friends if they wish as they work through things, and that they should "never feel compelled at any time to continue with any part of the process that doesn't feel right." Finally, the packet's introduction closes by stating that the process is "their" work and that the hope is that they feel validated, listened to, and affirmed and that they feel their voice is "being heard and respected." The next several pages of the packet present twelve questions that ask victims to record the initial impact of the crime on them and any related feelings they have. Each question focuses on victims' possible reactions or feelings, such as disbelief, numbness, confusion, helplessness, terror, vulnerability, and so forth. Though these twelve questions cover several pages, even one of the questions could take days or weeks to answer, depending on where the victim is in her or his journey. Some of the questions also ask victims to write about their experiences of reliving the trauma, anger, guilt, suspicion, shame, depression, and so forth. It asks them to sort out any connections they have with feelings of revenge and the connection these feelings have to their personal values, as well as any feelings of betrayal they have (by God, friends, family, community, and so forth). It also delves into the effects of the crime on their everyday life (e.g., sleeping, appetite, health, job performance, memories, relationships, marriage, and sexual interest) and ask if they experience grief over the loss of trust, purpose in life, and personal power and control. Next is a series of questions in which victims are asked about the crime: "Why did this happen to me? Could I have done anything to prevent this? Can this happen to me again? Do I need to fear for my safety? What happened to me as a result of the crime? Then and now, how does this impact my faith, my hopes and dreams, my future? What do I need in order to experience justice? Do I need revenge? Do I need compensation? Do I need answers to my questions? Do I need to have my feelings and experience validated? What do I need to feel empowered?"

The same set of questions is repeated, only this time the victim is encouraged to ask and answer these questions from the offender's perspective in order to personalize the offender[3] and to prepare for any possible feeling that could arise from the offender's response. The victim is then asked to write about the potential response of the offender when they meet face to face at the dialogue: "How will you feel/respond if the offender responds with: Quiet resignation? Anger and stubbornness? An emotional appeal for pity? An overly dramatic/manipulative response? Excessive reasoning as to why it happened? Projection of responsibility outside him-/herself or making excuses? Minimization ("it wasn't that bad")? Remorse, taking full responsibility, desiring to be accountable and do restitution/reparation? Complete denial? Refusal to talk?"

The subsequent component asks the victim to explore what healing means to her or him and what could bring about healing or begin a movement toward healing. This line of questioning is extended next to have victims think about the emotional, physical, mental, spiritual, social, and financial ways that the offender can "make right" what has been "wronged." The rest of the preparation packet continues in this vein, directing the victim to think about the kinds of symbolic or real efforts the offender can make to help in the victim's healing. It asks the victim to think about anything she or he wants the offender to commit to or promise as part of an affirmation agreement to confirm accountability and responsibility for what was done. Victims are also asked to consider what offenders can do to demonstrate that their past attitudes and behavior have changed. Finally, victims are asked to identify their goals and expectations for the face-to-face meeting, what they want to accomplish, and what issues or questions they wish to address.

For offenders, although there are some similarities with the questions posed in the victims' preparation packet, there are a number of areas constructed with specificity to offenders' perspectives. Even the introductory statements on the first page differ; offenders are urged to consider that "what you feel, what you think, what you do is what will provide the basis for healing change. Your attitude, your purpose, your motives, your resolve are what will make the difference in shaping a positive experience of growth for you." Also included is a short motivational message from David Doerfler, the original architect of the dialogue program for Texas, about the need for honesty and accountability.

The focus on the first four pages is on crime-impact questions. Offenders are encouraged to write their responses to each question on separate pieces of paper, in order to stimulate longer thought and reflection time. One question directs the offender to write a letter (not to be sent) to the victim that expresses the level of guilt felt and responsibility taken for the crime and its impact. When responding to this question, offenders are urged, "Make note of any ways you made it seem not so bad or found ways of excusing what you did, and/or attempted to project blame on the victim or others." This hypothetical letter becomes the foundation on which the facilitators build during the work that is done prior to the dialogue, because it reveals where the offender is in the beginning of the preparation process and what issues need to be worked through. For example, if an offender makes excuses or asks for forgiveness, facilitators would know to begin with these issues. Some of the impact questions address the following: "How do you remember the crime? What is your view of how you think the crime affected the victim's life (emotionally, physically, mentally, spiritually, socially, and financially)? How did the crime affect others (the victim's family, the community, the offender's own family and friends)?" Offenders are also asked to respond to questions similar to ones posed at the beginning of the victims' preparation packet, with a few additions, such as "Does anyone need to fear for his/her safety? What happened to me as a result of the crime? Why did I act the way I did at the time? What do I need in order to believe I have experienced justice? Why dialogue? How can talking with the victim help? How do the opinions/feelings/advice of others affect my thinking/feelings/behavior?"

The next component of the preparation packet asks offenders to put themselves in the shoes of the victim, a task that could be challenging in any number of ways, especially if they did not know the victim or what happened to her or him after the crime. Then, they are asked to answer, from the perspective of the victim, the questions posed to them as offenders on the previous pages (about twelve questions). Subsequently, offenders are asked to think about how they can "make things right" across a number of dimensions and what kind of real or symbolic restitution (other than money) they can make to their victim and any commitments or promises to the victim as part of an affirmation agreement to prove they are holding themselves accountable. A number of suggestions are offered beyond financial pledges, such as prayer, promises of safety, helping others within the community upon release, commitment to improve themselves through treatment and/or continuing education, periodic progress letters, formal apology and expression of remorse, talking and working with other offenders, and demonstration that they have changed their past attitudes and behaviors in some fashion. Another component asks offenders to establish some level of empathy or understanding for situations which would remind the victim of the offense. Offenders are asked to write as if they were the victim. Examples are provided to help guide offenders in taking on the role of the person they hurt, such as "When my own children reach the age when Dad yelled and hit me, I will be scared for their safety" or "Whenever I smell Brut aftershave, I become nauseous." Several pages are included in the offenders' packet that detail the possible ramifications of their crime on the victims' lives and what it means to accept guilt and responsibility. Here is a particularly powerful example:

> You have taken the victim's right to (1) grow and continue to be safe and secure, (2) move about his/her world, school, work without fear, and (3) realize his/her full potential. The past cannot be changed. Simply saying "I'm sorry" can do little to restore the levels of trust and potential that formerly existed. However, an offender's new resolve and commitment borne out of the acceptance of guilt and responsibility can make a difference. A new way of living on the part of offenders expresses greater accountability to their victims and communities can be helpful.

Preparing offenders for the upcoming dialogue continues in additional exercises. They are asked to make a list of several things: everything they need to do to not reoffend and to keep others safe, the goals and expectations for the face-to-face meeting and what they want to accomplish, and the issues and questions they want to address during the meeting. Some of the packet addresses the need for offenders to understand that a common question for victims is "Why me?" So offenders are encouraged to think about how to give victims relief from thinking that they have something "wrong" with them. Another common question that victims ask is why the offender committed the crime. The preparation packet includes the following to guide offenders in thinking about this question:

> Describe the things about you and the thinking process you followed to become an offender. Be careful to avoid "pity pot," "poor me" and "victim stance" attitudes. Write a clear, crisp explanation of why you offended and why you are responsible for the damage. This portion, like perhaps no other portion, should be a discussion of you, not a discussion of other people or other things. Think about the victim's understanding. If you say that you hurt a person because you were selfish, you must explain the goal of your selfishness. As an example, if you told a child you were selfish and stole the chocolate cake from the table, the child would have some grasp of why you took the cake. For most people, a crime is degrading, painful, and uncomfortable. It's not sufficient simply to say, "I did this because I was selfish." Most people don't understand why you wanted to hurt anyone in the first place.

Offenders also write a "letter of permission" that is given to their victim. The intention behind the letter is to give power to the victim by having the offender ask to meet with her or him.

Offenders are encouraged to complete a "finish each thought" exercise, covering the aftermath of the crime. Fourteen items are used in this exercise, with offenders asked to complete sentences such as "When I offended, employment was affected . . . (write down in what way); My family was affected . . . ; My children were affected . . . ; My self-esteem was affected . . . ; My ability to travel was affected . . . ; My health was affected . . . ; My hopes were affected . . . ; My use of alcohol, drugs or food was affected . . . ;" and so forth. Next, offenders consider the times in their lives when they were unable to protect themselves and someone hurt them, including instances of emotional abuse, physical abuse, sexual abuse, neglect, and abandonment.

Similar to how the facilitators prepare victims for possible responses from offenders during the dialogue, offenders are asked how they plan to respond if victims cry, apologize, forgive them, say hurtful or hateful things, or remember something about the offense that offenders do not remember. Offenders are encouraged to be prepared for other unplanned events and how they might handle themselves in ways that are respectful to the victims.

Also provided is a list of questions that victims often ask, so that offenders can practice their responses in honest, reflective, and respectful ways. The list of victims' possible questions includes "Why did you do those things to me? Will you ever do it again? Why me? What did I do? What do you know about the crime that no one else knows? How do you feel about my being angry with you? What would have happened if I hadn't turned you in (if applicable)? Why should I trust you? What help have you received in prison or from others?"

Once victims and offenders complete their respective preparation packets, they are given a fifteen-page "Grief Inventory." Similar to the preparation packet, victims and offenders work on the inventory independently and then give their responses to Kim. Often the participants express themselves better on paper than in person, especially in the beginning of the VVH program. With the exception of the final few pages, the inventories are similar for both victims and offenders. The questions and exercises push the participants to really think about the long-term consequences of the crime/victimization and how best to continue to heal and grieve (victims) or to take responsibility and have different responses to future events (offenders). Victims and offenders reflect on how others have reacted to the incident and to them and how relationships may have changed as a result of the loss/crime, as well as on how they might be challenged again postdialogue. There are a number of questions exploring the ways that they still may react to the crime (how they set boundaries, avoid talking about it or deny their feelings, self-medicate, and so forth) and how they have handled other losses or grief in their lives. Coping skills, ways of mourning, resources, and support networks are explored. Behavior, attitudes, value and belief systems, spirituality, and world views are often challenged or changed following trauma, and several pages of questions encourage participants to think about these effects. Exercises also help guide participants to think about how they will respond to each other during the face-to-face dialogues.

Some questions that appear most challenging center on asking participants to think about what they will take from the VVH program in helping them in the future. For instance, "How do you view the future? What remains for you to do, in order to grow in your grief/mourning, so that you will be doing the best you can? Have you made a decision to 'make it'? Do you want to be healed? What areas will be the hardest to rebuild in your life? What do you think is necessary to cope with or survive an experience like this? What will indicate you have done your best in growing through/coping/mourning the loss? What part does guilt play in your recovery/reconstruction/healing? Shame?" Other questions are broader: "What is your understanding of justice? Forgiveness? Revenge? The process of 'letting go'? And what are the values of all of these?"

For victims, their answers to the final questions reveal how attached they are to their story and if it is something they can give up attachment to and live a different kind of life. This area is explored in greater depth with victims, because it is important to them to have an identity without their victimization and to integrate their experiences into their lives. Offenders cannot "have a story" when they participate in the face-to-face dialogue because it is guided by what the victim remembers and deems important. Victims and offenders are no different from the rest of us; we all remember events differently. For instance, an offender may not "remember" that his sexual abuse of his sister began when the victim was only five years old, but the victim may have clear memories of it. For offenders, the final questions in their Grief Inventory ask them to consider possible ways that the victim could respond at their dialogue and what they would do, such as "If my victim was taking responsibility for the crime, I would . . . ; If my victim appeared to be angry/irritated/arrogant, I would . . . ; If my victim appeared to be finding reasons why it happened instead of feeling the trauma of the crime, I would . . ." Other questions ask offenders about any changes they see in themselves during the VVH process, such as if their story changed since the first time they told it and how; if they can allow themselves to see things from the viewpoint of their victim and, if so, what they see; if they have an identity without their prison ID number or as an offender; and what they have learned from their own experience of loss, and what they can still learn from it. Similar to the victims, offenders are asked if they want to be healed and if they want their lives to be different.

Once the paperwork is completed and the participants' responses are discussed at length in the individual meetings with the facilitator, work turns to the upcoming dialogue. This preparation could include role plays, victims talking with other victims who have completed the program, and so forth. Offenders are reminded that the dialogue is not about them, per se, so they should only answer what they are asked. If victims want more information or details, they will ask for it, so offenders need to refrain from telling them what they think victims would want to know. When it is clear that both the victim and the offender have worked through their issues and concerns and are ready to meet, the letter exchange occurs, generally about a month before the meeting. One of the key aspects of the letter exchange is for victims to tell offenders what they want to emerge at and from the dialogue. About two weeks prior to meeting, victims can tour the prison with the facilitator to see in advance how the day will unfold and where the dialogue will take place. This knowledge assists in decreasing anxiety about an unfamiliar situation. After the walk-through, the prison provides clearance for the one-time meeting, and the date is scheduled.

On the day of the dialogue, the victim meets the facilitator at the institution. The dialogue can be videotaped with consent from both parties, and the tape is held by the VVH program. Immediately following the dialogue, both parties complete an oral debrief in separate areas, conducted by the facilitator. This ensures that all parties are satisfied and monitors how they are handling the experience. Two weeks later, the facilitator meets separately with the victim and the offender for a follow-up visit, followed by a final follow-up visit two months subsequent to the dialogue. Both parties are sent a written evaluation form to complete and return to VVH, and the facilitator completes a final case summary. Regular contact with VVH ends at this point, although victims typically check in when something happens in their lives or if they want to watch the videotaped dialogue. Some minimal connection with offenders continues as well, since often the affirmation agreement includes a request for progress reports from the victims, and the VVH program coordinates these efforts.

Notes

NOTES TO CHAPTER 1

1. See Ronnie Janoff-Bulman (1992), *Shattered Assumptions: Towards a New Psychology of Trauma,* New York: Free Press.

2. Kathleen O'Hara (2006), *A Grief Like No Other: Surviving the Violent Death of Someone You Love,* New York: Marlowe, pp. 41, 45.

3. Although I see the victims of the crimes discussed in this book as survivors of crime, the program in which they participated uses the terms *victim* and *offender,* and paperwork and documentation follows this protocol. I primarily follow this terminology while recognizing the victims' position as survivors of crime.

4. O'Hara (2006), 19.

5. See Eviatar Zerubavel (2006), *The Elephant in the Room: Silence and Denial in Everyday Life,* New York: Oxford University Press.

6. Howard Zehr (2002), *The Little Book of Restorative Justice,* Intercourse, PA: Good Books, 21.

7. Although some programs are aimed at securing a particular outcome, such as diversion from the more formal and harsher mechanisms of the traditional criminal justice system, other RJ programs focus on the promise of achieving therapeutic goals, such as the one explored in this book.

8. See Zehr (2002), 8.

9. Unless specifically noted, all the names used in the book are pseudonyms. Many victims wanted me to use their real names because of their pride in how far they have come and their lack of shame about what happened to them. Some offenders, too, were comfortable with revealing their real names because they wanted to demonstrate accountability for their crimes. In the interests of privacy and consistency, however, I changed all the real names of victims/survivors, offenders, and other people in the stories to pseudonyms. One exception is the use of Kim Book's real name (used with permission). However, if the victims so desired, I have used the real first names of the deceased, as a way to honor their loved ones lost to crime.

NOTES TO CHAPTER 2

1. Turkey case reported in the *New York Times*: Julia C. Mean (2005), "Deal in Turkey-Throwing Case after Victim Calls for Leniency," August 16.

2. Kendra's case reported in the *New York Times*: Anemona Hartocollis (2006), "A Subway Nightmare Will Be the Focus of Yet a Third Trial," May 23.

3. Anemona Hartocollis (2006), "Nearly 8 Years Later, Guilty Plea in Subway Killing," *New York Times,* October 11, http: //www.nytimes.com/2006/10/11/nyregion/11kendra. html.

4. AP, "Amish Forgive, Pray and Mourn" (2006), *CBSNews.com,* October 4, http: // www.cbsnews.com/stories/2006/10/04/national/.

5. Donald B. Kraybill (2006), "Forgiving Is Woven into Life of Amish," *Philly.com,* October 8, http://www.philly.com/mld/philly/news/special_packages/amish/.

6. Ibid.

7. Gertrude Huntington, quoted in AP (2006).

8. For instance, Howard Zehr (2002, 37) speaks about RJ as "a process to involve, to the extent possible, those who have a stake in a specific offense and to collectively identify and address harms, needs, and obligations, in order to heal and put things as right as possible." Tony Marshall defines RJ as "a process whereby parties with a stake in a specific offence collectively resolve how to deal with the aftermath of the offense and its implications for the future" ([1999], *Restorative Justice: An Overview,* Home Office, United Kingdom, 5). Paul McCold offers a Venn diagram that illustrates the intersection of three circles that symbolize victim reparation, offender responsibility, and communities-of-care reconciliation, with the understanding that not all RJ programs will incorporate fully all elements (see Paul McCold and Ted Wachtel [2003], "In Pursuit of Paradigm: A Theory of Restorative Justice," *Restorative Practices Eforum,* www.restorativepractices.org).

9. See Zehr (2002).

10. B. Galaway and J. Hudson (1996), *Restorative Justice: International Perspectives,* Amsterdam: Kugler.

11. See the following examples of critiques of diversionary RJ programs and traditional victim-offender mediation programs for crimes of gendered violence: R. Busch (2002), "Domestic Violence and Restorative Justice Initiatives: Who Pays If We Get It Wrong?" in H. Strang and J. Braithwaite, eds., *Restorative Justice and Family Violence,* 223–248, Cambridge: Cambridge University Press; D. Coker (2002), "Transformative Justice: Anti-subordination Processes in Cases of Domestic Violence," in Strang and Braithwaite, *Restorative Justice and Family Violence,* 128–152; S. Hooper and R. Busch (1996), "Domestic Violence and the Restorative Justice Initiatives: The Risks of a New Panacea," *Waikato Law Review* 4:101–130; R. Lewis, R. Dobash, R. Dobash, and K. Cavanagh (2001), "Law's Progressive Potential: The Value of Engagement with the Law for Domestic Violence," *Social and Legal Studies* 10:105–130; J. Stubbs (2002), "Domestic Violence and Women's Safety: Feminist Challenges to Restorative Justice," in Strang and Braithwaite, *Restorative Justice and Family Violence,* 42–61.

12. Critics of any alternative programs that operate outside the criminal justice system are loathe to endorse a practice that appears to reprivatize these kinds of crimes, and critics believe that the programs give the impression that RJ is a "softer" option. (D. Coker [1999], "Enhancing Autonomy for Battered Women: Lessons from Navajo Peacemaking," *UCLA Law Review* 47:1–111). Still others question RJ's assumption that society is intolerant of violence against women and will provide sufficient funding to support the needs of victims and offenders. However, these concerns fail to distinguish between *diversionary* and *therapeutic* models of restorative justice programs.

13. A. Acorn (2004), *Compulsory Compassion: A Critique of Restorative Justice,* Vancouver: University of British Columbia Press. In this book, Annalise Acorn, a law professor, makes a strong argument against restorative justice practices wherein the seductiveness of remorse substitutes for punishment. Since the VVH program operates postconviction, offenders have already received traditional retributive-based justice through the formal criminal processing but have the opportunity to repair some harm to their victims through the process—thus, the VVH program operationalizes both accountability for wrongdoing and reparation for victims.

14. Zehr (2002).

15. Ibid., 16–17.

16. Very little research has been conducted on RJ programs designed for victims of severe violence to meet with their offender postconviction—and often occurring years after these crimes occurred. One exception is the pioneering work of Mark Umbreit and his colleagues in Texas and Ohio (see Mark S. Umbreit, Betty Vos, Robert B. Coates, and Katherine A. Brown [2003], *Facing Violence: The Path of Restorative Justice and Dialogue,* Monsey, NY: Criminal Justice Press). The exact statistics are challenging to compile since Pennsylvania counts indirect dialogues as completed cases, even though these dialogues involved letters only.

17. All these statistics were taken from the October 2009 report, "U.S. Corrections-Based Victim Offender Dialogue Programs in Crimes of Severe Violence," www.justalternatives.org.

18. If the offender does not want to participate in the VVH program, it is possible that the victim could meet with a "surrogate" offender if he or she desires, although no one so far in Delaware has exercised this option.

19. An example of a case that was not eligible for VVH involved the death of a child while she was in a home daycare facility in 2006. The owner of the home daycare left to attend a funeral, leaving her teenage daughter temporarily in charge of the children. A little girl suffocated between a headboard and a mattress while the owner was away, four hours after the little girl's mother had dropped her off for her first day at the facility. The owner is currently on house arrest, and the owner's daughter is on probation. The grandmother wanted to meet with the owner to find out whatever she could about her granddaughter's final hours. Although the owner of the daycare was willing to meet with the grandmother, she was terminated from the VVH program because she did not take responsibility for the death of the child. The owner also refused to take responsibility for leaving the daycare in the charge of her daughter, who was uncertified and unlicensed to take on such a responsibility. At this time, the grandmother still seeks to meet with the owner's daughter, who was the only person in the house at the time of her granddaughter's tragic death. The grandmother has written a note to the daughter, which she sent to Kim in the hope that someday it can be delivered, explaining that she cannot move on without having her questions answered and that she is no longer angry with the daughter. However, the daughter is prevented from participating in the VVH program until a wrongful-death civil lawsuit is settled.

20. As of August 31, 2010, Victims' Voices Heard will no longer be connected to People's Place II, Inc., but will continue as a nonprofit entity separate from an established organization.

1. For instance, according to national victimization data, in 2005, only 47 percent of all violent victimizations that occurred were reported to police. When you look at specific categories of crimes, auto theft has the highest reporting rate at 83.2 percent, robberies are 52.4 percent, while rapes are only 38.3 percent (Shannon M. Catalano [2006], "Criminal Victimization 2005," *BJS NCVS*, Washington, DC: U.S. Department of Justice, 10).

2. Since 1975, the National Institute on Drug Abuse (NIDA) has surveyed annually the extent of drug use among teenagers in the country. The 2009 survey results reveal that almost one-fifth (19.9 percent) of today's eighth graders, over a third (36 percent) of tenth graders, and about half (46.7 percent) of all twelfth graders have ever taken any illicit drug during their lifetime (results also show that drug use is roughly the same for males and females) (NIDA [2009], "NIDA InfoFacts: High School and Youth Trends," http://www.nida.nih.gov/Infofacts/HSYouthtrends.html). These trends reflect decreases since the peak years of drug abuse in the mid-1990s.

3. Two weeks prior to Nicole's murder, Nicole asked Kim how she could restart her medications. It seemed to Kim that Nicole was taking the first steps in getting her life together since she was turning eighteen soon and would no longer need her father's permission for medical care. Kim finds some solace in the fact that Nicole was starting to confront her self-defeating choices.

4. Restorative Justice Online (2006), "Making Victims' Voices Heard," http://www.restorativejustice.org/editions/2006/feb06/victimsvoices, February.

5. Carlos Holmes (1996), "Walker Received 38-Year Sentence for 1995 Murder," *Delaware State News*, April 19, p. 3.

6. J. L. Miller (1996), "A Mother's Plea for Justice Is Heeded," *News Journal*, April 19.

7. Letter to the editor (1995), "Devastated Families Are Forever Changed," *News Journal*, April.

8. Kim Book (1997), "Living Free in an Unforgiving World," *Delaware State News*, March 30.

9. Kate House (2000), "Story of Daughter's Murder, Mother's Forgiveness," *Dover Post*, October 4, p. 14A.

10. Beth Miller (1999), "The Joy of Forgiveness," *News Journal*, December 18.

11. The Texas program is described more fully in Umbreit et al.'s (2003) evaluation of two victim-offender severe-violence dialogue programs.

12. Restorative Justice Online (2006).

13. Research suggests that criminal justice majors demonstrate less empathy than nonmajors and are more punitive in their attitudes toward criminals and criminal justice issues (see K. E. Courtright, D. A. Mackey, and S. H. Packard [2005], "Empathy among College Students and Criminal Justice Majors," *Journal of Criminal Justice Education* 16 (1): 125–144.

NOTES TO CHAPTER 4

1. See Susan Estrich (1988), *Real Rape: How the Legal System Victimizes Women Who Say No*, Cambridge, MA: Harvard University Press.

2. I witnessed the ripple effect when Donna spoke about the rape and her experience with VVH at a statewide victim's tribute and recognition program during Victims' Rights Awareness month in 2006. Donna's sister, daughter-in-law, and granddaughter were in the audience, supporting her talk with enthusiastic applause and with genuine pride in Donna's healing and willingness to reach out to other victims and their families.

3. According to national data disseminated by the Bureau of Justice Statistics, rapists receive an average sentence of about 117 months (9.75 years) and serve an average of 65 months (5.4 years), which means they serve about 56 percent of their sentence before being released (L. A. Greenfeld [1995], "Prison Sentences and Time Served for Violence," *BJS Selected Findings (No. 4)*, NCJ-153858, Washington, DC: U.S. Department of Justice). Data from 2002 reveal that first-time released whites are sentenced to 75 months for rape, whereas first-time released blacks are sentenced to 92 months (www.ojp.gov/bjs/).

4. At this point in the interview, Donna told me, "So, if you are writing a book about this, and even one person picks that up and gets it, then, my God, look what you've done."

5. The warden at the prison suggested to Kim that the face-to-face meeting should wait until Jamel was moved back to the general population. He believed that the meeting would work better if Donna and Jamel were sitting at the table together, rather than with Jamel behind glass in an orange jumpsuit and shackles. The warden's sensitivity to these issues demonstrates a deep understanding of how severe-violence mediation programs work.

6. Sociologist Elijah Anderson ([1999], *Code of the Street,* New York: Norton), in his research on young men in disadvantaged neighborhoods, discusses how anger such as Jamel's manifests itself as part of the "code of the street" that emphasizes masculinity through toughness, violence, and heterosexual prowess confirmed by sexual conquest.

7. According to Kim's records, the case took three years to complete because of the fight between Jamel and another inmate two weeks before the scheduled dialogue was to take place. Jamel spent almost two years in a secured housing unit. Kim continued to meet with Jamel during this lockdown period on a monthly basis to monitor his progress; she also believes that the extra preparation time was helpful in that Jamel became even more committed to changing his life. These circumstances made this case unusual. All told, Kim met with Donna for thirty-six visits—about fifty-six hours of time—and Kim met with Jamel for fifty-two visits—about seventy-five hours of time.

8. Donna wanted to meet with Jamel's grandmother to let her know that she was not angry with her and that what Jamel did was not her fault. Donna told her that parents cannot be blamed for what their children do. In return, Jamel's grandmother expressed her deep sorrow to Donna about what Jamel did and said that she was sick after she found out that Jamel had raped Donna. Jamel's grandmother told Donna about going to prison to tell Jamel how angry she was and that he had not only hurt himself but he had hurt her too. She thanked Donna for agreeing to meet with her.

NOTES TO CHAPTER 5

1. For an insightful discussion of the enduring legal obstacles to prosecuting rapists, see law professor and prosecutor Andrew E. Taslitz's (1999) book, *Rape and the Culture of the Courtroom,* New York: NYU Press.

2. For instance, see J. McFarlane and A. Malecha (2005), "Sexual Assault among Intimates: Frequency, Consequences, and Treatments," final report submitted to the National Institute of Justice (NCJ 211678); M. L. Sturza and R. Campbell (2005), "An Exploratory Study of Rape Survivors' Prescription Drug Use as a Means of Coping with Sexual Assault," *Psychology of Women Quarterly* 29:353–363; Amy B. Silverman, Helen Z. Reinherz, and Rose M. Giaconia (1996), "The Long-Term Sequelae of Child and Adolescent Abuse: A Longitudinal Community Study," *Child Abuse and Neglect* 20 (8): 709–723; and Judith Herman (1997), *Trauma and Recovery,* New York: Basic Books.

3. See Nicola Gavey's (1999) chapter, "'I Wasn't Raped, but . . .': Revisiting Definitional Problems in Sexual Victimization," in Sharon Lamb, ed., *New Versions of Victims,* 57–81, New York: NYU Press.

4. Reentry research suggests that offenders' release from prison may revive victims' trauma, renew their fears, heighten tensions, and threaten their safety. See Susan Herman and Cressida Wasserman (2001), "A Role for Victims in Offender Reentry," *Crime and Delinquency* 47 (3): 428–445.

5. Andrew Karmen (2007), *Crime Victims: An Introduction to Victimology,* Belmont, CA: Wadsworth; Peggy Tobolowsky (1999), "Victim Participation in the Criminal Justice Process: Fifteen Years after the President's Task Force on Victims of Crime," *New England Journal on Criminal and Civil Confinement* 25:21; Taslitz (1999); and personal correspondence with career prosecutor in Wilmington, Delaware, April 11, 2008.

6. One of the most widespread criminological theories to address a person's attachments to conventional social institutions, such as family and school, is Travis Hirschi's (1969) control theory (*Causes of Delinquency,* Berkeley: University of California Press). For a more general discussion of offenders' motivations for committing crime, see Jack Katz's (1990) book *Seductions of Crime: A Chilling Exploration of the Criminal Mind from Juvenile Delinquency to Cold-Blooded Murder,* New York: Basic Books.

7. Rapists often speak candidly about their motives, including revenge, which is sometimes displaced onto a different person than the one with whom they are angry; see the following books for a discussion of rapists and their rationales or psychology: Timothy Beneke (1983), *Men on Rape: What They Have to Say about Sexual Violence,* New York: St. Martin's; Diana Scully (1990), *Understanding Sexual Violence: A Study of Convicted Rapists,* New York: Routledge; A. Nicholas Groth (1979), *Men Who Rape: The Psychology of the Offender,* New York: Basic Books.

8. For some young men, criminal activity is less instrumental (i.e., to achieve a particular outcome, such as money) than it is expressive. In other words, crime acts as a powerful vehicle through which masculinity and identity can be expressed. See James W. Messerschmidt's work: (2000), *Nine Lives: Adolescent Masculinities, the Body, and Violence,* Boulder, CO: Westview; (1997), *Crime as Structured Action: Gender, Race, Class and Crime in the Making,* Thousand Oaks, CA: Sage; and (1993), *Masculinities and Crime: Critique and Reconceptualization of Theory,* Lanham, MD: Rowman and Littlefield.

9. Criminologist Robert Agnew examines the relationship between strain and delinquency, suggesting that the theoretical concept of strain incorporates much more than simply a disjunction between aspirations and achievements ([1992], "Foundation for a General Strain Theory of Crime and Delinquency," *Criminology* 30:47–87). He identifies other sources of strain, such as the removal of positively valued factors in one's life (e.g., a relationship breakup), the presence of negative stimuli (e.g., child abuse or neglect),

among other things. Not all individuals who experience strain may act out criminally, however; individuals could attempt to minimize the strain, take revenge against those producing the strain, anesthetize themselves with drugs or alcohol to escape the strain, or rely on other coping resources, such as self-esteem or problem-solving skills or positive social support. For earlier studies more focused on relative deprivation, see Robert Merton (1975), *Social Theory and Social Structure,* New York: Free Press; Albert Cohen (1955), *Delinquent Boys,* New York: Free Press; and Walter B. Miller (1958), "Lower Class Culture as a Generating Milieu of Gang Delinquency," *Journal of Social Issues* 14:19.

10. Institutional resistance, as well as resistance from the community at large, is not unusual. Many people believe that victims' involvement can damage outcomes for offenders (see B. Shapiro [1997], "Victims and Vengeance: Why the Victims' Rights Amendment Is a Bad Idea," *Nation,* February 10, p. 264; B. Staples [1997], "When Grieving 'Victims' Can Sway the Courts," *New York Times,* September 22, p. A26). More recent scholarship, however, suggests that victims' involvement can contribute to reentry success for offenders by providing relevant input to decision-makers, offering experience and expertise, and so forth (see Herman and Wasserman [2001]).

11. James felt confused by Allison's continued interest in maintaining a connection with him. Kim assured him that the family was looking for peace but that they also wanted to feel safe. Kim wrote to him, "The main concern for all of them is that you not hurt them or anyone else ever again."

12. See Jeremy Travis (2000), "But They All Come Back: Rethinking Prisoner Reentry," in *Sentencing and Correctional Issues for the 21st Century,* 7, Washington, DC: U.S. Department of Justice, National Institute of Justice.

13. "Megan's Law" is used as a catch-all phrase to refer to statutes that require the mandatory registration and community notification of sexual offenders. Although there are no national standards that guide the application of community notification, states require convicted sex offenders to register their names and residential addresses with local law enforcement agencies upon conviction or release from prison (Michelle L. Meloy [2006], *Sex Offenses and the Men Who Commit Them,* Boston: Northeastern University Press).

14. For discussions of the challenges faced by inmates released from prison, see Craig Haney (2002), "The Psychological Impact of Incarceration: Implications for Post-prison Adjustment," working paper for From Prison to Home conference, Washington, DC: U.S. Department of Health and Human Services and the Urban Institute; see also Dina R. Rose and Todd R. Clear (2002), "Incarceration, Reentry and Social Capital: Social Networks in the Balance," working paper from "From Prison to Home" conference, Washington, DC: U.S. Department of Health and Human Services and the Urban Institute; Michael B. Jackson (2001), *How to Do Good after Prison: A Handbook for the "Committed Man,"* Willingboro, NJ: Joint FX; Marc Mauer and Meda Chesney-Lind, eds. (2002), *Invisible Punishment: The Collateral Consequences of Mass Imprisonment,* New York: New Press; Joan Petersilia and Jeremy Travis, eds. (2001), "From Prison to Society: Managing the Challenges of Prisoner Reentry," special issue of *Crime and Delinquency* 47; Joan Petersilia (2003), *When Prisoners Come Home: Parole and Prisoner Reentry,* New York: Oxford University Press; and Jeremy Travis and Sarah Lawrence (2002), *Beyond the Prison Gates: The State of Parole in America,* research report, Washington, DC: Urban Institute.

1. See the following classic works on battering: Lenore E. Walker (1979), *The Battered Woman*, New York: Harper and Row; Angela Browne (1987), *When Battered Women Kill*, New York: Free Press; Susan Schechter (1982), *Women and Male Violence: The Visions and Struggles of the Battered Women's Movement*, Boston: South End; R. Emerson Dobash and Russell Dobash (1979), *Violence against Wives*, New York: Free Press.

2. See the following scholarly journal articles: Olga W. Barnett, Tomas E. Martinez, and Brendon W. Bluestein (1995), "Jealously and Romantic Attachment in Maritally Violent and Nonviolent Men," *Journal of Interpersonal Violence* 10:473–486; Minna Piipsa (2002), "Complexity of Patterns of Violence against Women in Heterosexual Partnerships," *Violence against Women* 8:873–900; Ruth Fleury, Cris M. Sullivan, and Deborah I. Bybee (2000), "When Ending the Relationship Does Not End the Violence: Women's Experiences of Violence by Former Partners, *Violence against Women* 6:1363–1383.

3. See D. Follingstad, L. Rutledge, B. Berg, E. Hause, and D. Polek (1990), "The Role of Emotional Abuse in Physically Abusive Relationships," *Journal of Family Violence* 5 (2): 107–120; Trudy Mills (1984), "Victimization and Self-Esteem: On Equating Husband Abuse and Wife Abuse," *Victimology* 9:254–261. See also these books written for a lay audience: Beverly Engel (1990), *The Emotionally Abused Woman: Overcoming Destructive Patterns and Reclaiming Yourself*, New York: Ballantine; and Patricia Evans (1996), *The Verbally Abusive Relationship: How to Recognize It and How to Respond*, Holbrook, MA: Adams Media.

4. On the connection between religiosity and domestic violence victimization, see Marie M. Fortune (2001), "Religious Issues and Violence against Women," in Claire M. Renzetti, Jeffrey L. Edleson, and Raquel Kennedy Bergen, eds., *Sourcebook of Violence against Women*, 371–385, Thousand Oaks, CA: Sage.

5. When battered women are employed, abusers often harass them at their workplaces or sabotage their work at home through a variety of methods, such as causing bruises that damage their appearance, disabling the family car, changing their alarm clocks (see research by R. A. Moffit [2002], "From Welfare to Work: What the Evidence Shows," *Welfare Reform and Beyond*, Policy Brief No. 13, Washington, DC: Brookings Institution; and Jody Raphael [1996], "Domestic Violence and Welfare Receipt: Toward a New Feminist Theory of Welfare Dependency," *Harvard Women's Law Journal* 19:201–227). Some domestic violence scholars believe that abusers implicitly know that women with their own economic resources would have the financial means to leave (see R. M. Tolman and J. Raphael [2000], "A Review of Research on Welfare and Domestic Violence," *Journal of Social Issues* 5:667).

6. See Lundy Bancroft and Jay G. Silverman (2002), "Assessing Risk to Children from Batterers," www.smalljustice.com.

7. See Susan L. Miller and Elicka S. L. Peterson (2006), "The Impact of Law Enforcement Policies on Victims of Intimate Partner Violence," in Roslyn Muraskin, ed., *It's a Crime: Women and Justice*, 4th ed., 238–260, Englewood Cliffs, NJ: Prentice-Hall; Eve S. Buzawa and Carl G. Buzawa (2002), *Do Arrests and Restraining Orders Work?* Thousand Oaks, CA: Sage.

8. See Eve S. Buzawa and Carl G. Buzawa (2002), *Domestic Violence: The Criminal Justice Response*, Thousand Oaks, CA: Sage; Lawrence W. Sherman (1992), *Policing Domes-

tic Violence: Experiments and Dilemmas, New York: Free Press; Susan Edwards (1989), *Policing Domestic Violence: Women, the Law and the State,* London: Sage; H. Eigenberg, K. Scarborough, and V. Kappeler (1996), "Contributory Factors Affecting Arrest in Domestic and Non-domestic Assaults," *American Journal of Police* 15:27–54.

9. Although many battered women live in fear of injury or even death at the hands of their abusive partner, research shows that they are not uniformly passive but often act with courage, resistance, and resiliency when the opportunity arises (see Edward W. Gondolf and Ellen R. Fisher [1988], *Battered Women as Survivors,* New York: Lexington; and LeeAnn Hoff [1990], *Battered Women as Survivors,* London: Routledge and Kegan Paul).

10. See Jacquelyn C. Campbell and Karen L. Soeken (1999), "Forced Sex and Intimate Partner Violence," *Violence against Women* 5 (9): 1017–1035; Shannon-Lee Meyer, Dina Vivian, and K. Daniel O'Leary (1998), "Men's Sexual Aggression in Marriage," *Violence against Women* 4:415–435; Lauren R. Taylor with Nicole Gaskin-Laniyan (2007), "Sexual Assault in Abusive Relationships," *NIJ Journal* (National Institute of Justice) 256.

11. See G. Greif and R. Hegar (1993), *When Parents Kidnap,* New York: Free Press; D. Finkelhor, G. Hotaling, A. Sedlak (1990), "Missing, Abducted, Runaway, and Throwaway Children in America, First Report: Numbers and Characteristics, National Incidence Studies," Washington, DC: U.S. Department of Justice, OJJDP; and Amy Neustein and Michael Lesher (2005), *From Madness to Mutiny: Why Mothers Are Running from the Family Courts and What Can Be Done about It,* Boston: Northeastern University Press.

12. Among fathers who commit incest, threats like this are common tactics to scare their children into silence (see both of Judith Herman's books on this subject: [1992], *Trauma and Recovery,* New York: Basic Books; and [1981], *Father-Daughter Incest,* Cambridge, MA: Harvard University Press).

13. A Protection from Abuse order (PFA) is a civil law option that provides a court record of the abuse and stipulates a variety of conditions that must be followed by the abuser, such as staying away from the shared residence, not withdrawing money from the family bank accounts, and so forth; it is unlawful for the offender to violate a PFA, but its efficacy rests on a meaningful police response to violations.

14. According to the Delaware Victims' Bill of Rights, victims have the right to present a victim impact statement pursuant to §4331 of this title (69 Del. Laws, c. 167, §1; 73 Del. Laws, c. 60, §7).

15. In one study, McFarlane and Malecha (2005) found that 20 percent of the women raped in their marriages had rape-related pregnancies as well as an increase in sexually transmitted diseases and more posttraumatic stress disorder (PTSD) symptoms than women in abusive marriages who had not been raped.

16. Although some women who become pregnant as a result of rape feel as Laurie did, others choose not to carry their pregnancies to term. See research by Judith McFarlane for a discussion of how women control their sexuality within the context of abusive relationships: (2007), "Pregnancy Following Partner Rape," *Trauma, Violence, and Abuse* 8 (2): 127–134.

17. Once battered women reestablish a sense of personal efficacy, they are better able to make greater use of coping skills (see studies of resiliency among battered women by Gondolf and Fisher [1988] and Hoff [1990]).

18. Paul planned to tell Laurie about this incident during their face-to-face meeting. He did, in fact, tell her, and she expressed sympathy, but she also said that it did not excuse what he did to others.

19. The phrase "man up" began as a slang term used by young inner-city men to express the need to project a masculine identity (see Y. A. Payne [2006], "A Gangster and a Gentleman: How Street Life–Oriented U.S.-Born African Men Negotiate Issues of Survival in Relation to Their Masculinity," *Men and Masculinities* 8 (3): 288–297.

20. See D. Smith (1976), "The Social Context of Pornography," *Journal of Communications* 26:16–24. For batterers who use pornography and alcohol, as Paul did, the probability of a battered woman being sexually abused increases significantly. See Laurie Hinson Shope (2004), "When Words Are Not Enough: The Search for the Effect of Pornography on Abused Women," *Violence against Women* 10 (1): 56–72.

21. See Michelle L. Meloy (2006) and Scully (1990).

22. Anger often is the subtext in rapists' descriptions of their motivation. See Timothy Beneke (1983), *Men on Rape: What They Have to Say about Sexual Violence,* New York: St. Martin's; Diana Scully and Joseph Marolla (1985), "Riding the Bull at Gilley's: Convicted Rapists Describe the Rewards of Rape," *Social Problems* 32 (3): 251–263.

23. For some men who rape, the act is a symbolic opportunity to assert dominance over someone who has less power, in the way that one rapist describes: "Rape was a feeling of total dominance. Before the rapes, I would always get a feeling of power and anger. I would degrade women so I could feel there was a person of less worth than me" (Scully and Marolla [1985], 254). Many rapists also derive sexual satisfaction from the terror they inflict on their victims (see Beneke [1983]).

24. This is what Paul described in his interview with me; several years earlier, in his written description of the crime that was part of the VVH preparation process, he described his reason for not using the knife a little differently: "She started crying and as I looked down at Laurie, and I seen the hurt, and the pain. I said to her, 'You are not worth it,' and I got up." Yet another version came out during the dialogue. Laurie asked him if he was serious when he had the knife in his hand and told her that he was going to kill her. When Paul replied, "No," Laurie asked him to tell her why he threatened her life. Paul explained, "I felt less of a man. You were going to leave. I wanted to scare you and hold you at the same time."

25. The child-molestation charges were nolle prossed as part of the plea agreement.

26. Recent criminological research suggests that religious participation and beliefs can serve as a catalyst for offenders to transform their deviant identities and behavior (P. Giordano, M. A. Longmore, R. D. Schroeder, and P. M. Seffrin [2008], "A Life-Course Perspective on Spirituality and Desistance from Crime," *Criminology* 46 [1]: 99–132); however, it is unclear if the change is related to religious attendance, which could reflect increased prosocial opportunities and social support for offenders (and ex-offenders) or to the strengthened role of spiritual beliefs.

27. Although Paul never said this to me during our interview, he stated repeatedly to Kim that he felt that reconciliation between him and Laurie was possible in the future, although he understood that it was not the case that Laurie was coming to the prison to forgive him and then everything would be "okay" between them.

28. During the dialogue, Paul asked Laurie if she would accept some money from him each month to be used for the children. She agreed, and they signed paperwork in November 2002; Paul made his first restitution payment in January 2004 (twenty-five dollars). He never made another payment.

29. The court received letters from both of these friends in 2002, offering their support for Paul's early release because of his close connection to God and religion. Both individuals belonged to the same parish and frequently visited with Paul and attended his choir events. One of these friends has since passed away. The other friend wrote at some length about securing a trailer home for Paul to rent or buy upon his release, and he offered to help Paul find employment. This attempt to reduce Paul's sentence was unsuccessful. The status of these friendships and plans today is unclear.

30. Paul was released under the supervision of the Department of Corrections Probation and Parole in mid-2010.

NOTES TO CHAPTER 7

1. For research related to child molesters and cognitive distortions about victim harm, see W. L. Marshall, K. Hamilton, and Y. Fernandez (2001), "Empathy Deficits and Cognitive Distortions in Child Molesters," *Sexual Abuse: A Journal of Research and Treatment* 13 (2): 123–130.

2. Acquiescing to an adult's sexual demands never means that children's participation is willing or desired. Some children comply out of fear, since adult abusers try to make the sexual activity seem normal while simultaneously intimidating them with threats about what might happen to them or their family if they tell anyone about the abuse. Other children may participate because the attention—even this kind of inappropriate attention—may be the only kind of affection they receive from powerful adult caregivers in their lives (see Florence Rush [1980], *The Best-Kept Secret: Sexual Child Abuse of Children,* New York: McGraw-Hill; Herman [1981]; Groth [1979]).

3. See Rush (1980); Herman (1981). Research also reveals that often the general public assumes that in cases of incest, the entire family is dysfunctional and the mother must be blameworthy if she knows on some level what is going on and does not intervene and/or is in denial of the situation (T. Trepper and M. J. Barrett, eds. [1986], *Treating Incest: A Multiple Systems Perspective,* New York: Haworth).

4. T. Toray, C. Coughlin, S. Vuchinich, and P. Patricelli (1991), "Gender Differences Associated with Adolescent Substance Abuse: Comparisons and Implications for Treatment," *Family Relations* 49 (3): 338–344.

5. Melissa attributes her mother's unwavering belief in her as a crucial help in moving forward. Despite the loving support she received from her mother, brother, and other friends and family members, Melissa continued to feel much pain and guilt over the decision to disclose the abuse because of the ripple effect on her family. It is never easy for a child to send a parent to prison, even one who has committed despicable acts.

6. See both of Judith Herman's books on this subject: (1992), *Trauma and Recovery,* New York: Basic Books; and (1981), *Father-Daughter Incest,* Cambridge, MA: Harvard University Press.

7. Steven was released under the supervision of the Department of Corrections Probation and Parole in mid-2010.

8. Melissa remains convinced that she might not have been her father's only victim. Her mother told her that during her parents' first marriage, Steven visited brothels while stationed in Japan with the army. Children as young as ten or eleven years old were part of the prostitution market there. When her father came home from his tour of duty, he told her mother to get checked for sexually transmitted diseases (fortunately, he did not infect her).

9. See Meloy (2006) and Scully (1990).

10. Research reveals that most child sexual abuse begins with "innocent" activities such as bathing a child, tickling, or play wrestling; often these interactions work to gain the trust of the child and "normalize" adult-to-child touching (see John Crewdson [1988], *By Silence Betrayed: Sexual Abuse of Children in America,* Boston: Little, Brown).

11. See Scully (1990).

12. See Rush (1980); Katherine Brady (1979), *Father's Days: A True Story of Incest,* New York: Dell; Joanne Belknap (2001), *The Invisible Woman: Gender, Crime, and Justice,* Belmont, CA: Wadsworth.

13. Despite Steven's understanding of his comment, Melissa struggled with the anguish and pain it caused her for years; in fact, it became a key question that she wanted Steven to answer during their face-to-face meeting.

14. See Anna Salter (2003), *Predators: Pedophiles, Rapists, and Other Sex Offenders,* New York: Basic Books.

NOTES TO CHAPTER 8

1. It is traumatic for children to tell on a family member when abuse occurs because they may be conflicted, they may fear that their claim will be disbelieved or minimized (a fear created or reinforced by the perpetrator), and they may be manipulated through rewards and incentives. Victims also experience considerable shame and guilt, and they may be afraid of losing another family member's love (see Denise Kindschi Gosselin [2003], *Heavy Hands: An Introduction to the Crimes of Family Violence,* 2nd ed., Upper Saddle River, NJ: Prentice Hall). Research shows that children often delay disclosure until they are older (if they do disclose) because of the trauma involved as well as their socialization to obey adults and to fear social rejection and their fear of the criminal justice system (see Eli Somer and Sharona Szwarcberg [2001], "Variables in Delayed Disclosure of Child Sexual Abuse," *American Journal of Orthopsychiatry* 71:332–341).

2. For more information about SANE nurses, see the website of the International Association of Forensic Nurses www.iafn.org. And for research that demonstrates that SANE nurses not only improve the quality of forensics evidence collections but also provide help that benefits rape survivors' psychological well-being, see Rebecca Campbell (2004), "The Effectiveness of Sexual Assault Nurse Examiner (SANE) Programs," November, http://www.vawnet.org/category/Documents.php?docid=417&category_id=305.

3. Typically, child sexual abuse begins under "innocent" circumstances, such as tickling or bathing a child, but then progresses to more serious forms of noncontact sexual victimization and contact sexual abuse.

4. Making the victimization public is painful for sexually abused victims, an ordeal which is exacerbated for children since they are not exempt from defense tactics that are often abrasive and victim blaming (for a general discussion of obstacles related to fair, respectful, and effective prosecutions of sexual assault/rape cases, see Taslitz [1999]).

5. Another woman's testimony reinforced the veracity of the girls' story. She was an adult friend of the family who stepped forward and claimed that she was in the car with Bruce once, and he had reached over and touched her.

6. Kim assists any victim fully, regardless of religious affiliation or faith, and the program follows a secular design. For some victims, however, faith or religion plays a key role

in their determination to meet their offender and offers strength and comfort during the process (for more about faith, forgiveness, and restorative justice issues, see chapter 4).

7. Salter (2003).

8. See Rush (1980); Herman (1981).

NOTES TO CHAPTER 9

1. Research reveals that people in their late teens and early to midtwenties tend to drink most heavily (National Institute on Alcohol Abuse and Alcoholism [NIAAA], National Institutes of Health, April 2006), and these risky behaviors contribute to tragic consequences if these young people get behind the wheel of a car. Of the approximately five thousand people under the age of twenty-one who die as a result of underage drinking each year, about nineteen hundred deaths result from motor-vehicle crashes (NIAAA, January 2006). All states have a blood-alcohol concentration (BAC) limit of 0.08 percent for adult drivers and a BAC of zero for youth under age twenty-one (NIAAA, April 2006). At the time of the crash that killed Cameron, the nineteen-year-old driver, Jenny, had a BAC of 0.14.

2. Leigh recalled this time period when she spoke to my class in March 2008 and told my students that she had never felt such anger and hatred: "I could have pummeled her. I didn't think I could have so much hate. It wasn't until later when I realized that that hate would eat me alive. It was wasting my life. She already took my son. I can't let her hurt the rest of my family."

3. Research reveals that drinking alcohol is widespread among adolescents, with nationwide surveys showing that three-fourths of twelfth graders, more than two-thirds of tenth graders, and about two in every five eighth graders have consumed alcohol (NIAAA, January 2006). When binge drinking is examined (with binge drinking defined as heavy episodic drinking within the past two weeks that brings BAC to 0.8 percent or above), the national statistics indicate that this occurs with 11 percent of eighth graders, 22 percent of tenth graders, and 29 percent of twelfth graders (L. D. Johnston, P. M. O'Malley, J. G. Bachman, and J. E. Schulenberg [2006], *Monitoring the Future: National Survey Results on Drug Use, 1975–2005; Volume I, Secondary School Students,* NIH Publication No. 06-5883, Bethesda, MD: National Institute on Drug Abuse]).

4. Kim and Debbie approach life differently with regard to faith: Kim describes herself as a Christian and religious, and Debbie embraces a more general spirituality rather than an organized religion. Discussions of a victim's or offender's religious beliefs do not enter into the VVH process, however, except as one general question in a group of questions that asks participants how the crime affected them on different levels, including emotional, financial, physical, and spiritual. Both Kim and Debbie try to meet victims and offenders "where they are," so if they have a more religious way of understanding their social worlds, that is fine; but if the participants do not want to address religion, faith, or spirituality, there is nothing in the VVH program (preparation, dialogue) that necessitates a religious focus.

5. Jenny was required to pay restitution to cover costs such as Cameron's burial clothing and the family's counseling fees up until the date of the sentencing. She fulfilled her obligation, paying in small installments until it was completed.

6. In Jenny's VVH paperwork, she mentioned that she never looked at Leigh during the sentencing because looking at her would have caused too much fear. Jenny indicated that she would really "see" Leigh at the dialogue and not shrink away.

7. In Jenny's paperwork, she also promised that she would try to impress on others the dangers of drinking and driving and that she would pay as much as she could afford monthly toward the restitution she owed.

8. In fact, Cameron's family sued the bar that served Jenny so many drinks the night of the crash. Although they won a settlement of over a million dollars, the bar owner filed for bankruptcy, so the amount of the judgment was moot. However, Leigh is relieved that the settlement completed the circle required by the law, so if this should happen again, any bar could be held responsible for serving alcohol to a minor and for serving alcohol to a person who is intoxicated. Leigh contends, "This was the entire point of the lawsuit for me—to complete that circle."

NOTES TO CHAPTER 10

1. Julie's grandmother and grandfather were alcoholics, and a drunk driver had also killed her uncle. Kevin, the offender, also had an uncle who was killed by a drunk driver.

2. Deaths resulting from alcohol-related crashes account for approximately 33 percent of the total number of traffic fatalities (National Highway Traffic Safety Administration [2008], "Statistical Analysis of Alcohol Related Driving Tends, 1982–2005," Technical Report HS 810 942, Washington, DC: NHTSA). National Highway Traffic Safety Administration statistics report that 13,470 people died in alcohol-related motor-vehicle/ motorcycle crashes in 2006 (www.nhtsa.gov). The financial costs of these crashes are staggering for all citizens: research demonstrates that alcohol-related crashes cost the public over fifty billion dollars annually (see L. Blincoe, A. Seay, E. Zaloshnja, et al. [2002], "The Economic Impact of Motor Vehicle Crashes, 2000," NHTSA Technical Report HS 809 446, Washington, DC: NHTSA, http://www.nhtsa.gov/DOT/NHTSA/ Communication%20&%20Consumer%20Information/Articles/Associated%20Files/Econ-omicImpact2000.pdf). But these numbers do not begin to capture the immeasurable loss and grief associated with such preventable deaths.

3. For many victims/survivors of drunk-driving crashes, memorial signs placed at the roadside where the deaths occurred serve as important symbols that provide remembrance and comfort while displaying a public message. At least one judge (in Texas) requires some offenders to dig the holes for the markers if the families agree (J. H. Lord [1998], "Sacred Spaces," http://www.madd.org/victims/2471).

4. The court mandated an alcohol-abuse program, but Kevin's attendance and behavior were not monitored. Kevin looks back at that time now, understanding how much help he desperately needed, and wishes there had been more meaningful support in place (and consequences for noncompliance), similar to the weekly Alcoholics Anonymous meetings he attends now in prison.

NOTES TO CHAPTER 11

1. See Edward H. Fischer and J. W. Goethe (1998), "Anxiety and Alcohol Abuse in Patients in Treatment for Depression," *American Journal of Drug and Alcohol Use* 24 (3): 453–463.

2. In the 1970s, far less was known about the connection between depression and alcoholism. Wayne, the offender, also came from a family with members who suffered from alcoholism. His father was an alcoholic, and Wayne abused alcohol as well. Although

Wayne's first enlistment in the U.S. Marines ended in an honorable discharge, when he reenlisted, he was discharged because of his excessive drinking and fighting.

3. In Delaware, a Board of Pardons exists separately from a parole board. The Board of Pardons is an entity that has the authority to recommend cases to the governor for or against pardons, reprieves, commutations of sentence, and executive clemency. The governor is not bound to accept the board's recommendations but cannot grant a pardon or commutation without a recommendation from the board. A pardon does not remove the conviction record but just adds to the record that a pardon has been granted. A recent review of the past sixteen years of requests reveals that most prisoners serving time for violent crimes such as murder, rape, or robbery are denied by the Board of Pardons; only about 21 percent of the 265 requests were recommended for approval. For the 126 murder cases considered by the board, three pardons and eighteen commutations were recommended; only twelve have been granted—and only one of these cases was a first-degree murder. See Esteban Parra (2008), "Many Find Second Chance in Delaware Board of Pardons," *News Journal,* June 7, A1–2.

4. As in most states, at the time of Judy's murder, it was common for cases to be resolved with little or no contact between a prosecutor and the victim/survivor. Starting around 1985, the then attorney general in Delaware required all prosecutors to confer with victims before resolving their cases. Today, pretrial prosecutor-victim contact is part of the culture, mandated by policy of the attorney general's office and the Delaware Victims' Bill of Rights, which was enacted in 1992 (personal correspondence with a deputy attorney general, Delaware Department of Justice, April 11, 2008).

5. Within about a month of Kathleen's first contact with VVH, Kim also obtained a photo of Wayne (requested by Kathleen), talked to Wayne's counselor in prison to see what programs he had completed, discovered that he had never filed with the Board of Pardons, and arranged for the Department of Corrections to put a no-contact order into Wayne and Kathleen's brother's files so that they will not be incarcerated in the same institution.

6. Quotation from the trial transcript; case citation omitted to preserve anonymity. The medical examiner's testimony included a statement that although the consequences of the blow to Judy's head would have been the same regardless of the level of alcohol in her system, Judy probably did not perceive the pain as much because "as a result of the trauma, she'd go into shock because already there is some suppression of some centers of the brain, and if there is a trauma added to it, that individual may become unconscious much faster than someone who does not have any alcohol" (from the trial transcript). However, in Judy's case, the medical examiner believed that death was instantaneous because of the blow made by the heavy rock to her head.

7. From the trial transcript.

8. Wayne was kicked out of high school when he was sixteen years old. Soon after, he enlisted in the military and got married. The marriage ended when he was discharged from the military; he ultimately married two more times. Wayne says that his drinking and anger contributed to the failures of all three of his marriages.

9. One of Wayne's activities that impresses Kathleen the most is his construction of crosses for a victim's memorial. She feels that this demonstrates his growth in understanding victims' needs, and she likes that something positive came out of her mother's murder. She does not want Wayne to forget what he did, but she hopes that a better understanding of what put him in prison in the first place could help him to guide the paths of young offenders with whom he comes into contact in prison groups.

10. Since Wayne stopped drinking fifteen years ago, only once has he violated disciplinary policy while incarcerated. This incident involved his refusal to accept Christmas packages from a Salvation Army volunteer because he does not celebrate holidays out of respect for Judy. A guard insisted, which angered Wayne. His vocal and vehement refusal resulted in a write-up with sanctions.

11. According to a 2009 newspaper article, Wayne's daughter has reestablished contact with him (Esteban Parra [2009], "Confronting Offenders Lifts Burden for Some Victims," *News Journal,* April 26, 1).

12. The VVH program is victim initiated, however. Starting in 2008, offenders who wish to write a letter of responsibility and apology to their victims will be able to do so through a Letter Bank; more details are provided in chapter 14 of this book.

13. Their dialogue has since taken place; see chapter 13.

NOTES TO CHAPTER 12

1. The notoriety attached to this case is one reason the victim's son gave for his unwillingness to consent to an interview with me.

2. Research demonstrates that prior victimization experienced in childhood is often correlated with adult violence. See Kimberly A. DuMont, Cathy Spatz Widom, and Sally J. Czaja (2007), "Predictors of Resilience in Abused and Neglected Children Grown-Up: The Role of Individual and Neighborhood Characteristics," *Child Abuse and Neglect* 31 (3): 255–274; Abigail A. Fagan (2005), "The Relationship between Adolescent Physical Abuse and Criminal Offending: Support for an Enduring and Generalized Cycle of Violence," *Journal of Family Violence* 20 (5): 279–290.

3. Chris wrote about this story on a website, advertised by an organization (in another state) that offers an Internet mail service for a sixty-five-dollar fee. Since inmates have no access to email, they can rent an email address that someone else monitors and then sends any email the prisoner receives through postal mail to the prisoner. Chris used this service to construct a request for an advocate/lawyer to help him with his case. After Kim explained that the webpage offended his victim's family members, Chris took it down without hesitation.

4. The case attracted considerable attention around the state. The defense engaged expert witnesses who provided testimony on domestic violence drawing on their academic scholarship. On the basis of hospital documentation and affidavits from people who witnessed Greg's abuse, the state's Coalition Against Domestic Violence and other progressive justice-oriented programs support Andrea's version of her abusive relationship with Greg.

5. Andrea also received a sentence of natural life plus three years for conspiracy to commit murder. Chris received life plus five additional years for the use of a weapon and three for the conspiracy. Several years ago, the state permitted Andrea to transfer to an Arizona prison to serve out her time, because her daughter lives in Texas and she wanted to be closer to her daughter. In July 2010, the Delaware Board of Pardons recommended that the governor commute Andrea's sentence to a simple life term that would permit the possibility of parole; the governor has not announced his decision yet (Esteban Parra [2010], "Board Recommends Chance at Parole for Woman Who Killed Husband," *News Journal,* July 3, A1–2.

6. Chris's defense attorneys put on a vigorous defense, including entering an insanity plea.

7. In the court records, there is testimony from Andrea's co-workers and social workers with whom she met of Greg's sadistic abuse toward her. The divorce papers filed by Greg's first wife also mention physical and emotional abuse.

8. Chris was unable to attend her funeral since it was out of state.

9. Chris thinks that his brother, as a police officer, might struggle with his murder conviction. Chris told his brother about the VVH program, "and he really didn't say too much; he just said he thought it was good. And then, after the mediation took place, I wrote to him and told him that Brett O'Neil, the victim's son, had forgiven me and everything, and he hasn't responded to that letter yet."

10. Access to Pell grants for inmates was ended by Congress in 1994.

11. Chris wrote in his paperwork, "No one needs to fear for their safety around me. I am harmless. I have met bad people in prison, and I have been threatened by men I dislike, but I have hurt no one."

12. His case before the pardon board was denied on numerous grounds, including the short duration of time served, the serious nature of the offense, opposition by the state, opposition by the victim's family, opposition by the state police, and lack of support from the parole board.

13. All offenders are allowed to bring a support person with them, but the person Chris wanted to invite was deemed inappropriate. Kim and the correctional institution retain ultimate control over the presence of support persons because they have to consider larger issues related to institutional security, harm to victims, and so forth. Chris's support network today consists only of his brother, even though he has only visited Chris once in the last twenty-eight years.

14. In another dialogue that occurred in 2008, the offender only agreed to meet with the victim/survivor but refused to seek or continue any further contact after the dialogue. Kim respects these wishes and does not pursue further agreements from the parties, even if a no-contact order is not in place.

NOTES TO CHAPTER 13

1. See Kathleen Daly (2002), "Restorative Justice: The Real Story," *Punishment and Society* 4:55.

2. See both Daly (2002) and Acorn (2004) for a more detailed discussion of these different justice models.

3. Kathleen Daly (2006), "The Limits of Restorative Justice," in Dennis Sullivan and Larry Tifft, eds., *Handbook of Restorative Justice: A Global Perspective*, New York: Routledge, 134; A. Cretney and G. Davis (1995), *Punishing Violence*, London: Routledge, 178. Kathy Daly and Russ Immarigeon argue convincingly that by polarizing the concepts of the retributive and restorative justice models, it impedes an important discussion of the possible merits of each and how they could operate alongside each other. They suggest that "oppositional caricatures of justice models" place "everything in the 'retributive' column as nasty and brutish, whereas everything in the 'restorative' column seems nice and progressive," yet in reality, retributivist justifications for punishment entail proportionate responses to harm that could emerge as restitution and/or community service, rather than as revenge ([1998], "The Past, Present, and Future of Restorative Justice: Some Critical Reflections," *Contemporary Justice Review* 1:32–33).

4. O'Hara (2006), 134–135.

5. Zehr (2002), 71.

6. M. K. Harris writes that empowerment is most likely to occur in situations absent of domination and control so that individuals have greater opportunities for reflection, choice, and action. It is intuitive that people who feel powerless, such as inmates, may react with anger, fear, and aggression ([2004], "An Expansive Transformative View of Restorative Justice," *Contemporary Justice Review* 7 [1]: 134). Once individuals—victims and offenders—feel that they are in control of their lives and able to deal effectively with difficulties, then empowerment can be transformative. Certainly for the victims portrayed in this book, empowerment involved restoring a sense of self-determination, self-worth, and personal security. This transformation was also seen with offenders, who developed empathy and compassion for their victims through the VVH program, which encouraged "them to gain wisdom and strength in making choices and taking actions"—key components of empowerment (ibid.).

7. Harris (2004, 133) views empathy as an extension of a personal capacity to have compassion for another person to include a broader recognition of the need to restructure social and political institutions to be more responsive to other human beings. In the VVH program, both victims and offenders engaged in empathy, not just in their preparation exercise that asked them to put themselves in the other's shoes but also in how they responded to each other at the dialogue and in their ability to understand the other person's life.

8. See Estrich (1988) and Taslitz (1999).

9. In 2008, an offender who does not appear in this book tried to use his participation in the VVH program to his advantage at a parole hearing and was reprimanded for that attempt.

10. See Paul A. Miler and Nancy Eisenberg (1988), "The Relation of Empathy to Aggressive and Externalizing/Antisocial Behavior," *American Psychological Association* 103 (3): 324–344; M. S. Umbreit, R. B. Coates, and A. Roberts (2000), "Impact of Victim-Offender Mediation: A Cross-National Perspective," *Mediation Quarterly* 17 (3): 215–226; Nancy Weinberg (1995), "Does Apologizing Help? The Role of Self-Blame and Making Amends in Recovery from Bereavement," *Health and Social Work* 20 (4): 194–300.

11. See Cathy Spatz Widom (2000), "Motivation and Mechanisms in the 'Cycle of Violence,'" in David H. Hansen, ed., *Motivation and Child Maltreatment*, 1–38, Lincoln: University of Nebraska Press; Diane English, Cathy Spatz Widom, and Carol Brandford (2001), *Childhood Victimization and Delinquency, Adult Criminality, and Violent Criminal Behavior*, Final Report, NCJ 19221, Washington, DC: National Institute of Justice.

12. For example, research finds that when police act fairly when arresting domestic-assault suspects, suspects' rearrest rates were suppressed and similar to those suspects who experienced more favorable outcomes (Raymond Paternoster, Robert Brame, Ronet Bachman, and Lawrence W. Sherman [1997], "Do Fair Procedures Matter? The Effect of Procedural Justice on Spouse Abuse," *Law and Society Review* 31 [1]: 163–204; see also work by Tyler and colleagues that finds that if citizens view legal processes and procedures as fair, both positive and negative legal outcomes will be viewed as acceptable: Tom R. Tyler [1990], *Why Do People Obey the Law?* New Haven, CT: Yale University Press; Tom R. Tyler, Robert J. Boeckmann, Heather J. Smith, and Yuen J. Huo [1997], *Social Justice in*

a Diverse Society, Boulder, CO: Westview). Kathleen Daly (2006) contends that victims perceived high levels of fairness, or procedural justice, in restorative justice studies in Australia, New Zealand, and England, which is attributed mostly to their active engagement with fashioning case outcomes rather than to evidence of restorativeness.

13. In Umbreit and colleagues' (2003) work with victims of severe violence in Texas and Ohio, victims also reported the desire to have facilitators who are able to "connect deeply" and that they "would like to be in the hands of highly competent mediators who take time to get to know them, who listen profoundly, who validate their feelings and experience, who help them identify what they want to accomplish, and who then step out of the way during the actual dialogue, so that participants themselves can own the process" (335).

14. See Umbreit et al. (2003).

15. Cook and Powell raise possible negative implications for a more bureaucratized restorative justice program in that offenders' expression of remorse, regret, and apology might become more utilitarian than sincere if emotion is constructed more as a "product wheeled out to suit stage-managed circumstances" (Kimberly J. Cook and Chris Powell [2006], "Emotionality, Rationality and Restorative Justice," in Walter S. DeKeseredy and Barbara Perry, eds., *Advancing Critical Criminology: Theory and Application,* 83–100, New York: Lexington, 93). Similarly, greater involvement by community representatives or criminal justice system professionals could "steal" the events from the participants if the "events, outcomes, and process are 'owned' by the state" (ibid., 94). Bureaucratic demands might necessitate keeping the numbers up and the case-involvement time down—as is the case in south Australia—which could result in higher frustration and dissatisfaction from victims (and offenders) and place limits on the program's accomplishments. S. Williams also describes the dangers of succumbing to administrative demands that create assembly-line justice, even though it may be less expensive and more inclusive (S. Williams [1988], "Modernity and the Emotions: Corporeal Reflections on the (Ir) rational," *Sociology* 32:747–769). At the same time, however, Daly (2006) asserts that most RJ practices do not exist outside of the established formal justice system because police or courts still decide how to handle or refer a case.

16. Beth Richie ([2001], "Challenges Incarcerated Women Face as They Return to Their Communities: Findings from Life History Interviews," *Crime and Delinquency* 47 [3]: 370); Petersilia (2003), and others document the profound effects of imprisonment on offenders who leave prison with substance-abuse and mental-health issues inadequately addressed, with little or no family and community support and with few options for housing and employment. These consequences are compounded by the stigma of being an ex-offender and the cumulative effects of new laws and restrictions that hinder successful reentry while services are reduced, inevitably leading to rearrest (see Kamala Mallik-Kane and Christy A. Visher [2008], *Health and Prisoner Reentry: How Physical, Mental, and Substance Abuse Conditions Shape the Process of Reintegration,* Washington, DC: Urban Institute; Jeremy Travis [2005], *But They All Come Back: Facing the Challenges of Prisoner Reentry,* Washington, DC: Urban Institute).

17. Victims' valuing the passage of time in order for the dialogue process to succeed is consistent with Umbreit et al.'s (2003) research with victims of severe violence who participated in RJ dialogues in Texas and Ohio.

1. See Daly (2002); see also John Braithwaite (2007), "Encourage Restorative Justice," *Criminology and Public Policy* 6 (4): 689–696.

2. See Nils Christie (1977), "Conflicts as Property," *British Journal of Criminology* 17:1–15.

3. For instance, see Robert Elias (1993), *Victims Still: The Political Manipulation of Crime Victims,* Newbury Park, CA: Sage.

4. For example, see E. Villmoare and V. Neto (1987), *NIJ Research in Brief: Victim Appearances at Sentencing under California's Victims' Bill of Rights,* NCJ 106774, Washington, DC: U.S. Department of Justice; R. Davis, N. Henderson, and C. Rabbitt (2002), *Effects of State Victim Rights Legislation on Local Criminal Justice Systems,* New York: Vera Institute of Justice.

5. See Tobolowsky (1999).

6. J. Brienza (1999), "Crime Victims' Laws Sometimes Ignored," *Trial* 35:103–105; National Center for Victims of Crime (1999), "The NCVC Does Not Support the Current Language of the Proposed Crime Victims' Rights Constitutional Amendment," Arlington, VA: NCVC.

7. See Heather Strang (2002), *Repair or Revenge: Victims and Restorative Justice,* Oxford, UK: Clarendon.

8. See Braithwaite and Strang (2002).

9. The two exceptions were Jenny's sad and untimely death, and James, from whom I received no follow-up response. James has been released from prison, so I mailed him a letter using an address provided by his probation officer. He indicated his willingness to participate to Kim, but I did not receive responses to the written questions I sent him.

10. Melissa discovered this fact after Kim contacted all the victims to provide information about a new service called VINE (Victim Information and Notification Everyday), an Internet website sponsored by the National Victim Notification Service and currently available in forty-two states. It permits victims to verify release dates and obtain other up-to-date and reliable information about criminal cases and the custody status of offenders twenty-four hours a day (www.vinelink.com). In 2009, VINE notified Kim that her daughter's murderer was transferred to a prison in an adjoining state.

11. Melissa's wish came to fruition in early 2009 when Kim asked her if she could share her experiences and offer support to another victim of child abuse and incest who was in the process of going through the VVH program. Melissa spent a great deal of time talking with the victim, the victim took strength from her empathy and resiliency, and the dialogue occurred in spring 2009.

12. In spring 2009, through VVH, Kathleen received a letter from an inmate who heard her presentation at the prison. He was very moved by her talk, and it motivated him to write a letter to his own victim using the Apology Letter Bank (see note 13 and accompanying text).

13. Letters are screened for appropriateness before being placed in the bank. Criteria for rejection include offering excuses for a crime or requesting forgiveness from the victim.

14. See Daly (2002).

15. For examples of such programs, see James Ptacek's book: (2009), *Restorative Justice and Violence against Women,* New York: Oxford University Press.

16. Poor women, women of color, and lesbians are less likely to have their cases taken seriously by the criminal justice system, so restorative justice programs have the potential to mediate these effects (C. Q. Hopkins and M. P. Koss [2005], "Incorporating Feminist Theory and Insights into a Restorative Justice Response to Sex Offenses," *Violence against Women* 11 (5): 693–723). Such programs should be crafted with an eye to understanding how the experiences of these and other excluded groups may not be served by the traditional justice system or by existing restorative justice practices.

17. Sharon Lamb (1996), *The Trouble with Blame: Victims, Perpetrators, and Responsibility,* Cambridge, MA: Harvard University Press, 161.

18. For incest victims (and also for other victims of violence committed by a family member or an intimate partner), Sharon Lamb (1996) believes that forgiveness and empathy should never be expected.

NOTES TO APPENDIX A

1. T. Marshall (2003), "Restorative Justice: An Overview," in Gerry Johnstone, ed., *A Restorative Justice Reader,* 28–45, Cullompton, UK: Willan; see also S. Curtis-Fawley and K. Daly (2005), "Gendered Violence and Restorative Justice: The Views of Victim Advocates," *Violence against Women* 11 (5): 603–638.

2. For a provocative discussion about the use of care, feminist theory, and reintegrative shaming into a relational justice approach, see Guy Masters and David Smith (1998), "Portia and Persephone Revisited: Thinking about Feeling in Criminal Justice," *Theoretical Criminology* 2 (1): 5–27. Drawing on moral development work by Carol Gilligan (1982), Masters and Smith explore how concern about and inclusion of victims in restorative justice practices and the reintegration of remorseful offenders who understand and account for their actions, as described in John Braithwaite's reintegrative shaming theory ([1989], *Crime, Shame and Reintegration,* Cambridge: Cambridge University Press), combine to form relational justice. Similarly, restorative justice is relational and contextual, elevating victims' voices and experiences (as well as offenders') to the center of the process. See also Llewellyn's work on institutionalizing a comprehensive restorative justice program in Canada that connects these relational justice visions (Bruce Archibald and Jennifer Llewellyn [2006], "The Challenges of Institutionalizing Comprehensive Restorative Justice: Theory and Practice in Nova Scotia," *Dalhousie Law Journal* 29:297–343; see also J. Llewellyn and R. House [1998], *Restorative Justice—A Conceptual Framework,* Ottawa: Law Commission of Canada, 1–107).

3. VOM and victim-offender dialogue (VOD) typically use a facilitator who mediates between a victim and an offender in a face-to-face meeting, with support people (such as a family member or friend) present for victims and/or offenders; conferencing (often called group or family or community groups) follows a similar routine as VOM/VOD except that it includes a greater number of support persons, ranging from six to ten, often from the community; circles (often called peacemaking or sentencing or repair of harm circles) are fashioned after the conferencing models in that they include a larger number and different types of participants to support the victim and/or offender. Circles use a "talking piece" that is passed around to designate a speaker's turn; other kinds of RJ dialogue includes reparative boards and community-based programs that bring together victims and offenders in some fashion to develop a response to the crime (G. Bazemore and M. S. Umbreit [2001], "A Comparison of Four Restorative Conferencing Models,"

Juvenile Justice Bulletin, February, Washington, DC: U.S. Department of Justice, Office of Juvenile Justice and Delinquency Prevention).

4. L. Kurki (2000), "Restorative and Community Justice in the United States," in M. Tonry, ed., *Crime and Justice: A Review of Research,* 235–303, Chicago: University of Chicago Press.

5. The American focus on less serious offending contrasts sharply with the practice in other countries. In 1995, Germany used mediation with about 70 percent of crimes of violence committed by both adults and juveniles; it resolved about six thousand juvenile and three thousand adult cases in 1996. Family group conferences in New Zealand involve all youth crimes except murder and homicide. Austria's RJ programs handled 73 percent of adult crimes of violence and 43 percent of juvenile ones in 1997, and in that same year, Austria resolved over twenty-seven hundred juvenile and thirty-four hundred adult cases by victim-offender mediation (M. Kilchling and M. Loschnig-Gspandl [2000], "Legal and Practice Perspectives on Victim/Offender Mediation in Austria and Germany," *International Review of Victimology* 7:305–332). Only circle sentencing that takes place in New Zealand and South Australia uses RJ routinely in cases of juvenile sexual assault. Daly ([2006], "Restorative Justice and Sexual Assault: An Archival Study of Court and Conference Cases," *British Journal of Criminology* 46:334–356) examined close to four hundred cases of sexual violence in a diversionary program for a study that compared conferencing with formal court and found that more youth who went through the RJ-based conferencing were required to attend adolescent sex-offending counseling, which was associated with lower recidivism, whereas almost half the court cases were dismissed.

6. See Kurki (2000).

7. M. S. Umbreit and J. Greenwood (1999), "National Survey of VOM Programs in the U.S.," *Mediation Quarterly* 16:235–251.

8. Some programs allow offenders to choose not to deny their guilt, rather than admitting guilt, similar to a "no contest" plea in formal criminal justice proceedings.

9. Umbreit and Greenwood (1999).

10. M. Umbreit (1994), "Victim Empowerment through Mediation: The Impact of Victim Offender Mediation in Four Cities," special issue of *Perspectives* (American Probation and Parole Association), 25–28.

11. Ibid.

12. Jeff Latimer, Craig Dowden, and Danielle Muise (2005), "The Effectiveness of Restorative Justice Practices: A Meta-Analysis," *Prison Journal* 85 (2): 127–144; Strang (2002); Umbreit et al. (2003).

13. K. De Bues and Nancy Rodriguez (2007), "Restorative Justice Practice: An Examination of Program Completion and Recidivism," *Journal of Criminal Justice* 35 (3): 337–347; Nancy Rodriguez (2005), "Restorative Justice at Work: Examining the Impact of Restorative Justice Resolutions on Juvenile Recidivism," *Crime and Delinquency* 49:1–24; S. Truesdale (2005), "Family Bonding and Delinquency: A Multivariate Analysis Examining Minor and Serious Delinquency among United States Youth," *Dissertation Abstracts International* 65 (9): 3590-A; David Karp, Matthew Sweet, Andrew Kirshenbaum, and Gordon Bazemore (2004), "Reluctant Participants in Restorative Justice? Youthful Offenders and Their Parents," *Contemporary Justice Review* 7 (2): 199–216; M. S. Probanz (2001), "Using Protective Factors to Enhance the Prediction of Negative Short-Term Outcomes of First-Time Juvenile Offenders," *Dissertation Abstracts International* 62 (5): 1948-A; William R. Nugent, Mark S. Umbreit, Lizabeth Wiinamaki, and Jeff Paddock (2001), "Participation in Victim-Offender Mediation

and Reoffense: Successful Replications?" *Research on Social Work Practices* 11 (1): 5–23; Morgan Reynolds (2001), "Restorative Justice, American Style," *Intellectual Ammunition* (Heartland Institute), March/April; J. Katz (2000), *Victim Offender Mediation in Missouri's Juvenile Courts: Accountability, Restitution, and Transformation,* Jefferson City: Missouri Department of Public Safety; M. S. Umbreit (1995), "Restorative Justice through Mediation: The Impact of Offenders Facing Their Victims in Oakland," *Journal of Law and Social Work* 5 (1): 1–13.

14. Mark S. Umbreit, B. Vos, R. B. Coates, and M. Armour (2006), "Victims of Severe Violence in Mediated Dialogue with Offender: The Impact of the First Multi-site Study in the U.S." *International Review of Victimology* 13 (1): 27–48.

15. Zehr (2002).

16. D. Dyck (2006), "Reaching toward a Structurally Responsive Training and Practice of Restorative Justice," in D. Sullivan and L. Tift, eds., *Handbook of Restorative Justice,* 527–545, New York: Routledge; see also L. Presser and E. Gaardner (2004), "Can Restorative Justice Reduce Battering?" in B. R. Price and N. J. Sokoloff, eds., *The Criminal Justice System and Women,* 403–418, New York: McGraw-Hill.

17. Kathleen Daly and Julie Stubbs (2006), "Feminist Engagement with Restorative Justice," *Theoretical Criminology* 10 (1): 9–28.

18. Rashmi Goel (2005), "Sita's Trousseau: Restorative Justice, Domestic Violence, and South Asian Culture," *Violence against Women* 11 (5): 639–665.

19. Kimberly J. Cook (2006), "Doing Difference and Accountability in Restorative Justice Conferences," *Theoretical Criminology* 10 (1): 107–124.

20. Cook (2006), 121; see also John Braithwaite and Stephen Mugford (1994), "Conditions of Reintegration Ceremonies: Dealing with Juvenile Offenders," *British Journal of Criminology* 34 (2): 139–171.

21. Donna Coker (2006), "Restorative Justice, Navajo Peacemaking and Domestic Violence," *Violence against Women* 10 (1): 67–85 (quotation on p. 69).

22. See Daly (2002); K. Daly and H. Hayes (2003), "Youth Justice Conferencing and Re-offending," *Justice Quarterly* 20 (4): 725–264; Stubbs (2002).

23. Hopkins and Koss (2005).

24. Often domestic-violence cases are excluded from RJ programs; the Reintegrative Shaming Experiments (RISE), conducted in Canberra, Australia, in 1994, did include domestic-violence cases. This study found that conferencing produced a net reduction in reoffending of 38 percent compared to cases randomly assigned to the courts (Braithwaite [1999], "Restorative Justice: Assessing Optimistic and Pessimistic Accounts," *Crime and Justice: A Review of Research* 25 [ed. M. Tonry], 1–127). Some scholars have wondered if the exclusion of domestic-violence cases from most programs penalizes battered women, since the victims, offenders, and participants of conferencing perceive RJ as fairer and more satisfying than courtroom outcomes (Braithwaite [1999]). Moreover, Gale Burford and Joan Pennell's study of conference-based approaches to family violence in Newfoundland revealed significant reductions in both child abuse/neglect and abuse of mothers/partners and reduced drinking problems after conferences ([1998], "Family Group Decision Making: After the Conference," in *Progress in Resolving Violence and Promoting Well-Being: Outcome Report,* 2 vols., St. John's, Newfoundland: Memorial University of Newfoundland, School of Social Work). At the same time, however, Daly distinguishes between the ability to achieve fairness (procedural justice) and restorativeness (victim-offender mutual recognition, positive movement) (Daly [2002]).

25. Umbreit et al. (2003).

26. Mary P. Koss (2000), "Blame, Shame and Community: Justice Responses to Violence against Women," *American Psychologist* 55 (11): 1332–1343 ; Mary P. Koss, Karen Bachar, and C. Quince Hopkins (2003a), "Restorative Justice for Sexual Violence: Repairing Victims, Building Community, and Holding Offenders Accountable," *Annals of the New York Academy of Sciences* 989:384–396; Mary P. Koss, Karen Bachar, and C. Quince Hopkins (2003b), "Expanding a Community's Justice Response to Sex Crimes through Advocacy, Prosecutorial, and Public Health Collaboration: Introducing the RESTORE Program," *Journal of Interpersonal Violence* 19:1435–1463; Hopkins and Koss (2005).

27. Hopkins and Koss (2005), 696.

28. For a particularly cogent description of the second victimization experienced by rape victims and why they do not report rapes to police, see ibid., 694–696. For a more general discussion of potential harm to victims in RJ, see Jo-Anne Wemmers (2002), "Restorative Justice for Victims of Crime: A Victim-Oriented Approach to Restorative Justice," *International Review of Victimology* 9:43–59.

29. Hopkins and Koss (2005), 697.

30. Ibid.

31. See Stubbs (2002).

32. Hopkins and Koss (2005), 709.

33. See H. Astor (1991), "Mediation and Violence against Women," paper prepared for the National Committee on Violence Against Women, available from Violence Against Women and Legal Matters Section of the Office of the Status of Women, Department of the Prime Minister and Cabinet, 3–5 National Circuit, Barton, Australia; H. Astor (1994), "Swimming against the Tide: Keeping Violent Men Out of Mediation," in J. Stubbs, ed., *Women, Male Violence, and the Law*, 147–173, Sydney, Australia: Institute of Criminology.

34. See also Strang and Braithwaite (2002).

35. J. Davies, E. Lyon, and D. Monti-Catania,(1998), *Safety Planning with Battered Women: Complex Lives, Difficult Choices*, Thousand Oaks, CA: Sage, 33.

36. Stubbs (2002), 45.

37. See Adam Crawford and Todd Clear (2001), "Community Justice: Transforming Communities through Restorative Justice?" in G. Bazemore and M. Schiff, eds., *Restorative Community Justice: Repairing Harm and Transforming Communities*, 101–126, Cincinnati, OH: Anderson, as discussed in Stubbs (2002), 54.

38. It is helpful to keep in mind the distinction between the aim of restorative justice as "the establishment of equality in relationships and not as it is often presented in its more romanticized version the reconciliation of personal relationships typified by the sentimental goal of 'kiss and make up'" (Archibald and Llewellyn [2006], 305); similarly, restoration does not mean a return to the state of things before the wrongdoing but restoration "to our full potential as relational beings who flourish when accorded equal concern, respect and dignity" (ibid., 305–306).

39. Richard Tolman (1996), "Expanding Sanctions for Batterers: What Can We Do Besides Jailing and Counseling Them?" in J. Edleson and Z. Eisikovitz, eds., *Future Interventions with Battered Women and Their Families*, Thousand Oaks, CA: Sage; Mildred Pagelow (1981), *Woman Battering: Victims and Their Experiences*, Newbury Park, CA: Sage; Stubbs (2002).

40. Stubbs (2002).

41. Although the sheer length and intensity of the VVH program work against revictimization, it is still possible that an offender who deliberately quits participating in the program as a way to manipulate a victim's hope before the face-to-face meeting occurs can harm the victim by regaining power and control over the situation. However, many victims stated vehemently to me that the meeting was the "icing on the cake" and that they had already received so much from the program that they would not have been devastated if the meeting had been canceled. This attitude makes sense for those victims who had already received information about the offender and the incident and who felt they had been "heard," but the situation could be more debilitating for victims whose offender backs out before that happens.

42. W. Stewart, A. Huntley, and F. Blaney (2001), *The Implications of Restorative Justice for Aboriginal Women and Children Survivors of Violence: A Comparative Overview of Five Communities in British Columbia,* Ottawa, Ontario: Law Commission of Canada.

43. Julie Stubbs (2004), "Restorative Justice, Domestic Violence and Family Violence," Australian Domestic and Family Violence Clearinghouse, Issues Paper 9, http://www.austdvclearinghouse.unsw.edu.au/PDF%20files/Issues_Paper_9.pdf.

44. N. Johnson, D. Saccuzzo, and W. Koen (2005), "Child Custody Mediation in Cases of Domestic Violence: Empirical Evidence of a Failure to Protect," *Violence against Women* 11 (8): 1022–1059.

45. See L. Newmark, A. Harrell, and R. Salem (1995), "Domestic Violence and Empowerment in Custody and Vindication Cases," *Family and Conciliation Courts Review* 33 (1): 30–62.

46. Aileen Cheon and Cheryl Regehr (2006), "Restorative Justice Models in Cases of Intimate Partner Violence: Reviewing the Evidence," *Victims and Offenders* 1:369–394.

47. See L. Feder and L. Dugan (2002), "A Test of the Efficacy of Court-Mandated Counseling for Domestic Violence Offenders: The Broward Experiment," *Justice Quarterly* 19 (2): 343–375; Hooper and Busch (1996).

48. Koss et al. (2003a, 2003b); Cheon and Regehr (2006). See also Pamela Rubin's work with a Nova Scotia program for victims of sexual abuse and partner assaults in which facilitated dialogues occur between the victim, the violent offender, and the offender's support person in order to create sentencing recommendations ([2009], "A Community of One's Own? When Women Speak to Power about Restorative Justice," in James Ptacek, ed., *Feminism, Restorative Justice, and Violence against Women,* 79–102, New York: Oxford University Press).

49. Shirley Julich (2006), "Views of Justice among Survivors of Historical Child Sexual Abuse: Implications for Restorative Justice in New Zealand," *Theoretical Criminology* 10 (1): 125–138.

50. Hopkins and Koss (2005).

51. See Kay Pranis (2002), "Restorative Values and Confronting Family Violence," in H. Strang and J. Braithwaite, eds., *Restorative Justice and Family Violence,* Cambridge: Cambridge University Press.

52. See work by J. Pennell and G. Burford (2000a), "Family Group Decision Making: Protecting Children and Women," *Child Welfare* 79:131–158; J. Pennell and G. Burford (2000b), "Family Group Decision Making and Family Violence," in G. Burford and J. Hudson, eds., *Family Group Conferences: New Directions in Community-Centered Child and Family Practice,* 171–185, Hawthorne, NY: Aldine de Gruyter; and J. Pennell and S. Francis (2005), "Safety Conferencing: Toward a Coordinated and Inclusive Response to Safeguard Women and Children," *Violence against Women* 11:666–692.

1. See Michael Q. Patton (2002), *Qualitative Research and Evaluation Methods,* 3rd ed., Thousand Oaks, CA: Sage, 46.

2. See ibid.

3. Federal law (45 CFR 46) and university policy require that all research involving human subjects be reviewed and approved by an institutional review board (IRB) to ensure the protection of the rights and welfare of research participants. Research protocol must demonstrate that the benefit to the participant and the importance of the knowledge to be gained outweigh the risks to the participant to the extent that a decision to allow the participant to accept these risks is warranted, that the rights and welfare of participants will be adequately protected, that informed consent will be obtained by adequate and appropriate methods, and that research activity will be reviewed at regular intervals.

4. Many victims and offenders wanted their real names used in the book. The IRB approved using real names of deceased victims only, with the exception of using Kim and Ray Book's real names (as they requested), but the IRB would not allow other exceptions. I was disappointed by this decision, but I am bound by it.

5. For example, see Saundra D. Westervelt and Kimberly J. Cook's work with exonerated death-row inmates and their decision to give participants the opportunity to review the final copies of their interview transcripts to allow for changes, ensure accuracy, and give further input ([2007], "Feminist Research Methods in Theory and Action: Learning from Death Row Exonerees," in Susan L. Miller, ed., *Criminal Justice Research and Practice: Diverse Voices from the Field,* 38–54, Boston: Northeastern University Press).

6. Although some feminist scholars may view the methodological choices I made as indicative of a *feminist* research methodology, I differ. I believe that rigor in qualitative methods demands attention to a variety of standard research methods that I employ: facilitating researcher-participant rapport, encouraging reciprocity, honoring an individual's lived experience, and so forth. Too often, graduate-school methods training in the social sciences reflects a quantitative emphasis. Feminist influences in criminology have contributed to a backlash against an exclusive and acontextual quantitative focus, but this has had the effect of conflating feminist research and qualitative research methods. My work is explicitly feminist in its recognition of the power dynamics at play between the victims and offenders and the consequences of the crimes. This is why I chose to share chapter drafts with the victims. Honoring the storytelling of the victims can empower them and validate their experiences; my decision to explicitly seek input from victims illustrates my understanding of feminist methodology.

7. Patton (2002), 504.

8. All interviews with offenders took place in correctional institutions, but I followed the same semistructured interview approach that allowed for flexibility and elaboration.

9. Patton (2002), 226.

10. Patton (2002), 437.

11. See Clifford Geertz (1973), *The Interpretation of Cultures,* New York: Basic Books, 412–453; Norman K. Denzin (2001), *Interpretive Interactionism,* 2nd ed., Thousand Oaks, CA: Sage.

12. Norman K. Denzin (1989), *Interpretive Interactionism,* Newbury Park, CA: Sage, 83.

13. John Lofland and Lyn H. Lofland (1995), *Analyzing Social Settings: A Guide to Qualitative Observation and Analysis,* Belmont, CA: Wadsworth, 79–88.

14. Barney G. Glaser and Anselm L. Strauss (1967), *The Discovery of Grounded Theory: Strategies for Qualitative Research,* Chicago: Aldine.

15. Patton (2002), 235.

16. Ibid., 438.

17. Ibid., 248; see also J. Brewer and A. Hunter (1989), *Multimethod Research: A Synthesis of Styles,* Newbury Park, CA: Sage.

18. For further reading about qualitative methodology and triangulation, see Bruce L. Berg (2007), *Qualitative Research Methods for the Social Sciences,* 6th ed., Boston: Pearson.

19. Patton (2002), 293; see also Michael R. Hill (1993), *Archival Strategies and Techniques: Analytical Field Research,* Qualitative Research Methods Series 31, Newbury Park, CA: Sage.

20. One of the victims asked for Kim to review the videotaped dialogue and provide her notes to me, since she felt the descriptions of her father's sexual abuse were too personal; Kim reviewed the videotape in 2007 and gave me extensive notes.

21. See Patton (2002), 261–264.

22. The maximum-security unit houses about three hundred inmates, with each cell single bunked. Inmates are locked in their cells twenty-three hours a day, with one hour limited to shower and exercise time.

23. Lois Presser conducted in-depth interviews with violent male offenders, finding that self-constructed narratives provide an interpretive context for their behavior which is important in our understanding of "what they say and think of themselves" ([2008], *Been a Heavy Life: Stories of Violent Men,* Urbana: University of Illinois Press, 7).

24. In fact, Presser (2008) finds that feminist theorists and ethnographers advocate a reflexive approach to research methods, in that observations about participants are actively constructed in conjunction with the researcher's interpretation of the data, that "researchers are never just spectators to the activities that they study" (40). Presser chooses to acknowledge that although her presence is "a resource in [her] participants' identity work" that affects the interview exchanges in her investigations of the offenders' narratives, her analysis focuses on the violent men and not on her own self identity (44); see also L. Presser (2009), "The Narratives of Offenders," *Theoretical Criminology* 13 (2): 177–200.

25. See Diana Scully's (1990) work on convicted rapists, Michelle Meloy's (2006) work with male sex offenders on probation, and James Messerschmidt's work with violent teenage girls ([1999], *Nine Lives: Adolescent Masculinities, the Body and Violence,* Boulder, CO: Westview; [2004], *Flesh and Blood: Adolescent Gender Diversity and Violence,* Lanham, MD: Rowan and Littlefield).

26. See Anselm L. Strauss and Juliet Corbin (1998), *Basics of Qualitative Research: Techniques and Procedures for Developing Grounded Theory,* 2nd ed., Thousand Oaks, CA: Sage, 223.

27. See Lofland and Lofland (1995).

28. Patton (2002), 438.

29. Ibid., 454; see Glaser and Strauss (1967).

30. Strauss and Corbin (1998), 22.

31. Denzin (1989).

NOTES TO APPENDIX C

1. For those questions left unanswered by participants on the paperwork, I relied on the facilitators' case notes and interviews for a more complete understanding and analysis.

2. See Kathleen Daly (2008), "Girls, Peer Violence, and Restorative Justice," *Australian and New Zealand Journal of Criminology* 41 (1): 109–137.

3. This exercise is much harder for victims to do (i.e., to put themselves in the offender's shoes) than for offenders.

Index

Masculinity, 51, 53, 54, 58, 74, 78, 81, 150, 171, 176, 177, 206, 223, 239n6, 240n8, 244nn19, 23, 24

Meetings with family members, 53, 128

Megan's Law, 65, 241n13

Methodology: archival data, 219, 261n19; and collaborative process, 215-16; and control of respondents, 215; comparative case study approach, 6-7, 8, 218, 225; crime type, 219; crime type by race and gender of victim and offender, 220; crime type by relationship, 220; data collection, 4, 18, 216-17, 217-18, 219; feminist methodology, 260n6, 261n24; gender of researcher, 223; grounded-theory, 224; Institutional Review Board, 260nn3, 4; interviews, 216, 217, 218, with offenders in prison, 221-22; qualitative, 214, 218; respondent issues, 215; social desirability bias, 219, 222-23; "thick" description and analysis, 214, 217, 218, 225; triangulated design, 218-19, 223, 261n18; videos 219, 221, 234

Mothers Against Drunk Driving (MADD), 115, 119, 124, 127, 128, 218

Murder, 24, 182-183

"No contact" orders, 15, 20, 30, 60, 64, 164, 249n5, 250n3, 251n14

Non-profit programs, 174, 197, 204, 237n10

Offenders: and accountability, 16, 20; and anger 51, 58, 59, 69, 76, 80, 88, 135, 144, 171, 177; and childhood, 51, 77, 147, 170, 250n2; and letter writing 52, 118, 140, 229, 231, 233; and military, 147, 206; and offender-centered programs, 11, 14-15; and parole and pardon board, 138, 139, 143, 145, 152, 249n3, 251n12; and prison experiences, 54, 74, 75, 114; and punishment views, 57, 162, 171; and rationalizations, 78; and remorse, 50, 60, 77, 101, 114, 127, 139, 148, 151, 168, 169-70; and responsibility, 45, 51, 61, 64, 80, 91, 95, 102, 118, 142, 148, 168, 176, 188, 189, 191, 196, 213, 230, 231; and restitution, 114, 244n28, 247nn5, 7. See also Victims, and letters between victims and offenders

O'Hara, K., 4, 166

Pornography, 69, 78, 244n20

Power dynamics between victims and offenders, 15, 178, 181

Prison fellowship, 32

Procedural justice, 172, 252n12

Protection from Abuse order, 71, 242n13

Race and ethnicity, 41, 46, 52-53, 69, 200, 205-6, 255n16

Re-entry, 65, 67, 75, 81, 96, 105, 117, 132, 133, 156, 176, 177, 184, 197, 199, 224, 240n4, 241n14, 245n19, 253n16

Rehabilitation, 16, 54-55, 57, 60, 65, 113, 114, 117, 141-42, 151, 155, 171, 176, 177, 199, 249n9

Reintegrative Shaming Experiments, 257n24

Restorative justice: and communities, 205; and definition and issues, 7, 11, 203, 205, 210, 241n10, 253n15; and diversionary programs, 11, 12, 160-61, 191, 198, 204, 206-7, 236n11, 255n3; and empirical evaluations, 204-6, 207, 256n13; and general reasons for participation for offenders and victims, 168, 163; and larger context, 9, 16, 185, 203, 206, 256n5; and philosophy, 159, 255n2, 258n38; and post-conviction therapeutic programs, 11, 12-14, 169, 180, 186, 198, 206-07, 208, 209, 211, 212, 236n11

RESTORE program, 208-210, 258n26

Retribution, 159, 160, 185, 251n3

"Ripple effect," 53, 67, 132, 133, 145, 167, 169, 172, 192, 194, 200, 239nn2, 8, 245n5, 254nn11, 12

"Second victimization," 60, 62, 106, 137, 258n28

Sexual Assault Nurse Examiners, 98, 181, 246n2

Sexual offenders, 65, 67, 91, 102, 162, 171, 182, 208; and registry, 97, 99

Sexual violence, 12, 207-10, 212, 240n7, 243nn15, 16, 244n22

About the Author

SUSAN L. MILLER is Professor of Sociology and Criminal Justice at the University of Delaware. She is the author of *Victims as Offenders: Women's Use of Violence in Relationships* and *Gender and Community Policing: Waking the Talk*, editor of *Criminal Justice Research and Practice: Voices from the Field*, coauthor of *The Politics of Violence against Women*, and coeditor of *Rethinking Gender, Crime, and Justice: Feminist Readings*.